REBELS AN

Reflecting on #FeesMustFall

M000041722

ADAM HABIB

REBELS AND RAGE

Reflecting on #FeesMustFall

ADAM HABIB

JONATHAN BALL PUBLISHERS
JOHANNESBURG & CAPE TOWN

Originally published in South Africa in 2019 by
JONATHAN BALL PUBLISHERS
A division of Media24 (Pty) Ltd
PO Box 33977
Jeppestown
2043

ISBN 978 1 86842 896 0
ebook ISBN 978 1 86842 897 7
Every effort has been made to trace the copyright holders and to obtain
their permission for the use of copyright material. The publishers apologise
for any errors or omissions and would be grateful to be notified of any
corrections that should be incorporated in future editions of this book.

Twitter: www.twitter.com/JonathanBallPub
Facebook: www.facebook.com/JonathanBallPublishers
Blog: http://jonathanball.bookslive.co.za/

Cover by Sam van Straaten
Design and typesetting by Catherine Coetzer
Printed and bound by CTP Printers, Cape Town
Set in Adobe Caslon

Contents

Abbreviations

ANC	African National Congress
ANCYL	African National Congress Youth League
ASAWU	Academic Staff Association of Wits University
BEE	black economic empowerment
CALS	Centre for Applied Legal Studies
CCMA	Commission for Conciliation, Mediation and Arbitration
CFO	chief financial officer
CHE	Council on Higher Education
COO	chief operating officer
COSATU	Congress of South African Trade Unions
CPI	consumer price inflation
CPUT	Cape Peninsula University of Technology
DASO	Democratic Alliance Students' Organisation
DBE	Department of Basic Education
DHET	Department of Higher Education and Training
DUT	Durban University of Technology
EEF	education endowment fund
EFF	Economic Freedom Fighters
FNB	First National Bank
GDP	gross domestic product
GEMP	Graduate Entry Medical Programme
GEO	Gender Equity Office
HBU	historically black university
HEI	higher education inflation
IEC	Independent Electoral Commission
NECF	National Education Crisis Forum
NEDLAC	National Economic Development and Labour Council
NEHAWU	National Education, Health and Allied Workers' Union

NPA	National Prosecuting Authority
NSFAS	National Student Financial Aid Scheme
NUMSA	National Union of Metalworkers of South Africa
NWU	North-West University
PASMA	Pan Africanist Student Movement of Azania
PSC	Palestinian Solidarity Committee
PYA	Progressive Youth Alliance
SABC	South African Broadcasting Corporation
SACC	South African Council of Churches
SAPS	South African Police Service
SASCO	South African Students Congress
SAUS	South African Union of Students
SERI	Socio-Economic Rights Institute
SRC	Student Representative Council
TUT	Tshwane University of Technology
TVET	technical vocational education and training
UCT	University of Cape Town
UDF	United Democratic Front
UJ	University of Johannesburg
UKZN	University of KwaZulu-Natal
UN	United Nations
UNAM	National Autonomous University of Mexico
UNISA	University of South Africa
UP	University of Pretoria
USAf	Universities South Africa
UWC	University of the Western Cape
VAT	value added tax
WISER	Wits Institute for Social and Economic Research
YCL	Young Communist League

Preface

WE are a haunted executive at Wits University – haunted by the fear that we will not rise to the strategic challenge of our era. We do not have the ideological comfort of those at the barricades where there is a certainty in the critique. Neither do we have the emotional serenity of the mainstream corporate executive who is comfortable with the world as it is. Instead, we occupy a lonely nether world where we recognise that things can and must change, yet know that we have to operate within the financial and political constraints of the present. Our strategic task is to craft a bridge between the limits of the present and the possibilities of the future, a bridge we can only build by striking an appropriate balance between our competing institutional priorities.

Long before any of us arrived at Wits, the university adopted a vision of being research intensive. In a sense, it was this vision that attracted us to the job. Part of this may have to do with the academic vanity of leading an institution that has significant research output and postgraduate throughput. But it also has to do with our collective commitment to addressing inequality within the global academy. If we truly believe in an egalitarian world, then we need to work towards a global academy of commons. Such an academy requires South Africa to have its own cohort of research-intensive universities. Otherwise, research and scientific production will remain concentrated in the North; in the context of a globalised, knowledge-based economy, the inequality within our world will continue to prevail.

But our responsibility as Wits executives is also to address the inequality in our national context. Universities can only successfully contribute to addressing inequality if, on the one hand, they produce enough professional graduates that these skills do not command a premium in the market and, on the other, they enable access for students from poor communities. These two goals require universities of sufficient quality to enable throughput – but that are either priced appropriately or have sufficient financial aid to allow poor students to access them.

Both of these competing priorities have to be addressed simultaneously in a financially sustainable way. There are, of course, some who believe that our financial fiduciary responsibilities can easily be traded in favour of our academic and social ones. But we need to think through the wisdom of this strategy, in particular because it is premised on a widespread assumption among the far left that the state would be compelled to bail universities out were they to get into a financial crisis. Yet this strategy has been tried before, with devastating consequences. In the late 1990s, what was then the University of Transkei effectively embarked on a strategy to address its historical infrastructural disparities by deliberately pursuing a financial deficit. Within years, the institution was on the brink of insolvency; while the state did eventually bail it out, it did not do so at the levels required or within the timeframes necessary. The net effect was the academic destruction of what was then one of the country's strongest historically black universities: the financial crisis prompted the departure of top academics and students. The university has never truly recovered.

The tragedy of this strategy is not that it is likely to fail, but rather that it repeats past failures simply because it is dislocated from any understanding of the history of the transformation of the higher education system in this country. It reminds me of a lesson that noted educationist and political activist Neville Alexander once taught me and some of my colleagues. He often remarked that, while he may have been a noted Marxist theoretician and scholar, his socialism only developed political relevance when ANC notable Walter Sisulu taught him African history while they were imprisoned on Robben Island. It is this nationally responsive and contextually relevant Marxism that lies at the core of Neville's magnum opus, *One Azania, One Nation*, written soon after his release from Robben Island. This is the lesson that the advocates of fiscal complacency need to learn: if we do not understand our history, and the relevance of our context, we risk repeating the failures of our past.

The strategic imperative of our time is to strike the balance between equally compelling priorities. When I concluded my installation address at Wits University in the Great Hall on 24 August 2013, I underscored the importance of balance in executive decision-making at universities. Reflecting on the experiences and writings of great activists and organic intellectuals – Kahlil Gibran, Antonio Gramsci and Steve Biko – I stressed that striking the balance between competing priorities is a prerequisite for human progress. This lesson continues to apply to contemporary South Africa. Whether we are speaking of growth and redistribution in the economy, or service delivery and transformation in the state, or national responsiveness and global competitiveness in universities, balancing competing priorities is the precondition for breaking out of our structural impasse and achieving progressive outcomes.

It is this struggle for balance that has governed the practice of Wits's executive management in recent years. In driving research, we appointed top professors and created incentives for the general academic to publish. Our recruitment of top students targeted those at the apex of the schooling system as well as those in quintile 1 and 2 schools through the Vice-Chancellor's Scholarships and the Vice-Chancellor's Equality Scholarships respectively. Student recruitment in our Faculty of Health Sciences similarly underscored merit by prioritising students with the best results, yet simultaneously reserved 20 per cent of seats each for top students from rural schools and from urban quintile 1 and 2 schools. The overall goal in our student recruitment was to achieve a strategic balance between demographic representativeness and cosmopolitan orientation.

This strategic approach to managing the institution has had some success. Wits is one of the most demographically representative of South Africa's research-intensive universities, yet we remain cosmopolitan by attracting students across the race, class, cultural and national divides. Our research output has increased by 56 per cent in the past four years, and 86 per cent of our journal articles published in 2017 were in high-quality international journals. Our throughput of both undergraduate and postgraduate students has also increased steadily. Our postgraduate numbers are now at just under 14 000 in a total student cohort of 37 000. It should also be noted that, although I remain sceptical of the methodologies and assessments of university ranking systems, Wits has steadily improved in many of the global rankings, and is ranked as either first or second on the continent.

Yet despite these successes, serious challenges remain and came to the fore most dramatically in two sets of events: the #RhodesMustFall and #FeesMustFall protests. Collectively, these became the largest student social movement since the dawn of South Africa's democracy in 1994. The protests emanated from two major challenges facing higher education: alienation and access. The #RhodesMustFall movement, in which students at the University of Cape Town (UCT) demanded the removal of the statue of Cecil John Rhodes, captured the alienation of the largely black student population at UCT and reflected valid concerns about institutional racism and/or the slow pace of transformation at all of our universities. Transformation movements developed at all of the historically white universities. While they focused on specific institutional challenges, all questioned the identity of the university and what it meant to be an African institution in the 21st century. The #FeesMustFall movement began at Wits and spread across the country, culminating in student marches to Parliament and the Union Buildings. Its high point was when President Zuma, after negotiating with student leaders and vice-chancellors at the Union Buildings, conceded that the state would cover the student fee increase for 2016. In that moment, the students achieved in a matter of ten days what vice-chancellors had been advocating for at least ten years: bringing down the costs of higher education. The #FeesMustFall movement, whose principal concern was access for poor black students to affordable, quality education, gave notice that Zuma's fee concession was merely the first step in a broader struggle for free education.

The students' discontents were undeniably legitimate. It was unacceptable for black students not to feel at home at South Africa's public universities. Neither was it acceptable for talented students from poor communities to be denied access to higher education. All stakeholders needed to address both challenges urgently – including university management, academics, students and government. Addressing these challenges was not only positive for the students, but was also necessary for enabling the agenda of inclusive economic development and helping to challenge the high levels of inequality in our society.

Yet despite the legitimacy of the students' demands, their struggles had to play out in ways that did not undermine the university as a safe and free space for ideas. Moreover, the decisions that university executives made in response to these demands could not compromise universities' long-term sustainability: this would simply compromise the educational prospects of future generations of poor South Africans. Achieving a strategic balance between allowing this legitimate social movement to evolve and maintaining the free, safe space and the long-term financial sustainability of the university became the principal task of the Wits executive in managing the student protests. We recognised that the students' social and political awakening created opportunities for opening up the systemic and institutional constraints on finances and spending priorities – opportunities we could use effectively to progress towards the intellectually vibrant and humane university that we collectively envisioned. Yet we were also aware that, if this did not unfold in a measured and thoughtful way, it could engender academic flight and a financial crisis. We recognised that striking this strategic balance was not the responsibility of any other internal stakeholders – students, academics, professional and administrative staff – but ours, supported by our Council. Ours was the responsibility for making hard choices and deliberating on trade-offs, of crafting second-best solutions in the existing world rather than a world we wished existed.

We knew we would be pilloried and attacked by many who were not responsible for crafting this strategic balance; criticised by some for being too hard, and by others for being too soft; accused by some of being neoliberal, and by others of being fiscally irresponsible. As an executive team, we were not always of one mind on all issues, and had to reach strategic consensus in the cauldron of protest. We knew that public support would not always be forthcoming, even though we could always rely on some very special individuals to provide counsel. As the events unfolded, we as an executive came to rely far more on one another, and on the counsel of a small number of Council members and academics – Randall Carolissen (chair of Council), Brian Bruce (former deputy chair of Council), Isaac Shongwe (current deputy chair of Council), Theunie Lategan, Cas Coovadia, Rob Hamer, Len Sizani, Barney Pityana, Mavuso Msimang, Dikgang Moseneke, Mary Scholes, Shireen Hassim, Cathi Albertyn, Sharon Fonn and Achille Mbembe. Of course, we did not always agree, and our disagreements were spirited, but every one of us was directed by a desire to ensure that Wits University continued on its path of transformation, yet remained an intellectually vibrant institution serving South Africa and the world. I also came to rely far more on my fellow vice-chancellors, all of whom confronted similar challenges.

This is the story I tell in the pages that follow. When Ester Levinrad of Jonathan Ball Publishers first approached me to write this book, I was sceptical: I recognised that I could not be dispassionate, being a prominent participant in the protest events. I have written extensively on the protests, particularly in the *Daily Maverick* (and have borrowed liberally from these writings for this book), but wrote to advocate non-violence and, as a participant, to correct misconceptions. I imagined that a book had to be so much more – dispassionate, comprehensive and analytical. But as Kanina Foss, my then chief of staff, and I discussed it further, the idea grew on us. Why could this not be a book about a participant in the events, detailing why we made our choices and how we think the system can be fixed? Such a book could be a corrective to the crude caricatures of bipolarity between conservative university executives and revolutionary protesters that sometimes animate the public discourse and even the pages of books that were hurriedly produced in the protests' wake. This book could contribute to the corpus of reflections on the student protests, and serve as one of the sources for the more dispassionate analytical studies that would emerge in the years to come.

Ester concurred that it would be a participant's account. But another problem emerged: how to find the time to write it? Kanina and I agreed that the best way to do this would be for me to get away from the office for a couple of months – impossible, given the challenges we confronted and their urgent need for institutional and systemic solutions. And then fortune struck. I was coming to the end of my first term as vice-chancellor and had just been offered a second term. The Council agreed to give me a six-month sabbatical between the two terms to write this book. Sarah Nuttall facilitated a link with Skip Gates, whose Hutchins Center at Harvard University agreed to host me and provide an intellectually stimulating space; the Ford Foundation, and Nicolette Naylor in particular, agreed to sponsor my sojourn in the United States.

A final challenge emerged in the writing of the book – whom to name and whom to anonymise. This was especially important, given that I would be serving another executive term. After giving due consideration to the issue, I followed some general rules. First, I have retained the names of all those who have put themselves out into the public domain, reflected and critically engaged on the issues. Second, where matters might be sensitive to individual colleagues, I have only mentioned their names with their explicit consent. Finally, I have anonymised individuals in cases where correspondence was directed for my personal attention, and when individual students are not known and could be irreparably harmed as a result of specific conduct or incidents. These general rules, I believe, enable the telling of a story that needs to be told, yet allow me to do so respectfully and responsibly.

I offer this book as one contribution among many to enable an understanding of the student protests, their structural and immediate causes, their character and implications, and the potential solutions and trade-offs confronting us as South Africans. I recognise that I have a particular window into the student protests, and that as a result I do not represent a full or comprehensive picture of the events. But I offer the book as one among a plurality of accounts, precisely to enable a comprehensive understanding of events. I also reflect on the lessons to be learnt from the universities' challenges. These are lessons about the leadership of our government, the management of our public institutions, and the mobilisation of our people – lessons that all of us need to learn if we are to heal the divides of our past and build the society that our Constitution envisions. If this book contributes in some small way to that end, then the difficult events upon which it reflects, and the sacrifices that have been made, would truly have been worth enduring.

Adam Habib
December 2018

MAJOR ROLEPLAYERS

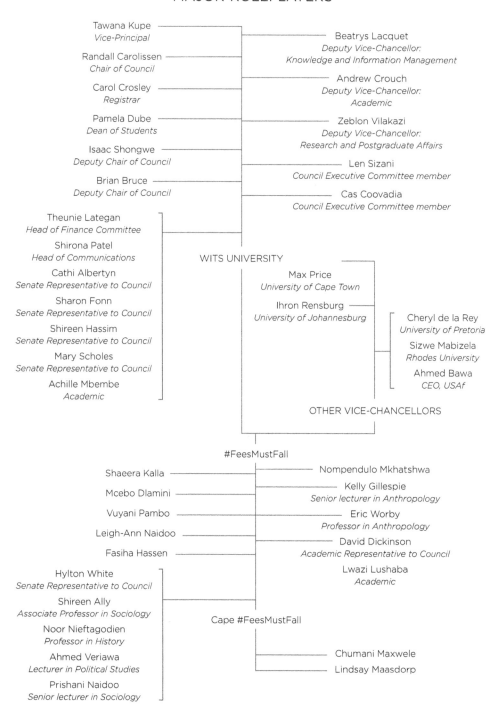

Tawana Kupe
Vice-Principal

Randall Carolissen
Chair of Council

Carol Crosley
Registrar

Pamela Dube
Dean of Students

Isaac Shongwe
Deputy Chair of Council

Brian Bruce
Deputy Chair of Council

Beatrys Lacquet
*Deputy Vice-Chancellor:
Knowledge and Information Management*

Andrew Crouch
*Deputy Vice-Chancellor:
Academic*

Zeblon Vilakazi
*Deputy Vice-Chancellor:
Research and Postgraduate Affairs*

Len Sizani
Council Executive Committee member

Cas Coovadia
Council Executive Committee member

Theunie Lategan
Head of Finance Committee

Shirona Patel
Head of Communications

Cathi Albertyn
Senate Representative to Council

Sharon Fonn
Senate Representative to Council

Shireen Hassim
Senate Representative to Council

Mary Scholes
Senate Representative to Council

Achille Mbembe
Academic

WITS UNIVERSITY

Max Price
University of Cape Town

Ihron Rensburg
University of Johannesburg

Cheryl de la Rey
University of Pretoria

Sizwe Mabizela
Rhodes University

Ahmed Bawa
CEO, USAf

OTHER VICE-CHANCELLORS

#FeesMustFall

Shaeera Kalla

Mcebo Dlamini

Vuyani Pambo

Leigh-Ann Naidoo

Fasiha Hassen

Nompendulo Mkhatshwa

Kelly Gillespie
Senior lecturer in Anthropology

Eric Worby
Professor in Anthropology

David Dickinson
Academic Representative to Council

Lwazi Lushaba
Academic

Hylton White
Senate Representative to Council

Shireen Ally
Associate Professor in Sociology

Noor Nieftagodien
Professor in History

Ahmed Veriawa
Lecturer in Political Studies

Prishani Naidoo
Senior lecturer in Sociology

Cape #FeesMustFall

Chumani Maxwele

Lindsay Maasdorp

1

The night on the concourse

FRIDAY the 16th in October 2015 was a hot and humid evening, made even more so by the throngs of students who occupied the multi-storey concourse in the middle of Wits University's main admin block. Hundreds of students hung over the balconies that overlooked the ground floor, surveying us and the events below. The ground floor was also bursting with students, and some staff. We were seated at the chairs and tables on the south end of the concourse, with our backs to the lifts. There were some students behind us as well.

The heady atmosphere was made all the more intoxicating by the sounds of 'Iyho Solomon', the haunting song that commemorates the life of Solomon Kalushi Mahlangu, a young Umkhonto weSizwe militant executed by the apartheid state in 1979 at the tender age of 22. I had heard the song echo all day, and for many days before. But it seemed to have an even more poignant effect on this humid evening, with the press of students and the cameras. I wondered for a while at the relevance of the song. After all, Solomon Mahlangu was not linked in any way to university struggles. But he was a young man when he was executed, about the same age as many of the students who now sang about him. He too was involved in a noble cause; it is said that, before he was led to the gallows, he uttered to his mother the final words: 'My blood will nourish the tree that will bear the fruits of freedom. Tell my people that I love them. They must continue the struggle.' Given this mythology, and his age, it is not surprising that Solomon Mahlangu became the mythological mascot of South Africa's #FeesMustFall protest.

I sat with my executive team and members of the university's Council. Beatrys Lacquet, Deputy Vice-Chancellor: Knowledge and Information Management, Infrastructure and Operations sat to my left, while the Chair of Council, Randall Carolissen, was to my right. Andrew Crouch, Deputy Vice-Chancellor: Academic was also nearby, as was Pamela Dube, Dean of Students. All three executive members had been with me the entire day. Carol Crosley, our registrar, was also there, but had come in with some of the other Council members in the evening. Randall had come in slightly earlier. When he called earlier and volunteered to join me, I warned him that he would be obliged to stay for hours. Yet he did not hesitate.

The other members of Council came after hastily convening a Council meeting. The students had wanted me to overturn the fee increase that had been decided at Council a week earlier. I had refused, informing them that I could not overturn a Council decision. They had then insisted that the Council convene in the concourse, in front of them, and rescind the decision. This did not happen, but members of the Council did meet on the 11th floor above the concourse. Then, after they were engaged and invited down by some of the student leaders, some Council members decided to join us on the concourse. Again, I warned them that, if they decided to come down, they would be with us for hours. And yet they came. Cathi Albertyn, Rob Hamer, Len Sizani, Cas Coovadia, Conrad Mueller and Adele Underhay, all very different individuals with diverse experience and histories, came down and spent the night on the concourse. Some saw this as a way of demeaning the Council. It may well have been, but I could not have been prouder to be sitting beside these individuals. Collectively, we sat that evening, uncowed. Each of us explained – individually, patiently, repeatedly – that the fee increase decision could not be rescinded. If any party were to make a concession, it would have to be the state, whose decision to lower our subsidies continuously was the root cause of the fee increase.

I was tired by this time, of course. It had been a long day. I had woken up at 03h30 that Friday in Durban to make a 05h30 flight to Johannesburg. The protest had begun early on Wednesday morning, when students had stood in front of the university gates and refused to let vehicles leave the premises. They lay down in front of the gates and challenged vehicles to drive over them if they wanted to leave. It was an ingenious strategy, which paralysed the university; it was accompanied, of course, by protesters shutting down classes.

There had been a curtain-raiser earlier in the week – on Tuesday evening, at our Management campus in Parktown – when students had protested against the expansion of the Wits Business School and the closure of a residence, despite a commitment to source alternative accommodation and ensure that there would be no reduction in the number of beds available to students. They had insisted that I collect a memorandum, which I did, but the evening classes at the Business School had been significantly impacted. The next morning, the students had moved to the campus in Braamfontein; the demand became to rescind the fee increase that had been decided a week earlier at the Council meeting.

Throughout Wednesday, we had tried to negotiate with the protesting students about the fees issue and to allow free vehicle mobility on and off campus. But this was to no avail. We called the police in, but asked them to maintain a discreet presence at the gates so as not to inflame the situation. We managed, eventually, to get all vehicles off the campus by opening additional exits surreptitiously. But there had been massive disruptions not only to our academic programmes, but also to people's personal lives. Parents had been prevented from picking up their children from school. A staff member who had a serious medical condition had been prevented from seeing his doctor. There were countless other infractions against both staff and students.

Towards the end of Wednesday evening, another challenge emerged. I was meant to be in Durban on Thursday and Friday for a ministerial conference on transformation in universities, but how could I leave under these conditions? The executive team insisted that I should go, however, and that they would manage the protests and get the academic programme back on track. And so I left for Durban on Wednesday evening, but I might as well not have gone. For all of Thursday at the conference I remained glued to the phone, keeping track of developments on campus. Students at the conference also read a memorandum from the leaders of the protesting Wits students, demanding that the conference take a position against the fee increase. While this obviously did not happen, developments at Wits continued to overshadow the conference. By Thursday evening, confronting another challenge of staff and students having to leave the campus, the executive team decided to send in the police to disperse the student protesters. But just as the police were to move in, the student leaders petitioned the executive to ask me to return so that they could engage me directly. I agreed, and took the first morning flight to Johannesburg. After a brief stop at Savernake, the vice-chancellor's official residence, where I quickly freshened up, I went to the campus first for a short briefing with the executive team. By 08h00 we were collectively ready to engage with the protesting students, but waited for Pamela Dube to give us the signal that they were ready to receive us.

Just before 09h00, Pamela indicated that the students were ready for us, but wanted to meet at the Yale/Empire Road entrance. I agreed to this and Andrew Crouch, Pamela and I proceeded to walk across campus to the students. We were accompanied by Protection Services officers; as we approached the entrance, protesting students started singing and chanting. Initially, the protesters simply surrounded us, making it hard to get any engagement going with student leadership. Eventually, we collectively agreed to move to the gate itself, where there was an elevated structure on which we could stand and address the students. I was not expected to speak. The student leaders – Nompendulo Mkhatshwa and Shaeera Kalla – wanted to be the only ones speaking, and I was simply to hear them out. For a while, with the crowd's approval, I even held aloft the loud hailer for Nompendulo. The message, of course, was the same. 'The students cannot afford the increase,' Nompendulo said. 'The fee increase must be rescinded.'

This went on for about an hour, before another group of singing protesters arrived, led by two other student leaders, Mcebo Dlamini and Vuyani Pambo. At that point, Shaeera turned to me and recommended that I leave. But I demurred. After a short period of speeches, chants and toyi-toying, Vuyani turned to me and complained about the heat. He asked whether what was then known as Senate House, now Solomon Mahlangu House, could be opened so that the students could get out of the sun. I agreed to instruct security to open the building. As the protesters turned to march there, Pamela once again recommended that we leave. We were right next to the Yale/Empire Road entrance, with security, and a car was available to whisk us away. But again, I did not heed the advice. It was time to see this matter through, so I decided that we should go with the students.

On arriving at the concourse, I was offered a chair. But I deliberately decided to sit on the floor as I had done on multiple other occasions, the most recent having been earlier that week at the Tuesday evening protest on the Management campus. This would become a matter of controversy in the days ahead. What had been a perfectly innocent act was blown out of all proportion by the *Saturday Star*, which alleged in its headlines that I had been forced to sit on the floor. Not only was this blatantly untrue, but it also provided factions of the student movement with ideas. And so, on Monday the following week, when the protests spread to UCT, some student leaders forced the deputy vice-chancellors to kneel and sit as an act of humiliation. Vuyani, a leader in the Wits Economic Freedom Fighters (EFF) Student Command who had a penchant for spectacle, would also try it a few days later on Gwede Mantashe in a student march to Luthuli House (ANC headquarters). Vuyani was deliberately and publicly rebuffed by the secretary-general, who saw it as an act of humiliation. Vuyani's attempt exposed divisions within the student leadership, with the other three Wits leaders at the march objecting, all of whom were organisationally associated with the ANC – an organisational tension that would continue to haunt the #FeesMustFall movement.

A few days later, the head of Journalism at Wits, Anton Harber, would criticise Gwede for not sitting down. He drew a distinction between humility and humiliation and suggested that my decision to sit on the floor was an act of the former, but not the latter. But this was only true so long as it was a voluntary act, not forced on me by anyone else. Once it became an act of compulsion, forced by student leaders, the simple act of sitting on the floor transformed into an act of humiliation. Gwede was perfectly within his rights, then, to refuse to sit. Indeed, I would have done the same in a similar set of circumstances.

The rest of Friday morning and afternoon was marked by both good-natured interaction and spectacle. Soon after we arrived at the concourse, and while Andrew and I were sitting and talking to Mcebo, Beatrys kindly brought us some nuts and coffee, which we shared with those around us. Yet, a few hours later, Nompendulo would make a spectacle of the fact that I needed to get away from the noise and walk to one of the side corridors to call my wife, Fatima, to inform her that all was well. When it got slightly hot in the concourse, a number of the students and I walked to the courtyard behind the concourse to get some fresh air; later, when I walked to the toilet in the early evening, Nompendulo would again make it a spectacle and pass a disparaging, ageist remark. During the afternoon, when private security decided to come onto the concourse on their own and immediately caused an altercation, a number of students, including Mcebo and Vuyani, surrounded me to ensure I was protected. Yet a few minutes later, Vuyani or Mcebo would make one or other disparaging statement about me to one of the journalists. It was these little acts of personal kindness, coupled with acts of political spectacle, that not only marked the day and night on the concourse, but were also to become a hallmark of the entire #FeesMustFall campaign.

Throughout the day while we sat together, I informed both Mcebo and Vuyani that, while I recognised the onerous burden of the fee increase, the Wits executive was powerless to do anything else given the continuous annual decline in state subsidies. I had said to both students that, if academic quality was to be maintained, there was no option but to increase fees. And, I indicated, 'I cannot and will not rescind the fee increase.' In any case, it was a Council decision which I had no power to reverse. If anything was to be done, the concession would have to come from the state. But I also expressed my reservations about whether the state would come to the party. I indicated that the vice-chancellors had been engaging the ANC government for years on the declining subsidy, to no avail, and expressed scepticism about whether this historical moment would be any different. This firm position not to rescind the fee increase was shared by almost all of Council, and would be the distinguishing feature of our collective response that night.

Four student leaders would become the face of the Wits #FeesMustFall movement. At least three of them – Mcebo, Shaeera and Vuyani – I had interacted with, sometimes substantively, prior to the October protests. The other student leader, Nompendulo, had just been elected Student Representative Council (SRC) president for the coming year and was to take office on 1 November 2015, two weeks after the protest got going. In the weeks and months ahead, I would get to know her as well as I knew the others. Each of these students would significantly influence the #FeesMustFall campaign, both at Wits and the national level, and each would in turn be significantly affected by the movement.

Mcebo's interaction with me officially began when he was elected and assumed office as SRC president in November 2014. Outgoing SRC leaders had cynically wished me luck when we were informed that he had been elected president, which suggested that he already had quite a reputation. He also had a charge of assault of another student hanging over his head when he stood for and won the SRC office – a problem which we have often contemplated solving by passing a rule that prevents candidates from contesting office when they have a pending charge. But this would prejudice the students, since they must at least be presumed innocent until found guilty. In any case, this issue would come to haunt us when, in February 2015, he was found guilty of the charge by a disciplinary hearing. The SRC constitution requires anyone found guilty of an offence to stand down, and I had an engagement with Mcebo in this regard. Initially, I made a concession that allowed him to remain in office for a further 14 days because he was taking the decision of the disciplinary committee to review. But when the matter began to drag out, I called him in and asked him to step down voluntarily or I would be forced to dismiss him. Three days later, Mcebo publicly made his notorious statement: 'What I love about Adolf Hitler is his charisma and his capabilities to organise people ... There is an element of Hitler in every white person.'

I have often wondered whether he made this statement deliberately to make it politically inconvenient for me to dismiss him as SRC president. After all, the charge that would subsequently be levelled against the executive and me by the student activists associated with Mcebo is that we fired him because we were beholden to Zionist interests. But as abhorrent as I found his views on Hitler, our legal advice suggested that his remarks fell within the parameters of the constitutional right to free speech. In any case, pulling the race or ethnic (Zionist) card was not going to dissuade us in any way from removing Mcebo as SRC president. The SRC constitution demanded that he be removed, and it was necessary at a university like Wits to ensure that student leaders were subject to the same policies as the rest of the student body. And so the decision was made, even though we knew it would be heavily contested by student political parties associated with the ANC, EFF, and Black Consciousness and Pan-Africanist traditions.

For the next few months, Mcebo took to the airwaves to paint himself as a victim of a management insensitive to 'the black child', a patronising term that was to become popular among student activists in the university arena. The mainstream media, addicted as it is to sensationalism, partnered in this public spectacle on race and ethnic baiting. Within the university itself, debate raged on our motivation for removing Mcebo and, even after I personally engaged in public debates with the student body in which I demonstrated that the decision to remove him was made prior to his Hitler comments, significant sections of political activists would just not concede. In this world of 'fake news', evidence was just not going to be allowed to detract from a preconceived conclusion.

As matters settled, however uneasily, Mcebo got embroiled in another altercation. The incident took place at the annual electoral debate where candidates for SRC elections are grilled on their experience and suitability for the position. In August 2015, in the midst of a hotly contested election between the ANC-aligned Progressive Youth Alliance (PYA), the EFF and a moderate political alternative under the label Project W, a fight broke out. Video footage clearly showed Mcebo involved in a physical altercation with a student from Project W. In a subsequent preliminary suspension hearing, Mcebo showed no contrition for the incident; as a result, he was one among a number of students who were suspended. The university was subsequently taken to court on the matter by legal representatives who were arranged by the national EFF, and, while the court did not overturn our decision to bar implicated students from participating in the SRC election, it did overturn our decision to suspend these students until their disciplinary hearings. This was motivated on the grounds that the affected students' right to education would be infringed. While I disagreed with the court decision, believing that the right to education had to be balanced against the constitutional right to safety of all students – which was itself compromised by the altercation's violent actions – the university abided by the court ruling and decided not to appeal this decision.

Mcebo thus entered October 2015 with a political score to settle, and the fee protests provided the perfect opportunity. Ironically, our personal relationship remained cordial. In one-to-one interactions, Mcebo was always polite and engaging. He insisted that our political differences were not personal, and he would often send me personal messages to clarify this in the midst of heated political contestation in the public domain. But the 'public' Mcebo was a different person, especially if there were cameras around. On television or radio, Mcebo would make the most scurrilous of statements about me or other members of the executive, and would often knowingly articulate completely false stories. He also had an interesting ability to coin a phrase; he once suggested on television that I had 'an uncircumcised heart'. Until today, I am still unsure whether this was meant as a compliment or an insult. In any case, Mcebo behaved as if he had separate public and private personalities. This was to remain a feature of his engagement throughout the #FeesMustFall campaign.

The other person who clearly had a score to settle was Vuyani. His relationship with me dated back to the end of late 2013 when, as the convener of the EFF Student Command at Wits, he sought official student club/society status. Initially, he and a number of students undertook a sit-in of my office, demanding recognition as a student club/society. They had been denied access by the SRC, which was largely made up of individuals from both the South African Students Congress (SASCO) and Project W, on the grounds that they had missed the application deadline. I called in the SRC and requested them to consider registering the EFF as a student club/society. The SRC president, Shafee Verachia, petitioned Council expressing concern that I as vice-chancellor was interfering in matters that were the purview of the SRC. My response was that it was inappropriate for the SRC to use an administrative rationale to deny a constitutional obligation, namely the EFF's right to be recognised as a duly constituted political alternative. It was eventually decided that the EFF would be granted recognition and that this would be formally done through the office of the SRC, which reluctantly agreed to fulfil its governance obligation in this regard. Vuyani, of course, is of the view that the EFF's formal recognition arose as a result of the sit-in – this not only misrepresents the power of that demonstration, but also fails to recognise that people in authority can sometimes act out of political principle.

In late 2014 and early 2015, Vuyani was one of the few students who participated in a consultation exercise on the challenge of transformation and how a transformation programme should be thought through in relation to Wits. His ideas were particularly valuable not only because they presented a student perspective, but also because they highlighted both the anger that had emerged from the alienation of certain black students from the institution and the importance of class in understanding their experience. Soon thereafter, though, Vuyani's engagement became far more belligerent. It coincided with the EFF's deciding to compete in the SRC elections. The hallmark of the EFF's strategy seemed to be to demonstrate their radicalism through engaging in spectacle, foul language, and the breaking of institutional and legal rules. The first manifestation of this was when a number of EFF student members broke into a dining hall, assaulted and threatened staff, and basically helped themselves to food on the grounds that no one should be obliged to pay for what is an essential need. All the individuals involved in the incident were subsequently charged. Their campaign in the 2015 elections was incredibly belligerent, and seemed to centre on public statements about university officials that were often replete with expletives. This approach to campaigning culminated in the election debate where the EFF students were in the main guilty of creating circumstances that ultimately led to violence. Almost all of the EFF candidates standing for election were suspended – many, including Vuyani, until their disciplinary hearings.

Vuyani's suspension emanated from the fact that video footage depicted his involvement in a physical altercation. When I subsequently interviewed him to hear his side of the events, he simply refused to engage on the grounds that he did not have legal representation present. His suspension and that of others was endorsed by Council, as was the decision to suspend the EFF's operations at the university until such time as they renounced violence on campus. This prompted the national leadership into action, and Floyd Shivambu, the EFF's deputy president and a student leader at Wits in previous years, called me early on a Sunday morning in September. The next day, Randall Carolissen, Tawana Kupe (Deputy Vice Chancellor: Advancement, Human Resources and Transformation) and I met the EFF delegation, which comprised Floyd Shivambu (deputy president), Dali Mpofu (national chair), Godrich Gardee (secretary-general), Vuyani and a number of other student leaders. After quite a bit of haggling, the EFF did formally indicate that they did not condone violence, which allowed us to rescind the suspension of their operations. But when they requested us to also rescind the suspension of those who had been violent or acted in a manner that led to violence at the election debate, and allow them to participate in the SRC, we refused on principle. As a result, the meeting ended with Gardee suggesting that we had 'made an enemy of the government in waiting', and Floyd indicated that they would 'meet us on the streets'. Clearly the Student Command's exhibitionism and bravado had its roots in the parent body.

As indicated earlier, the courts did overturn the suspension on the students who had been violent or acted in a manner that led to violence at the election debate in August 2015, a decision that truly emboldened the affected students. In the evening after the court arrived at its decision, Lwazi Lushaba, a doctoral student, part-time lecturer and self-proclaimed guru of radical students on campus, came to see me, requesting that I meet the suspended students who had now been reinstated. I agreed to meet a delegation of the students in a meeting room at a particular time, since I had to be at another event across the city soon thereafter. Thirty minutes after the allotted time and just before I had to leave for my other appointment, Lwazi returned, demanding that I receive all of the aggrieved students on the concourse. I refused, not only since I now had to be elsewhere, but also because it went against our earlier agreement. Lwazi responded by suggesting that punctuality was a bourgeois sensibility and that it would be imprudent for me not to meet what he suggested was 'the revolutionary conscious vanguard of the student body'. I again refused and left, a decision that I am sure did not endear me to this cohort of students, of which Vuyani was an important leader. I am told he took the suspension personally, and his conduct throughout the #FeesMustFall events of the next two years would bear this out.

The third leader was Shaeera Kalla, who became SRC president after our decision to remove Mcebo. Shaeera had served as Mcebo's deputy and was responsible for almost all of the engagements with the executive in the early months of the SRC's tenure. Mcebo, it seemed, was less enamoured by the daily grind of SRC management and therefore delegated this to his able deputy. She, on the other hand, while relatively efficient, did not have a substantive independent political base within the ANC student structures, even if she did have it within the Muslim Students Association. Shaeera was one among a cohort of Muslim student activists, mainly women, who had become radicalised into the broader political struggle both as a result of their solidarity work on Palestine and because of an alliance established with SASCO, the ANC Youth League (ANCYL) and the Young Communist League (YCL) to form the PYA.

My initial interactions with Shaeera were relatively amiable and, while differences emerged given our respective positions and mandates, these were always addressed in a broadly respectful manner. Others in my executive team, however, and especially our chief financial officer

(CFO), Linda Jarvis, found her particularly duplicitous. Linda suggested that, in the fees negotiations, Shaeera would receive all the information required to make a decision, but would often lie to Council and me that it had not been made available. Eventually, I ensured that all e-mails were copied to me so that I could track whether the full set of financial information had been made available to the SRC. In the course of the next two years, the rest of the team, me included, did come to realise that Shaeera could never be trusted to stand by a decision to which she had been a party. Repeatedly, she would enter into an agreement or be informed of a decision, but would not subsequently acknowledge it.

Shaeera particularly incensed my wife Fatima after an interaction with us in December 2015 in Umhlanga, a seaside resort near Durban. We were on our morning walk when we bumped into her and a group of friends or family members. As we greeted each other and walked on, she turned and said, 'VC, I just wanted to say that I am sorry. It was never personal.' I smiled and informed her that it was perfectly okay and that there were no hard feelings. Yet in the year that followed, our relationship did indeed become more strained. Her attacks did seem to become personal, both on Twitter and in the rest of the public domain. This particularly angered Fatima, whom I constantly had to warn not to engage Shaeera if they were ever to come across each other.

The strained relationship seemed to have been sparked by an incident associated with the planning of Israel Apartheid week. This is an annual event hosted by the Palestinian Solidarity Committee (PSC) at Wits and always turns out to be a tense affair as supporters of the Palestinian struggle and Israeli state confront one another. Although I am particularly supportive of the Palestinian struggle, given the atrocities that the Israeli state has been party to, I am especially mindful of the importance of ensuring that all voices are allowed to be heard on campus. Moreover, since my first year at Wits in 2013 when the PSC disrupted a concert of an Israeli pianist, we have insisted that the events of Israel Apartheid Week must be negotiated by the Dean of Students with all parties, including the PSC, PYA, SRC and the South African Union of Jewish Students. In early 2016, however, Shaeera's behaviour and that of some of her colleagues was particularly scandalous. After having agreed to a set of events at specific times, they mischievously launched a set of activities a couple of days earlier, largely by duplicitously getting a sports club to reserve the library lawns for what was ostensibly to be a sporting event. The matter created a great deal of consternation; we exchanged particularly sharp words at a hastily convened meeting of all parties concerned. We as the executive were especially disturbed by the event as it compromised the security of the broader university. But the incident pointed to a bigger problem about means and ends. Too often, progressives involved in a noble struggle, but blinded by the righteousness of their cause, lose perspective, violate the rights of others, and adopt strategies and tactics that delegitimise the cause itself. This was a problem that was to recur repeatedly during the months ahead.

The final leader was Nompendulo, whom I knew least well at the fateful protest of October 2015. She had been elected SRC president just a few weeks earlier and was only to take office on 1 November. But she quickly became one of the most recognisable faces of the #FeesMustFall campaign, appearing on the cover of *Destiny* magazine and being feted by the media in the weeks that followed. Yet it quickly became apparent that Nompendulo was not emotionally ready for the glare of publicity that was to follow. Soon after coming to the attention of the broader public, she became the subject of media investigations highlighting her working relationship with the ANC. She quickly developed a reputation for being prickly and having an inflated ego, walking off live interviews on television and radio when she felt uncomfortable about the questions she was asked. Nompendulo was also subject to significant criticism from factions within the student movement, sometimes unfairly, because she was seen to have hogged the spotlight and made herself the spokesperson of the #FeesMustFall movement.

In the months that followed, however, I got to know Nompendulo well. I found her charming and amiable, and I personally got on well with her. She did disappoint me when she publicly defended the burning of the Law Library at the University of KwaZulu-Natal at a student consultation hosted by the Department of Higher Education and Training (DHET) on the grounds that it had only contained the archives of Roman-Dutch law. But aside from such isolated thoughtless comments, especially when she felt compelled to grandstand in front of the television cameras, Nompendulo was very pleasant and interacted well in face-to-face engagements. On one occasion, she even surprised Council by suddenly voluntarily expressing recognition of the progressive credentials of the vice-chancellor and the executive team, and saying that she was sure that this would be recognised in due course. By the end of her tenure, however, Nompendulo seemed utterly demoralised about the movement and her own experiences within it. This is perhaps why, when asked to comment on the protests at the end of 2016, she replied, 'I am willing to speak in about six months' time or a year. Only because [my view] won't be understood as I want it to be understood.'

These four student leaders were not the only ones to play a significant role, but they were perhaps the most recognisable faces associated with the #FeesMustFall movement. As such, they not only influenced the evolution of the movement both institutionally and nationally, but were also most dramatically impacted upon by this struggle and its consequences. Some of this was at the most obvious level. Other than Vuyani, almost all of the student leaders' academic performance was poorer than it should have been. But there were also more subtle impacts. Relationships both among them and with others in the university community changed significantly as a result of their behaviour and choices. Although they often claimed to represent the student community, this could increasingly be questioned as the struggle continued into 2016. And as they came to represent smaller and smaller sections of the student community, they reacted with hostility by either racially or ideologically pigeonholing all those who disagreed with them. The net effect was a self-reinforcing logic in which the leadership became increasingly marginalised from its own base, insisting that its constituency adapt to its choices rather than itself reflecting the views of those it was meant to represent.

These leaders also tended to separate their private and public personas artificially. While some separation between these two identities was sensible given their emergence into the public arena, such a distinction can become dangerous when it is pushed too far. I and many other executives of higher education have often bemoaned the tendency of student leaders to say one thing privately and hold another view publicly. We have spoken about how amiable individual leaders are in one-to-one interactions, but how scandalous their behaviour can be in a crowd or in front of television cameras. I have personally expressed the concern that 'some of the prominent leaders among this new generation of activists are displaying behavioural traits that are typical of the most venal of the current politicians'.

Some of these leaders have often claimed that they were unhappy about what they perceived as my 'brash responses' to their commentary in the public domain. Yet what they have not considered is the tenor of their own interactions in the public discourse. This is something that has not received sufficient reflection, even by journalists and scholars who rushed to publish the first books on #FeesMustFall. In an engagement with Rehad Desai, who produced a documentary on #FeesMustFall, I suggested that it was disingenuous for student leaders to complain about brashness when their own populist behaviour in the public domain often violated ethical parameters. I also suggested that politically it was untenable to expect higher education leaders to continue to remain silent in the face of continuous abuse. Sometimes leadership does require drawing a line in the sand by not only challenging the propagation of false information, but also holding those responsible for it accountable. Civility in public engagement was a matter that concerned me greatly, so much so that I was moved to reflect on it in a video communique to the university community at the end of the first semester in 2017. Sensing an increasing discomfort within the university community about personal interactions on a day-to-day basis, I appealed to students in particular, and the university community in general, about the importance of being measured in engagements with those whose views we do not share. I suggested that uncivil engagement only served to fracture the institutional community, the net effect of which would be the weakening of the university itself. 'Respect', I held, 'begets respect', and it is in our collective interest that we relate to each other 'as members of a common humanity'. This is an issue, I believe, that continues to require attention, not only in higher education, but more broadly in public discourse and engagement in South Africa.

These four leaders of the university's #FeesMustFall movement, then, were the ones who were locked in engagement with us during the night on the concourse, each alternating between rallying the hundreds of students who looked on from every available space on the ground floor and the balconies above, and then appealing to us on an individual level to rescind the fee increase. The executives and Council members present faced an impossible tension between a cause that we knew to be legitimate and a fiduciary responsibility that we could not abdicate.

Without a doubt, the #FeesMustFall movement has a legitimate complaint about the cost of university education. For more than two decades, ANC leaders and politicians have spoken about free education and its importance for addressing inequality and poverty, yet they have effectively created a set of circumstances and adopted policies that have led to the opposite. Soon after 1994, the ANC adopted a Higher Education Act that had as its core priority the massification of higher education. This was perfectly sensible, given the need to address the historical racial injustices of our past and develop the skills that are required to enable economic growth and inclusion. As a result, the university system expanded from about 420 000 students in 1994 to about 1.1 million in 2014. But there was no concomitant increase in university subsidies. The net effect has been a continuous decline in the per capita subsidy for students for two decades. Universities compensated for this by raising fees, the highest of which were at the research-intensive universities. These inevitably tended to be the historically white universities, which meant that the cost of university education became highly unequal across the higher education system.

Government did indeed establish the National Student Financial Aid Scheme (NSFAS), and subsequently expanded it more than fourfold to enable access to higher education by poorer students. But students could only qualify if their annual family income was less than R122 000. For those with an annual family income of more than R122 000, there were no public scholarships based on need – even though the full cost of study at Wits, inclusive of accommodation and subsistence, exceeded this amount. Students in this category had to rely on student loans from banks and other financial institutions, and their parents and/or families had to put up assets to access such loans. This created much distress, not only among the poor, but also within the working and middle classes. Of course, none of this seemed to dissuade politicians from both the ruling and opposition parties from continuing to parrot the call for free education. ANC party conferences that deliberated on the matter fudged differences, tweaking resolutions by attaching phrases such as 'for the poor' to the call for free education. But this did little to change party propaganda and politicians' rhetoric. Governing politicians were particularly disingenuous, playing to their audiences with calls for free education when they were on party platforms, but talking about realism, fiscal prudence and measuredness in their government capacities. The net effect was a crisis of expectations that began to build across society – and, in particular, among 'missing middle' students in the university system.

Vice-chancellors and higher education executives knew that the system was no longer sustainable and had been complaining for years about declining per capita subsidies. But the challenge had become particularly acute. Not only did the subsidy increase no longer match university expenditure as a result of currency fluctuations and inflationary pressures, but the DHET had also begun increasingly to top-slice an ever-diminishing subsidy grant for special projects. These projects, such as the capacity grant for the historically black universities (HBUs) and funding for the National Institute of Humanities, were important, but the problem was that they were being culled from a diminishing subsidy grant rather than constituting new monies negotiated from Treasury. This state of affairs would create huge tensions between government leaders and vice-chancellors. When the protests fully ignited, the ANC's Secretary-General Gwede Mantashe, Minister of Higher Education Blade Nzimande and even President Jacob Zuma would try to deflect attention to the vice-chancellors and universities without any sense of reflection on their own complicity in establishing a system of higher education in which there had to be an increasing reliance on higher student fees to maintain quality academic programmes and research projects within the universities. But this time, some of the vice-chancellors, me included, would publicly challenge these government leaders and highlight the systemic deficiencies that forced universities to raise student fees. The result was an uneasy relationship between government and university leaders, with each recognising the necessity of a productive engagement but also refusing to allow the other to deflect attention from their own complicity in enabling the crisis.

The matter came to a head in 2015. Even before the October protests, there were disruptions at the beginning of the year which suggested that the ground was beginning to shift: general economic difficulties and increasing university costs were beginning to bite into the pockets of students and their families. The protests at Wits at the beginning of 2015 were about admissions, fees and upfront payments. They were particularly strident, although manageable, and saw Mcebo's first rise to prominence. This was soon followed by protests at UCT that brought Chumani Maxwele to national attention after he threw faeces on the statue of Rhodes. These developments prompted many in university leadership into action through two separate initiatives – the first directed at the big banks, and the second at government. On the former, I initiated separate discussions within both the Wits University Council and the board of what was then Higher Education South Africa (HESA), now Universities South Africa (USAf), on the wisdom of trying to engage the banks in developing a low-interest loan scheme for students to enable access to universities. There were concerns, of course, in both forums about whether the banks would have the appetite to look beyond the narrow bottom line. The scepticism was more pronounced in the engagements of the HESA board, in part because the Wits Council had more bankers on it – including Cas Coovadia, head of the Banking Association of South Africa. But both the Wits Council and the HESA board eventually agreed that an exploration of the idea was warranted, and I wrote to the CEOs of the four largest banks requesting a meeting to discuss the idea.

All four banks were open to engagement. I personally met the CEOs of Standard Bank and First National Bank (FNB), Sim Tshabalala and Sizwe Nxasana respectively, had a telephone conference call facilitated by Cas Coovadia with Mike Brown, CEO of Nedbank, and met a team of senior Absa executives. The idea that I originally put to all of them was the possibility of providing student loans to students in sought-after professions – doctors, engineers, actuarial scientists and the like – as a means to attract them early as customers, because they were likely to become high-income earners. My hope was that universities could then redirect resources currently dedicated to such students to others who were unable to receive student loans as easily. It was Sim who then broached the idea of banks creating a student loan scheme. While he was open to my idea, he wanted to push me to consider an alternative: convince government to use the NSFAS money, standing at R10 billion per annum, as collateral that the banks could then use to raise money on the open markets. The net effect would be that the banks could raise enough resources to cover the fees of all students in the higher education system. The downside would, of course, be that students would come out of universities with debt; over time, this could balloon into a student debt crisis along the lines of that in the United States. I discussed this idea with Sizwe, who provided further detail on the ratios required to raise money on the open market and the kinds of interest rates required to sustain it. But he, too, was open to exploring the possibility, and was fortuitously appointed as chair of the NSFAS board by Blade Nzimande when he retired as CEO from FNB. When #FeesMustFall exploded onto the scene a few months later, Sizwe would take this idea and develop it into the Ikusasa Student Financial Aid Programme, a mechanism directed towards addressing the resourcing requirements for 'missing middle' students in higher education.

The second intervention was directed at President Zuma. For months the vice-chancellors had been engaging Minister Nzimande and the DHET about the challenge of the declining subsidy. While the minister and the DHET had acknowledged this, their constant refrain was that the problem lay with Treasury, which was just not open to making more resources available for higher education. When USAf broached the idea of directly engaging and lobbying Treasury and the Presidency, given that the DHET was not being successful in this regard, DHET officials would balk at the idea. Essentially, the DHET had become an obstacle to a more aggressive institutional challenge to the declining subsidy. Eventually, at the September 2015 USAf board meeting, the vice-chancellors decided that this state of affairs could no longer be allowed and that I would make a direct appeal on our collective behalf for a meeting with the president. Minister Nzimande was copied on the letter, but it was not addressed to him so that the DHET could not become an obstacle to the meeting. President Zuma agreed to meet the vice-chancellors on 30 September 2015, just over two weeks before #FeesMustFall erupted. Minister Nzimande was invited to the meeting, but was not thrilled that we had bypassed him. Gwebinkundla (Gwebs) Qonde, the director-general of the DHET, would subsequently grumble about many of us, complaining that we had been unappreciative of the political divides and had essentially given President Zuma the opportunity to go after Minister Nzimande. Yet what Gwebs did not truly appreciate was not only that his department was failing to arrest the decline in subsidy, but that our collective interest was less in the ruling party's palace intrigues and far more in how to address the challenge of declining subsidies, and therefore increasing fees, at our universities.

Only the USAf executive came to the meeting on 30 September. President Zuma was accompanied by a few officials and ministers, in particular the director-general in the Presidency, Cassius Lubisi. Our central message on the day was that the declining subsidy and the concomitant fee increases that we had been forced to levy were no longer tenable. I described the challenge as 'heading for the eye of the storm', a phrase that President Zuma was to remember some three weeks later when we met again in the midst of the #FeesMustFall crisis. Of course, we had anticipated that the storm would break in January 2016 when a new cohort of students would enter the university system. President Zuma allowed a significant amount of discussion at the meeting and also gave Minister Nzimande the opportunity to speak on the issue. Minister Nzimande's intervention was largely supportive of our concerns. In the end, it was agreed that a task team would be established with the director-generals of both the Presidency and the DHET, USAf representatives in the persons of me and Mvuyo Tom, vice-chancellor of the University of Fort Hare, and student representatives from the South African Union of Students (SAUS). The task team was to provide a report with recommendations to the president by the end of November 2015. The meeting concluded with a press conference at which President Zuma essentially announced the agreement.

Two days later, on 2 October, the Wits Council had to turn its attention to the issue of student fees. This was despite the fact that we were aware that the continuous double-digit fee increases were unsustainable. While I had been mandated to try to address the systemic challenge in this regard, the immediate imperatives of running the institution sustainably required us to increase fees. The percentage increase in subsidy for Wits stood at 4 per cent in an inflationary environment close to 6 per cent. The Council on Higher Education (CHE) estimates that higher education inflation (HEI) stands at approximately 2 per cent above normal inflation. This meant that the subsidy increase was 4 per cent below our annual increase in expenditure, which effectively required our student fee increase to be pitched at about 12 per cent. The Wits executive management's proposal to the Council meeting was an 11 per cent increase, whereas the SRC insisted that it should be below 10 per cent – and preferably 9 per cent. There was no suggestion of there being no increase at this Council meeting. This became a demand only after the protest was launched. In the hope of bringing the SRC on board, the chair of the Finance Committee, Theunie Lategan, proposed that Council agree to a 10.5 per cent increase, and this eventually won the day. The compromise meant that the university would sustain a budget deficit for the year. The SRC, however, voted against the proposal. Only one other party opposed the increase: David Dickinson.

David represented academics on the Council. His constituency was a separate category from the Senate, which comprises professorial academics, heads of schools and representatives of stakeholder groups. His membership of Council was meant to enable non-professorial academics to have a voice on Council. Dickinson was a former academic union leader at Wits and had been there for some years. His ideological orientation was far left and, like many of us, he believed that universities were seriously underfunded. But unlike most others on the Council, he was willing to sacrifice the principle of financial sustainability in the vain hope that doing so would provoke a systemic crisis and force government to capitulate. As he explained in the academics' report to Council of 2 October 2015, on why he voted against the fee increases in council:

> It was not an easy decision to make. Voting 'yes' to the increase, however uncomfortable, would secure stability, at least in regard to the institution's finance. Voting 'no' would throw budget planning into chaos, and force some difficult decisions to be made as to where the shortfall was to be found. I chose the latter option, on the grounds that double digit student fee increases have to be stopped at some point … Without a fuss, the logic of balancing books, with ever decreasing government support, will likely go on indefinitely but with enormously damaging social consequences. So, there was a fuss.

I was sceptical, of course, about this strategic approach, having witnessed its consequences at the University of Durban-Westville, where I had worked and been active in the 1990s. My scepticism also emanated from my previous research on the academic collapse of the then University of Transkei, whose management had followed a similar strategic approach. The problem with this approach was that it was devoid of any under-standing of the context and history of our higher education system. As a result, it ran the risk of destroying Wits as a research-intensive university.

David tended to write communiques after each Council meeting. Most Council members were critical of this; the chair had once intervened to prevent it. The concern was not only that it reflected on matters contained in the minutes, which risked creating confusion about Council decisions, but also that he often passed disparaging comments about other Council members obliquely. It seemed, to me, that David regarded himself as the only radical on the Council. In any case, fearing a damaging, polarised debate on academic freedom, I brokered an agreement with another union leader, David Hornsby, to allow David Dickinson to continue with his communiques – but only within strict parameters that did not contradict the minutes and were respectful of others. But David often did not honour the agreement; when he did so, it was only the letter of the agreement, but never its substantive intent.

In the months to follow, he would violate the agreement in multiple ways, ultimately forcing the Council to institute an investigation that culminated in a decision at the end of 2016 to withdraw his ability to produce communiques. Piqued at the decision, he resigned, which most Council members appeared, to me, to accept with much relief.

In any case, Council decided on a 10.5 per cent fee increase at its October 2015 meeting. I was uneasy about announcing the decision immediately, given the general foment in higher education institutions. I suggested that the secretariat hold off for a few weeks. But David insisted on detailing the increase in his communique. Given this situation, I reluctantly agreed that the secretariat could announce the increase. As I feared, this prompted the SRC to call for a protest the following week. In subsequent reflections on the protest, I highlighted the role David played in forcing our hand to announce the fee increase a few weeks before the final examinations in 2015. I do not believe that he caused the protest, of course. It would have happened anyway, given the structural pressures emanating from the system. My concern in highlighting his role was more to identify the dangers of his attitude, which a small cohort of far-left academics and activists shared. This attitude involved a willingness to use Wits University as a proxy for promoting a systemic crisis by advocating extreme solutions and being unwilling to consider trade-offs. The net effect of this zero-sum game, I feared, would be to destabilise the institution and plunge it into financial crisis, leading to a loss of top students and staff, and ultimately threatening its research-intensive character. The loss of the last cohort of research universities on the African continent would reconsolidate the inequalities in the global academy, where research institutions are concentrated in the global North and teaching institutions in the global South. In effect, it would create the very outcome that these scholars and activists were hoping to challenge. I would cynically come to refer to this group of scholars and activists as the Pol Pot brigade – one that would create an equality in poverty, in effect.

The night on the concourse was a dramatic, historic moment. Thousands of students confronted a vice-chancellor, the executive and senior members of the Council of one of the African continent's top universities about the costs of higher education. The executive and Council were essentially in concert, holding the line that the fee increase was unavoidable given existing university subsidies, and could only change if government was prepared to invest more in higher education. Effectively, the political economy of post-apartheid higher education was being put on trial – live, in front of the nation and the world.

The student leaders set the rest of the protesting community up for disappointment when they made the simple demand for us to rescind the fee increase. It was not possible for any of us to do this without violating our respective mandates and responsibilities, and none of us would have done so. For a part of the evening, students gave each Council member the opportunity to address them. Each member patiently explained why they could not rescind the fee increase; each one was subsequently howled down. The most painful moment may have been when Len Sizani stood to take the mic. The students applauded, assuming that a black African Council member would hold a different position. But when he, too, patiently explained why we could not make the concession, not only was he howled down, but there were shouts from some that he was an Uncle Tom and a stooge. I saw the pain in his eyes and wondered at the irony: a group of students who claimed to believe in decolonisation forgetting their commitment to ubuntu and their own cultural values by treating a man who was old enough to be their father or grandfather in this way. In this small incident, I also witnessed the racial chauvinism and intolerance implicit in a part of the student movement – a part who imagined one's views to be determined by the colour of one's skin. Anyone who did not accord with their ideological viewpoint was to be condemned and humiliated.

Other small incidents that evening exposed the implicit prejudices and/or lack of ethics of at least sections of the protest movement. One of the Council members – Adele Underhay, who was also a leader of the Administrative, Library and Technical Staff Association, which organised professional and administrative workers at Wits – had a health scare. We feared a heart attack brought on by the stress of the evening. Adele was taken to the ambulance that was on standby. At the ambulance, she was confronted by Shireen Ally and Prishani Naidoo, two academics in Sociology, who informed her that her leaving would be viewed as a sign of disrespect by the students on the concourse. They then escorted her back to the concourse. Only when the matter was brought to our attention and we insisted that she be allowed to leave was she allowed to go back to the ambulance and be taken to hospital. In another incident, a young master's student – Jafta Kolisang, who was to figure prominently in events of the following year – deliberately targeted Beatrys by blowing a vuvuzela in her ear and only backed off when I personally stood up to confront him. Both incidents reflect how activists involved in a struggle for social justice can, in the heat of the moment, lose their sense of humanity in relation to other human beings with whom they disagree. This would recur time and again in the months that followed.

But, to be honest, these were isolated incidents and did not define the evening. Overall, students were good-natured; hundreds of little conversations happened between the students and me, and between other Council members and students. Cathi described her evening as one in which she 'learned an enormous amount about their (ordinary students') perspective, as well as trying to explain (to them) the financing processes and limits' that informed Council's decision in this regard. I recall Zimitri Erasmus, an academic in Sociology, coming over at one point to check whether I was okay and whether I needed anything. Several other students did so as well. I experienced many similar small acts of kindness, as did the others. The atmosphere was generally amiable, if a little boisterous.

The problem was that we were at a stalemate. The student leaders had effectively cornered themselves into making a demand that we could simply not deliver on. I recall Mcebo coming to me at some point that evening with a plea: 'Please just give us something so that we can all go home.' It was quite a way beyond midnight. I told him that we could not rescind the fees, and he accepted this, but asked for some concession to be made. Slowly, small conversations began at the margins, between Mcebo, Vuyani, Randall and me. I recall that none of the conversations involved Nompendulo or Shaeera, but I do know that they were part of the subsequent leadership consultations. At various moments of the evening, I had conversations with Ahmed Veriava, who taught in the Politics department at Wits, was a supporter of the student struggle, and served as a broker in engagements with student leadership. In fits and starts, we slowly arrived at a provisional agreement.

The agreement we documented essentially allowed us all to call it a night and live to fight another day. We agreed to convene Council and consider a revision of the fee increase. We also agreed that Council would report to a university assembly on Monday at noon. The term 'university assembly' would subsequently become a matter of contention. There was no such term in our official lexicon. We do have a General Assembly, which is chaired by our chancellor and called on very special occasions to pronounce on one or other matter of national importance. We have only held a few General Assemblies in the life of the university. But this was not what the students wanted. They essentially expected us to report to a gathering similar to the one that was there that evening. This terminology preoccupied us in Council deliberations for a while. At one point in the evening, the executive and Council members asked for time out and went to one side of the concourse to caucus and deliberate on the provisional agreement. We quickly came to a collective consensus; it was then up to the student leadership to sell the deal. Given that the student leadership had promised a rescinding of the fee increase, it was not an easy sell. Ultimately, it fell to Mcebo. After a bit of cajoling and political grandstanding, he won support for the agreement.

At just after 04h00, we agreed to call it a night. The student leaders – Mcebo and Vuyani in particular – and many of the other students came to shake hands with all of us at the front. When Mcebo came to me, I said to him, 'You guys have overplayed your hand. We can't have another engagement like this again, and no other VC would agree to one.' He shrugged and smiled, exhausted by the day's and night's proceedings. We all were exhausted. After arrangements were made to transport students to the residences on the other campuses, and when I had informed the rest of the Council members that we would be in touch during the course of the day about a meeting over the weekend, we parted ways.

In the days that followed, many would congratulate me for staying all night and engaging the students. But others, including some vice-chancellors and political leaders, were critical. In the months ahead, Derrick Swartz, vice-chancellor of the Nelson Mandela University and a noted activist in his own right, and I would have heated debates about the wisdom of my strategy on that fateful day. In retrospect, I think it was a mixed blessing. Our decision to stay earned us political kudos that would be useful in the coming months. Students could not legitimately claim that we were not prepared to engage. But it is also true that some student leaders seemed to have interpreted our willingness to spend the night as a sign of weakness; in the year ahead, we would have to make hard decisions in this regard.

I went home immediately. As soon as I saw her, I knew that Fatima had not slept. Irfan, my eldest son who was at UCT, had been feeding her with information throughout the night through friends who were on the concourse. Zidaan, my youngest son, was more complacent about the events and had gone to bed some hours earlier. Fatima and I had a cup of tea and I went to bed at about 06h00, falling into a restless sleep. I remember thinking, as I dozed off, that Fatima had paid a far greater emotional price. At least I had had the advantage of adrenalin coursing through my veins. Fatima and others had been watching the events on television, unsure what was going on and whether their loved ones were safe. The many calls from family and friends heightened her unease. It saddened me that Fatima should suffer the consequences of a job I had decided to take. Is it fair to our loved ones to accept these responsibilities?

I also sensed that, as the night on the concourse had ended, the terms of engagement had shifted fundamentally. The historic moment was only beginning; higher education would never be the same again.

2

A movement divided

I WOKE a few hours later, at about 11h00. I went for a run to clear my head and think things through: how to respond to a legitimate social struggle on one hand, while avoiding an eventual decline in the university's academic standards on the other. I was all too aware that the road to hell was paved with good intentions.

After a long shower, I discussed scheduling a Council meeting with Carol Crosley. We needed to develop a formal position on the students' demand, even though we had collectively insisted that meeting it was fiscally unsustainable. We agreed to let everyone take Saturday to recover, and scheduled the meeting for Sunday at 11h00. The meeting was held in the Council Chamber on the 11th floor of Solomon Mahlangu House. It was attended by 25 of the 29 members. Shaeera Kalla in her capacity as SRC president did not attend, although the Postgraduate Association representative, Zuhayr Tayob, was there. He declared a conflict of interest, stating that he was there explicitly to make the students' case on the matter and that he would be reporting to the other student leaders. There was a concern raised about whether there was adequate official student representation, but the Council nevertheless felt that it could not abdicate its responsibility and proceeded with the meeting on the assumption that management would apprise the SRC of the outcome of the deliberations.

Two sets of issues dominated the Council meeting: the concessions that were possible regarding the fee increase, and an esoteric conversation on the meaning of 'university assembly'. The university had only a General Assembly, preceded by an engagement of all of the institution's stake-holders in which they reach a collective consensus on the issue at hand. The first time such an event had been called was in 1959, to protest the state's imposition of the Extension of University Education Act, which formalised the segregation of higher education. There was another one in early 1992, two years before South Africa's first democratic election, when the university community pronounced in favour of a democratic society. In 2001, at the height of officialdom's Aids denialism, the university condemned the state's approach and pronounced in favour of the provision of antiretroviral drugs at a General Assembly. The final event was in 2013, during my tenure, when Nelson Mandela passed away and the university held a memorial service to honour the life of its most illustrious son.

The matter preoccupied Brian Bruce, our deputy chair of Council. Brian, a previous CEO of the construction group Murray & Roberts, was concerned about the fact that we had committed to a 'university assembly' in the document. He recognised that the conditions on the concourse had been trying, and that it was understandable that people had not picked up the discrepancy, but he was worried about the legal implications. I was more sanguine, seeing the document as a political rather than a legal agreement. I suspected that what the students had meant by a university assembly was essentially a reconvening of the student meeting on the concourse, which we had committed to addressing on Monday at noon. In the end, we need not have bothered, for the matter was overtaken by events on the ground. It was to re-emerge, however, a year later when we invoked the General Assembly as a mechanism to break a deadlock with protesting students.

The more substantive issue at the Council meeting was the concessions the university could make regarding the fee increase. Here again, the debate revolved around the institution's fiscal sustainability. We had little room to manoeuvre. The 10.5 per cent increase had been decided against the backdrop of a declining economy and above-inflation increases in expenditure. Electricity price hikes were firmly in double-digit figures and the value of the rand had declined by 22 per cent in the previous year or two, dramatically increasing the costs of library journals, books and research equipment. Coupled with all of this was the fact that the Wits ICT network needed to be overhauled at a cost of R500 million if we were to remain competitive in teaching and research.

In the ensuing debate, we considered instituting an austerity budget and cutting back on all non-essential expenditure. It was decided that I would continue to engage government about helping to make up the financial shortfall. I also personally committed to redirecting to poor and academically deserving students any variable pay, based on performance, which was due to me in 2015. I had done something similar every previous year during my tenure at Wits, dedicating 50 per cent of my variable pay to students in need. After a long debate, it was decided that the fee increase would be suspended and negotiations with the student leadership would be reopened. Council chose a negotiating team and called on the student leadership to do the same. There was a commitment that all financial and other information would be made available to the students' negotiating team.

We discussed one final matter before concluding the meeting. Beatrys Lacquet expressed her concern about using the concourse again for the meeting with the students, because it violated university policy as well as national health and safety regulations. It was one thing to have been part of the student protest on Friday. It was completely another for university leadership to violate the health and safety regulations knowingly. We made a call to Shaeera to express our concerns about the use of the concourse and to recommend that the meeting be held on the piazza outside the Great Hall. Shaeera agreed; after a short discussion on the security protocols to be followed, the Council meeting ended.

The next morning, Monday 19 October, found me at the office early with some members of the Council ExCo – Randall Carolissen, Brian Bruce, Cas Coovadia and Len Sizani – planning the announcement to the students. Beatrys was to call us just before noon, and security would escort us to the steps of the Great Hall. Of course, we anticipated that there might be an attempt to repeat Friday's events, and had put measures in place to prevent this.

We had also begun to receive reports that protests had started at universities across the country. Max Price, the vice-chancellor of UCT, was not in the country, but I had received reports that students there had started boycotting classes and that deputy vice-chancellors had been taken hostage and forced to sit on the floor. There were similar reports from Fort Hare, KwaZulu-Natal, Limpopo, Nelson Mandela Metropolitan, Pretoria, Rhodes, Western Cape and even Stellenbosch universities. I had spoken to a number of the vice-chancellors during the morning and there was no doubt that the #FeesMustFall movement had begun to spread. This did not bode well for the outcome of our engagement with the students.

Just before noon, Beatrys came to the office with a few security officers to escort us to the Great Hall. Suddenly, we received a report from security at the Great Hall telling us to wait, because students were refusing to be addressed there. Shaeera had agreed to the venue, but was incapable of carrying the students with her. This was to happen repeatedly in the coming days. We were also informed that a security officer had overheard an interaction between a senior academic and some students about surrounding executive management and Council members and compelling them to agree to a new set of concessions. Soon, we heard that the more belligerent student protesters were pushing through the security cordon, and then that they had broken the locks to get into the Solomon Mahlangu concourse. This breach of the agreement and violation of health and safety regulations could not be allowed to continue. Council ExCo refused to address the students and all of us left the premises.

Council ExCo and management reassembled at the offices of the Banking Association of South Africa, where Cas Coovadia was the

CEO. Here, we deliberated on our next steps, which essentially revolved around how to reinstitute security and get the academic programme back on track. In between these deliberations, I dealt with a range of media interviews, supported by university spokesperson Shirona Patel. We faced an all-out media war: student leaders were misrepresenting our decision not to address them as a violation of Saturday morning's agreement. I had to correct the facts and clarify that we had agreed with the leadership to a meeting outside the Great Hall, and that the continuous violation of health and safety regulations could not be allowed to continue. Disconcertingly, we were now receiving reports that students had taken their march off campus and were harassing motorists. In one case, a vehicle had been overturned as the driver had tried to drive through the crowd of protesters. Mercifully, no one had been injured; the motorist had been rescued and taken away by the police.

During the meeting, I got a call from officials at USAf indicating that Minister Blade Nzimande had called a meeting with the vice-chancellors and student leaders in Cape Town the next morning. Clearly, the quickly spreading protest had begun to concern government, and they were suddenly keen to fashion a settlement that would bring it to an end. Management and Council ExCo agreed that I should go to Cape Town and that Andrew Crouch should manage matters at Wits. We hoped that some resources would be made available to facilitate a national resolution that would bring the crisis to an end.

I flew to Cape Town on Monday evening and stayed at the Townhouse Hotel near Parliament, where the meeting was to be held. The vice-chancellors began Tuesday with a caucus in which we each reported on the protests on our campuses, then developed a consensus view on the causes of the protest and what to do. We collectively held the view that, since universities had been forced to declare double-digit fee increases because of below-inflation subsidy increases, government should come to the party by making a contribution to defray institutional costs. The Minister and the DHET were not difficult to convince. They, too, had recognised for some time that the per capita subsidy decline was not sustainable, and had made repeated proposals to Treasury in this regard. But Treasury officials had, until then, held the view that, because 55 per cent of university students did not graduate, the sector was not providing sufficient returns on investment.

The Minister first convened separate meetings with the student leadership and the vice-chancellors, and then chaired a joint meeting with both constituencies. The students were represented by the SAUS, a national body representing the official student leadership on all university campuses. One of the leaders was Tebogo Thothela, a Wits student and a president of its SRC prior to my arrival. He was a thoughtful and sensible leader with whom one could have a rational conversation and come to a productive outcome. But he was also a member of SASCO, ANCYL and the YCL, as were many of the other SAUS leaders. Despite the rhetorical bravado of some of them, they were confronting a legitimacy crisis: they were seen as too closely aligned to, and therefore susceptible to co-option by, the national ANC leadership.

The joint meeting of the vice-chancellors and the student leadership, chaired by the minister, resolved to propose a national fee increase of 6 per cent, with the state making up the difference. This would have meant that students would have to pay an inflationary increase of 6 per cent, while the DHET would have been responsible for the 4 to 4.5 per cent difference. The proposal came from Nzimande and was generous in that it constituted post-budget expenditure and would therefore require the DHET to effect cuts elsewhere. It was to be sold to the student public by indicating that, since it was largely in line with inflation, in effect it constituted no real increase in student fees. But in retrospect, the proposal was too nuanced – and, frankly, too little of a concession too late in the political game.

The minister did not cover himself in glory either in the press conference immediately after the meeting. In what was an attempt to be lighthearted, but became one of those gaffes that politicians tend to make, Minister Nzimande announced the inflation-linked fee increase proposal and then stated – on live TV – that, 'If the students don't accept this, we will start our own movement #StudentsMustFall.' I cringed as he uttered the words, fearing that they would be completely misread in this volatile political moment. Mercifully, while I was required in my capacity as chair of USAf to sit at the main table with the minister, I was not in the camera frame when the statement was made. He did laugh after the statement, indicating that it was an attempt at humour, but it was nevertheless interpreted as callous and dismissive. A meme of the incident immediately went viral and the statement was condemned by both student leaders and observers.

Soon after the press conference, I left for Johannesburg. By the time I landed at OR Tambo International Airport, reports were coming in that the student leadership had rejected the proposal and were planning to march on Parliament the next day. We also began picking up on social media that some student leaders at Wits were encouraging a march to Savernake, where I lived. We quickly decided to move Fatima, Zidaan and me out of the house. Fatima was not keen; we had a huge argument over the matter. 'Zidaan is in the middle of his Grade 11 examinations and it is just not fair to put him through having to move out of the house,' she argued. I sympathised, but feared that we would have to have stringent security at Savernake and that, if the protesting students did indeed march to the house and try to occupy it, someone would get hurt. Eventually, Fatima relented. We packed in a hurry. In the meantime, Kanina Foss, my chief of staff, arranged an apartment in Killarney. Late that evening, we moved out of Savernake to spend the first of many nights outside of our official home.

Our new abode immediately became a problem. Both residents and staff recognised me easily, which compromised our security, so we had to move out the next day. Imraan Valodia, the dean of Commerce, Law and Management, whose family at the time still stayed in Durban, offered us his more discreet apartment and volunteered to move into the Killarney one. And so our second move happened on the Wednesday morning. It was in Imraan's apartment that Fatima and I sat and watched students from the universities in Cape Town march on Parliament during the October Medium Term Expenditure Review. We had had an argument with Irfan that morning because he had insisted on going to the march. I had no objection in principle. But I was concerned about his security if it were to come out that he was my son. In the end, we lost the battle; we watched the TV coverage with trepidation as police repelled students with teargas and stun grenades as they tried to overrun the parliamentary precinct.

The scenes outside Parliament were not pretty. Earlier, students had demanded that Minister Nzimande address them, but then refused to hear him out. Again, he had done himself no favours by trying to address them from behind the parliamentary barricades. By the end of Wednesday afternoon, 30 students had been arrested, including the sons of Frank Chikane, Archbishop Thabo Makgoba and Max Price. Student activists Chumani Maxwele and Lindsay Maasdorp were also among those arrested. One of the more positive features of the march was its non-racial character. Black and white students, rich and poor, marched together for the collective goal of a no fee increase and an accessible higher education system. It was to represent the high point of the social movement and would later be looked upon nostalgically.

Parliament was criticised for continuing proceedings after the protesting students had been dispersed, but the incident clearly rattled government. Late on Wednesday afternoon, I received a call from President Zuma's spokesperson, Bongani Ngqulunga, who broached the idea of the president convening a meeting of all stakeholders. He also asked what I thought would be the best response. I replied without hesitation: concede the 0 per cent, but this would have to be made up by the state. The next day, when it was announced that the president convened a meeting of all internal stakeholders on Friday morning, USAf released a public statement making the same call, that government concede to the protesting students and make up the lack of increase in fees.

Thursday was also eventful. This time, students from the University of Johannesburg (UJ) and Wits marched on Luthuli House. It was here where the fateful standoff between student protesters and Gwede Mantashe occurred. Mantashe had been asked to receive a memorandum and EFF student leader Vuyani Pambo tried to humiliate him by demanding that he sit down on the ground. Mantashe refused; it was only the intervention of ANC-aligned Mcebo Dlamini that broke the logjam. The memorandum demanded that funds be released both for effecting the no fee increase in 2016 and for the insourcing of all vulnerable workers, and that a plan be put together for free, quality higher education. The proceedings ended peacefully and were marked with a memorable picture of the four Wits leaders – Nompendulo, Mcebo, Shaeera and Vuyani – leading the march. The photo would be emblazoned on the cover of the *Financial Mail*.

I spent Thursday night at the Sheraton Hotel, opposite the Union Buildings in Pretoria. The vice-chancellors and chairs of council were to caucus there early the next morning in preparation for our meeting with the president. We kicked off at about 07h00 and were driven to the Union Buildings at 08h00. There we were given a venue to have a second caucus during which, together with the chairs of council, we developed our collective recommendations for addressing the crisis. Our proposal was premised on the recognition that the double-digit fee increases were prompted by the failure of state subsidies to keep up with higher education inflation (HEI). The CHE assessed that HEI was approximately 2 per cent above consumer price inflation because universities had special expenditure requirements, including highly specialised staff, academic journals and research equipment. Inflation was at 6 per cent per annum in 2015 and many institutions had received a state subsidy increase of only 4 per cent. In this context, universities had compensated for the real decline in per capita subsidy by increasing fees above 10 per cent. This was to keep institutions financially stable and avoid a decline in the quality of our academic offerings.

Yet the vice-chancellors and chairs of council also recognised the legitimacy of the students' concerns. Double-digit fee increases were no longer sustainable, especially given most families' dire economic circumstances. The only option, we proposed, was for the state to make available the resources for effecting a no fee increase. The vice-chancellors also raised two other concerns. The first related to the infrastructural deficit that some universities, especially the HBUs, had inherited. We held that this had to be acknowledged and addressed in future financial arrangements. The second concern related to the importance of institutional autonomy and academic freedom. While some government officials and politicians were sanguine about these constitutional principles, and some student leaders had even asked for them to be scrapped, we collect-ively held that they were important. We had warned activists of the dire fate of universities in other parts of the continent, and the fact that their academics and students now bemoaned the loss of their freedom and autonomy. All in all, our request was that the state accede to the demands of the protesting students, but that this be done in a manner that enabled respect for universities' academic freedom and autonomy.

It is worth noting that the no fee increase was unanimously support-ed by the vice-chancellors and the chairs of council who were present at the Union Buildings on that fateful Friday morning of 23 October. This is worth underscoring because, since then, some of the vice-chancellors, together with officials from the Democratic Alliance, have questioned the wisdom of the zero per cent fee concession by President Zuma. They hold that it created a precedent that students insisted on in ensuing years, which was financially unsustainable. They have also suggested that the president's concession represented a significant in-cursion into the governance authority of university councils, eroding the autonomy of universities.

I remain sceptical of this critique. Not only is it decontextualised from the political circumstances of that moment, but it also ignores the fact that President Zuma only made the decision after a full consultation with students and vice-chancellors, all of whom supported the concession. Moreover, the president's concession was framed as a recommendation that would only take effect once councils had formally agreed to it. The decision also amounted to the injection of an additional R1.9 billion subsidy into the university system at a moment when vice-chancellors and chairs of council were bemoaning the fact that their institutions were grossly underfunded, although it must be said that the subsequent distribution of these resources penalised institutions like Wits and UCT. Perhaps most importantly, the assumption that setting national fees necessarily erodes universities' academic freedom and institutional auton-omy must be questioned. After all, this is standard practice in many Western democracies, including the UK, yet British universities and academics are not perceived to have lost their autonomy and freedom. Ultimately, we need to understand that academic freedom and institutional autonomy operate in democracies within a framework of social accountability.

In any case, the president's meeting convened at about 10h00 that morning. After we had all handed in our mobile phones, which were duly locked away – a measure I assume was necessary to ensure that discussions were not communicated to others outside the meeting – the proceedings began, with President Zuma introducing the challenge at hand. Represented in the room were not only the vice-chancellors and chairs of council, but also all the student formations, including those of the opposition parties – the Democratic Alliance Student Organisation (DASO) and EFF Student Command – and a number of Cabinet ministers, including those of Higher Education and Training, Science and Technology, Social Development, Intelligence and Police. In his introductory comments, President Zuma described us as being in 'the eye of the storm' and turned to me to acknowledge that I had warned of this moment using the same description at our meeting three weeks earlier.

He then allowed the student groups to articulate their concerns. They all highlighted the financial burden that fees imposed on students and their families. He gave me an opportunity to respond on behalf of the vice-chancellors and chairs of council, and I articulated the collective position we had developed that morning. This was followed by a general discussion in which many others, including students, vice-chancellors and ministers, spoke. It soon became apparent that no one really objected to the proposal of a concession being made to the students, although some student leaders and Cabinet ministers made belligerent remarks about university executives.

As we spoke, enormous crowds massed outside the Union Buildings. The student groups that had planned to march to the Union Buildings that morning were supported by many societal stakeholders, including the political parties. The Wits executive had not only encouraged the university's academics and professional and administrative staff to support the march, but had also personally come out. Initial reports suggested an almost festive, carnival atmosphere, but some students soon started getting restless. We heard teargas canisters being fired in the distance. A number of the meeting's participants urged the president to go outside and announce the decision. Eventually, he agreed, and the meeting was closed. As we broke, we saw distant plumes of black smoke.

As officials ushered the president away and made preparations for the announcement, we all returned to wait at the Sheraton. The lobby was abuzz; students were milling around in groups, political notables were huddled in whispers, and there was a general sense of anticipation in the air. Most of the vice-chancellors sat together, occasionally engaging students and officials. I recall having a spirited but pleasant conversation with a number of students, and taking selfies afterwards. But underlying this almost festive atmosphere was unease. Small groups of students in the gardens outside the Union Buildings, mostly associated with the EFF, were taunting police and burning tyres. Every now and then, the police responded with teargas. We all sensed that matters could easily get out of hand.

Then Zuma came onto the TV screens to announce the no fee increase concession. We had all expected him to address the students. Instead, he simply announced the decision to the journalists in the Union Buildings. This was the opportunity for the small group of irate students to turn violent. Mobile toilets were set alight and police were stoned. The police responded with teargas and stun grenades, and the protesters scattered. In the midst of this, Sizwe Mabizela, the vice-chancellor of Rhodes, ran into the crowds outside the Sheraton to try to calm tempers. He phoned me from within the mayhem to say that the police were overreacting. I phoned Cassius Lubisi, the director-general in the Presidency, to complain that a moment of celebration and collective victory was being squandered. His reply was that the seat of state – the Union Buildings – was under attack, which essentially constituted a coup. It could not be allowed to stand. I protested, saying that a small group of anarchists were looking to create mayhem, and that the police's overreaction was letting them get their way. Cassius promised to look into it, but I knew then that the moment was lost. The matter would be resolved by force, by both the police and the small group of violent protesters for whom the struggle for free education was merely a pretext to create general political mayhem.

When I went outside to observe the events, I came across a few scared Wits students. In the mayhem, they had become separated from the rest of the group. They reported that a small group of EFF students from the Soshanguve campus of the Tshwane University of Technology (TUT) had attacked their bus and threatened to set it alight, accusing them of being privileged and aloof from the protests. I phoned Ahmed Veriava, who I knew was assisting with the organisation of Wits students in the march. He confirmed that there had been an incident, but assured me that it was under control and that they were getting the students together to head back to campus. I returned to the Sheraton, where I lamented the lost opportunity with some colleagues for a short while, then decided to call it a day. En route back, I received confirmation from Prishani Naidoo, another Wits lecturer, that all of our students were safe and headed back to campus. I was relieved, but also irritated; I sensed implicitly that an opportunity had been lost to bring a decisive political end to the national student protest that had emerged just over a week earlier.

The Wits executive decided not to begin the academic programme immediately on Monday. We assumed that there would be divisions among the protesting students and that some would either not be keen, or be under political instruction not to return to the academic programme. This turned out to be largely correct. The divisions among the student leadership emerged as soon as they returned to campus, and were accentuated after reports emerged that there had been a meeting between the PYA leadership and some emissaries from the ANC that Friday evening. There were suggestions that Shaka Sisulu, grandson of one of the ANC's most beloved elder couples, Walter and Albertina Sisulu, had engaged the PYA leadership with a view to taking charge of the student movement and getting students back to class. Scraps of paper with scribbled notes from the meeting gave some credence to the allegations. There were also suggestions that money had changed hands, with R40 000 having been made available to assist the process. The allegations split the student movement at Wits, delegitimised its SRC (which was PYA-aligned), and complicated management's future efforts to consult with students.

There is no doubt that government, and therefore the ANC, were keen to get students back to class. The protests had become an embarrassment to the ruling party. Indeed, the ANC had, for some days, been intervening to try to influence the protests. At the behest of some of the ANC-aligned students, Luthuli House had arranged for food to be distributed to protesters by the NGO Gift of the Givers. So confident was the ANC that the protests were now in hand that Blade Nzimande had personally told me at the Union Buildings, 'You should not be too concerned about the march because the Congress-aligned student structures are now in charge.' There is some legitimacy, therefore, to the complaints by some student leaders that the ruling party was meddling in the student movement.

But the ANC was not the only party doing this. The EFF was as complicit in trying to manipulate the student leadership. It continued to influence the direction of the student protests through its own student leaders, Vuyani being the primary figure at Wits. This is why Vuyani was so keen to make Gwede Mantashe sit down on the ground at Luthuli House. This incident was inspired not by #FeesMustFall, but the EFF's desire for spectacle and the humiliation of leading figures of the ruling party. This is why Julius Malema so proudly highlighted the event on the BBC current affairs programme *Hard Talk* in December 2015. Indeed, the EFF's manipulation of the student movement was most cogently revealed in the same interview when Malema bragged about how his people – Vuyani and Mcebo – had led the movement. 'Look at the picture of Wits where it started,' Malema says. 'There is guy [*sic*] called Vuyani and Mcebo. Vuyani is the EFF leader and Mcebo is the ANC Youth League leader. Both of them were inspired by this leadership of the EFF.' Of course, this was at a time when Malema believed Mcebo was about to switch sides to the EFF. Little did he realise that Mcebo was playing the EFF as much as he was being manipulated by its commander in chief. In the end, Mcebo remained in the ANC, even though his ideas – and sometimes even his behaviour – were indistinguishable from his colleagues across the political aisle.

What all of this suggests is that the student movement was not divided as a result of the interventions of vice-chancellors and executive management at universities, as Vuyani and other student leaders were fond of arguing. Rather, #FeesMustFall became divided by student leaders' own complicity in the political agendas of their respective political parties to capture the movement. Rekgotsofetse Chikane, another student leader and the son of Frank Chikane, perhaps best describes the variety of political factions within #FeesMustFall and their arbitrariness and complexity in his book *Breaking a Rainbow, Building a Nation: The Politics Behind #MustFall Movements*. In a sense, the #FeesMustFall movement and the universities were merely a political football for the ANC and EFF in what, by then, had become a personal and emotional battle between contending political elites.

Be that as it may, the central issue that now confronted the Wits executive was when to begin the academic programme. Throughout the weekend, the executive made attempts to consult the SRC. But the SRC was reluctant to engage and incapable of making a decision. Having been caught in political subterfuge with emissaries from the ANC, the SRC members were terrified of being branded as sellouts, so they abrogated their responsibility to provide any level of leadership. In the meantime, stakeholders from outside the political parties were beginning to organise. An online petition calling on the university to begin the academic programme garnered more than four and a half thousand signatures from students, far in excess of anything that the student political parties were able to put together. Perhaps because of this, and the fact that the executive had, by then, indicated to the SRC that it would proceed unilaterally with beginning the academic programme, the SRC eventually relented. We jointly agreed to resume classes on Wednesday 28 October.

Management also decided to convene a meeting of the Senate the next morning so that we could brief the senior professoriate on the events of the past week and decide on a restructured academic programme. The Senate meeting was a milestone in three distinct ways. First, there was an attempt to disrupt the meeting from within the academy itself. Largely organised by a group of far-left scholars in the Faculty of Humanities, a number of junior academics, and some retired ones, gatecrashed the Senate meeting and demanded to be part of the deliberations. This was ostensibly part of a political strategy by this group of academics, aligned with the student protesters, to reject the academic governance structures of the university and reimagine them so that all substantive decisions would be made in an assembly where students would be in the majority. In the midst of this 'academic invasion', a compromise was quickly fashioned. I requested the 'academic invaders' to step out of the chambers temporarily while I sought the permission of the Senate to allow them in. This was quickly granted, even though there were some dissenting voices, and the group was then formally invited in to be part of the deliberations.

Second, the meeting was truly astonishing in that this group of far-left academics, led by some of the senators and, in particular, David Dickinson, proceeded in the most patronising of tones to lecture the rest of the senators about their complicity in 'whiteness' and their lack of sensitivity to the decolonisation project. The astounding feature of this engagement was that the ones lecturing the Senate were not only white, but, in many cases, also expatriates. There was not a hint of irony in their intervention, and I could not help but think of two texts that I had come across in my political past. The first was a text produced by Nosipho Majeke (Dora Taylor) of the Unity Movement titled *The Role of the Missionaries in Conquest*, which highlights how those filled with the righteousness of their cause can so easily be led astray and enable political outcomes that are diametrically opposed to what they ostensibly stand for. The second was Vladimir Lenin's *Left-Wing Communism: An Infantile Disorder*, a polemical text in which the leader of Bolsheviks lays into ultra-left traditions in the communist movement for their failure to appreciate the importance of tactics and strategies and the necessity of compromise in the struggle to advance the revolution.

Finally, not long into the meeting I was informed that a group of students were trying to break into the Senate chamber. They had somehow been informed that the Senate meeting was underway, and wanted to disrupt it. Security had locked the chamber; the students were now banging on the doors and trying to break them down. The incident was also noteworthy because of an altercation between Beatrys Lacquet from the executive management team and Kelly Gillespie, an academic from the Anthropology department who was part of the far-left cohort. Kelly's partner, Leigh-Ann Naidoo, was a doctoral student at Wits and a leader among the student protesters. Beatrys found Kelly banging the door from the foyer, trying to break it. There were a number of witnesses to their physical altercation, which was also caught on our cameras; this became the subject of much controversy in the days that followed. By this time, I had adjourned the meeting and informed the senators who would like to leave that they could do so from the rear entrance. Quite a few did, but many others remained. I then instructed security to open the doors and awaited the influx.

Within minutes, the chamber was overrun with protesting students. After the initial confusion, I asked the students what they wanted. They expressed disquiet at decisions being made without their involvement, and demanded that the meeting be chaired by someone other than me. Eventually, they decided on Lwazi Lushaba as the chair. The meeting proceeded incoherently, until it was decided that the space was too cramped and the meeting was shifted to the concourse. I went along and listened to the complaints of the protesters, some students, other outsourced workers and yet other academics. The substance of the complaints revolved around the injustice of outsourcing services. There were calls for the termination of all legal contracts with service providers, the immediate insourcing of all employees working in outsourced service companies, the dissolution of the position of vice-chancellor, the disbanding of the Senate and Council, and the reimagining of the university so that all substantive decisions were made in an assembly with all stakeholders, including the students. I took copious notes. After about an hour, I departed, and the meeting continued on the concourse.

The Senate meeting was significant precisely because it heralded the beginning of a backlash against much of the far left. Until then, much of the Senate had simply resigned itself to the rhetorical polemics of some of the far-left senators, allowing them the illusion that they spoke for the academy. But the active disruption of the Senate and the political arrogance of some of the chief architects of the incident galvanised other senators into active engagement. No longer would the far left remain unchallenged by other senators. Their views would be actively contested, and a progressive pragmatism began to dominate Senate deliberations – one in which achieving socially just outcomes was still important, but in which these outcomes were to be achieved in a way that preserved the essence of what it meant to be a university and recognised that we operate in the world that exists, rather than one we wish existed.

That Tuesday evening was perhaps one of the most difficult of 2015. As the resumption of the academic programme loomed on Wednesday morning, some of the more desperate of the remaining protesters resorted to violence. Under the cloak of darkness, a vehicle was torched and part of the campus bookshop burnt. The symbolism of burning books at a university was lost on these protesters for free education, as it was on some of their defenders. None of the executive slept much that night, receiving continuous reports about running battles with a small group of protesters. Just after midnight on Tuesday, I received a call from Fasiha Hassen, a PYA leader who was also the incoming secretary-general of the SRC. With fear in her voice, Fasiha indicated that residence students were being threatened. She urged security reinforcements to be brought in. She also informed me that students from Men's Residence were forming a security cordon around the residence. In the heat of the moment, I lashed out at Fasiha, saying: 'You try to ride a tiger and then when it turns on you, you run to us.' Immediately, I regretted it. Fasiha remained silent and, chiding myself, I softened and said that we had just approved the deployment of additional private security. What I did not tell her was that we had also approached the police to deploy at the entrances of the campus. The rest of the night proceeded without incident, although the entire executive remained on tenterhooks until the morning.

I was at the office early on Wednesday morning, as were the rest of the executive. Some Council members were also there, including Brian Bruce and Isaac Shongwe. Brian decided to go to the gates and assist with operations there, while Isaac remained with me. A small group of protesters were out as well, but this time we were well prepared and ensured that there was a free flow of traffic through the entrances. The protesters were allowed to protest but the presence of police and private security deterred any violence. Classes did begin, even though there was less than 50 per cent attendance. We had expected this – and assumed that, for each day we held the campus, attendance would improve and academic operations would normalise.

At about noon, Imraan Valodia got in touch to inform me that he had been approached by an individual who claimed to be an emissary from the student protesters who could broker an agreement if I was prepared to engage them in Yale Road just behind the Jorissen Street entrance. Sceptical, I agreed, at Imraan's urging; Imraan then went and fetched the young man. A group of us, including Imraan, Isaac and some security personnel, accompanied the young man to Yale Road. As we approached the protesters, we saw the police were across the road, keeping a wary eye out. As soon as we reached the protesters, the young man blended into the crowd. We had been set up.

What followed was a verbal altercation with the student protesters. Vuyani was there. In his usual verbose style, he started berating us about dividing the students and securitising the campus. Characteristically, he took no responsibility for, and ignored the fact that the police and private security deployment was necessitated by, the violence of the previous evening. Others spoke, too. Two outsourced workers spoke of their hardships, as did a young man, Jeremia Lelosa, who was associated with the Zionist church branch at Wits University. All were far more courteous than Vuyani, and Jeremia would eventually send me an e-mail apologising for the rudeness of some students during the engagement. Leigh-Ann Naidoo was also there and spoke of the challenge of in-sourcing and the importance of addressing it. I, of course, responded firmly, informing the group that, while I sympathised with the issues and would allow the protest, 'the violence will not be tolerated and the police and private security will remain for now'. I also indicated executive management's willingness to consider how to address the human rights violations associated with insourcing. But there was a verbal standoff. After a short back and forth, Isaac whispered in my ear that it was time to return and shepherded me away from the group and back to the office.

The rest of that Wednesday proceeded without incident, as did the night. Clearly, the police and private security had stabilised matters, leaving an uneasy calm. Attendance on Thursday was far better and there was a tentative sense that normality was returning. Sometime in the morning, three of the academics associated with the far left, including Kelly Gillespie and Humanities professor Eric Worby, came to the 11th floor of Solomon Mahlangu House. They came across me in the corridor and asked that we consider an engagement with the remaining group of protesting students with a view to reaching a political settlement. Again, I indicated that we were open to this, but that our position on violence was non-negotiable. After a short while, they departed, indicating that they would try to convince the leadership of the remaining student protesters to enter into a negotiated outcome with management.

A couple of hours later, Leigh-Ann and Lwazi came to the 11th floor and asked for a meeting. After adjusting my diary, I agreed. The meeting began oddly when Leigh-Ann introduced herself as the daughter of Derek Naidoo, an activist colleague of mine from some years back. I expressed surprise and indicated that her father and I had worked closely together. She replied that she knew. Then, with the arrogance character-istic of many of the Fallist activists, she promptly asked: 'So what happened to you?' Irritated, I responded equally arrogantly: 'Someday, when Derek is around, perhaps we can talk to you about earlier struggles and teach you about strategy and tactics.' Having at least symbolically drawn our respective lines in the sand, we proceeded in earnest. Lwazi indicated that, if I was willing to come down and address the protesting students and workers on the concourse, and open to establishing a negotiated engagement on the issues, they would be willing to go back to class and bring an end to the protest. I was in agreement, but made it clear that I would not engage endlessly on the concourse. We agreed that I would come down for an hour, and then leave. After getting the rest of the executive team's consent, a group of us, including Tawana Kupe and Deputy Vice-Chancellor for Research and Postgraduate Affairs Zeblon Vilakazi, both of whom had missed many of the events of the previous weeks because they had been out of the country on official business, went to the concourse to address the remaining protesters.

Lwazi chaired the meeting, which we almost walked out of at the beginning: one of the SASCO-affiliated student leaders joined the meeting and effectively tried to upstage the others. Lwazi walked up and assaulted him. I got up to leave, indicating that I would not be party to this kind of violent behaviour. A number of the students and workers mobbed me, asking me not to leave, and promised that this would not happen again. Reluctantly I sat down, and Leigh-Ann remarked about the assault with a smirk: 'It was well deserved and long overdue.' The incident underscored the dangers of party-political factionalisation and was a precursor of a wider challenge to emerge in the year ahead.

The rest of the meeting went well. A number of workers spoke about their personal circumstances, the unfairness of outsourcing arrangements, and their low wages. Students also spoke about the importance of resolving this thorny issue. Vuyani was there, but remained silent. Eric spoke about the importance of a university such as Wits meeting its human rights obligations by ridding itself of outsourcing. What his remarks did not convey, of course, was that we had agreed at Senate some months back about the importance of our human rights obligations in this regard, but that I had warned that it would come at a financial cost that, collectively, we would have to be willing to pay. Eric had been asked to think through proposals for how the university could do this without compromising its financial sustainability. When he failed to do so and I confronted him in Senate about this, his response was that it was not his task to do so, but an executive management responsibility. This was not uncommon. Very few of the activists ever wanted to confront the choices and trade-offs we had to make. Demands were simply meant to be acceded to without confronting the challenge of limited resources.

After a while, I addressed the crowd and indicated that we were open, in principle, to addressing the outsourcing challenge in a way that did not put the university at financial risk. I proposed that the meeting choose representatives who could engage a management team led by Tawana and Zeblon. This team could think through how to address the outsourcing challenge and the processes to be followed, and would report to the workers on the coming Sunday, 1 November. The meeting agreed to consider the proposal and officially respond to me in an hour or two, after which we left.

By the end of Thursday, there was light at the end of the tunnel. The remaining protesters had agreed to the proposal and talks were underway.

These engagements with Tawana and Zeblon had yielded an in-principle commitment to insource vulnerable workers on terms that were compatible with the university's financial sustainability, and a task team comprising representatives of all of the institution's stakeholders was to be established to work out the modalities. The in-principle commitment arose, in part, as a result of UCT having conceded on this matter early on the morning of 28 October. Until then, the vice-chancellors had been of the view that, collectively, they should hold out against insourcing until the state was willing to underwrite its costs. However, as soon as Max Price sent me an SMS in the early hours of the morning confirming the concession, I knew that Wits would have to make a similar concession. The issue that now began to preoccupy us was the terms on which the insourcing would happen, how to pay for it, and what the consequent trade-offs would be.

By the following week, classes had resumed in earnest and Wits was back on track academically. Stability had returned and students were preparing to sit for their examinations. But the turmoil in the higher education system would continue for some weeks, which did not bode well for the new academic year. It seemed that 2015 had merely been a curtain-raiser for a much more violent 2016.

Wits University may have been where #FeesMustFall began in 2015, but it was definitely not where it ended. While Wits had returned to its academic operations, other institutions continued to be embroiled in protests and violence. This prompted Tyrone Pretorius, vice-chancellor of the University of the Western Cape (UWC), to joke with underlying seriousness at a USAf board meeting that 'Wits starts the trouble, goes back to its academic life and then leaves us all to have to clean up the mess'. And what a mess it was. Arson attacks continued, impacting North-West University (NWU), the Cape Peninsula University of Technology (CPUT), and UWC most severely. Both CPUT and UWC cancelled their 2015 examinations, using the year assessments to progress all students except those in their final years. At UWC, final-year students wrote their examinations off campus, while at CPUT, examinations were postponed to January 2016. The DHET calculated the total cost of the damage to the infrastructure of South African universities in 2015 to be R1 billion.

In Gauteng, as Wits University stabilised, so protests began to take off at UJ. Until then, UJ had been relatively quiet. A number of observers argued that this was because Vice-Chancellor Ihron Rensburg and his executive management had corralled its ANC-aligned SRC to avoid student protests. But in early November, the protests arrived at UJ with a vengeance. UJ was far more prepared, and had developed a more stringent security response. Protesters who disrupted operations or were violent were locked out of campus. Simultaneously, UJ announced a commitment to insourcing cleaning staff and established a task team under Deputy Vice-Chancellor Mpho Letlape to negotiate the process and timelines in this regard. On 6 November, about 140 protesters were arrested outside the Kingsway campus and spent the night in a cell at the Brixton Police Station for violating the court interdict prohibiting protesters from coming within 500 metres of the entrance of the campus. Many of those arrested were students and outsourced workers from UJ, but there was also a significant group of Wits students among them.

That same evening, I received a call from Bonita Meyersfeld, director of the Centre for Applied Legal Studies (CALS) at Wits, enquiring whether Wits University had any official objection to CALS assisting protesters who had been arrested at the Kingsway campus. I indicated that it was within their mandate to support these individuals, and that we were comfortable with their doing this. I also received a visit from Shafee Verachia and Vuyani Pambo, both of whom were providing support to those held at Brixton. They asked if I would facilitate an engagement with Ihron, but I demurred, although I did agree to engage him on the matter. Ihron and I had been in regular contact throughout our respective protests, not only keeping each other abreast of developments, but also commiserating on having been forced to move our families from our official residences. On one occasion, I informed him about the request we had received through Nompendulo, the Wits SRC president, to provide UJ protesters with a venue to consult with students. Ihron and I agreed that he would allow them the use of premises at UJ to prevent undue external interference in their processes. By the middle of November, UJ seemed to have brought its protests under control – an agreement with the National Education, Health and Allied Workers' Union (NEHAWU) and an outsourced worker representative committed it in principle to insourcing and agreed that the task team would conclude its deliberations by February 2016. A couple of days later, it also agreed to temporarily lift the suspensions on six students, including Khutso Rammutla, UJ's outgoing SRC president.

UJ was perhaps the first university to come under heavy criticism for securitisation. Not only was this continuously raised by student leaders such as Leigh-Ann Naidoo, but it was also voiced by sympathetic academics as well as journalists such as Greg Nicolson. Yet neither the student leaders nor the sympathetic academics and journalists were willing to confront the reality of the protesters' engaging in the large-scale violation of the rights of others, and some of them resorting to violence, including arson that involved a bus and some infrastructure at UJ. A few months later, in May 2016, UJ would lose its Sanlam auditorium to arson and suspend 17 students for being implicated in the incident. It is this blasé attitude towards violence that has come to haunt both the #FeesMustFall movement and the universities, and it is perhaps the single greatest curse afflicting South Africa's contemporary political system.

While these developments played out, the vice-chancellor of Fort Hare, Mvuyo Tom, and I continued to serve on behalf of USAf on the Presidential Task Team on Short-Term Funding Challenges that Jacob Zuma had established at the beginning of October 2015. The protests delayed the start of the task team's deliberations, but we got going properly in November 2015. The meetings, chaired by Cassius Lubisi and the director-general of the DHET, Gwebs Qonde, met mainly over weekends and had full representation from national student structures, USAf, the business sector, the DHET and Treasury. Its mandate was to find a solution to the challenge of historical debt, a looming crisis for the 2016 registration process. It concluded its deliberations in early December and essentially proposed that the state make available R4.5 billion to pay for NSFAS students who had been unfunded or underfunded in 2013, 2014 and 2015, and to ensure that the unfunded students were paid for in the 2016 and 2017 years. It also recommended that a new funding model be established with funds from the private and public sectors to finance the cost challenges for 'missing middle' students. Zuma received the recommendations favourably and formally announced the report's recommendations as presidential decisions on 15 December 2015, thus adding to the R2.3 billion that he had committed in October towards financing the no fee increase – bringing the state's total additional contribution to higher education in the 2015/16 financial year to a whopping R6.8 billion.

November 2015 at Wits University was far quieter than any other time that year. Students were preoccupied with examinations, and almost all of the academic staff with assessments. But the challenges of the previous months had left their imprint on the university community. Unsurprisingly, they surfaced first among the far left. David Dickinson, in his capacity as academic representative on Council, authored what purported to be a review of the events of the past few months. As usual, his account lacked any sense of propriety or understanding of context or moment, and was written in the style of a belligerent commentator who presents his hindsight as 20/20, unburdened by institutional constraints or the responsibilities of office. The review deliberately misled by omitting information that did not suit its conclusions and was filled with gratuitous insults against almost everyone with whom Dickinson had served in any governance structure. It was particularly disparaging of the chair of Council and me: in a subsection titled 'We need to talk about Adam', it bemoaned the fact that we 'did not align ourselves with the students' against the state, and described our responses to the shifting political circumstances as a 'line of action [that] had become as convoluted as a plot line in The Bold and the Beautiful'. I can only imagine that the review was written as bait to draw me personally into a verbal fracas, but, cognisant of my role as vice-chancellor and my responsibility for maintaining the dignity of the office, I decided not to engage David publicly, even though not doing so took every ounce of my strength.

In retrospect, this was the best response: his public review alienated not only the vast majority of academics and the Senate, but also the Council members, who were appalled. The Council's view was perhaps best described by Barney Pityana – a contemporary of Steve Biko, the first chairperson of the democratic South Africa's Human Rights Commission and a former University of South Africa (UNISA) vice-chancellor – who, in a letter to David, said: 'As a black member of Council ... whose life has been spent in opposition to apartheid, ... [who] was banned, jailed and tortured by agents of the ... system, and who has been a student leader in my time, I am offended by the aspersions you cast on us collectively ...' Barney then proceeded to dissect David's review, underscoring the responsibility of a Council member to take his fiduciary responsibility seriously and to refrain from using his position to get Council 'to bring down the institution or operate outside the laws and policies set by government', and the importance of Council not being held hostage by institutional stakeholders so that it can rather 'listen, consider options ..., apply its mind and resolve only that which is best for the institution'. He then proceeded to rebut each of David's claims by providing counter-examples, and concluded that the purpose of his review had never been to engage the chair or the vice-chancellor but 'to insult, demean their characters and label'. 'I fear', Barney concludes, 'that you are taking liberties and that you take collegiality to extremes.' Ultimately, David's review exposed him for what he had become: an individual so filled with the righteousness of his cause that he took on no obligation of responsibility along with all the rights he claimed, and was prepared to destroy the very institution that paid his salary at the altar of his politics and ideology because he would never truly have to bear the consequences.

But the protests had not only left an imprint on Wits University and other similar institutions. Tensions also continued to play out within USAf. This body was never as coherent as the protesters believed it to be. After all, each vice-chancellor takes on the mantle of an institution's ambitions which, given South Africa's legacy of historical inequality among institutions and in an environment of resource scarcity, inevitably pits each against her or his peers. The USAf environment is therefore one of continuous tension and collaboration, institutional ambition and collective interest. The student protests and the subsequent societal response accentuated these divides.

This manifested itself most significantly at a USAf meeting on 10 December 2015, when Mahlo Mokgalong, vice-chancellor of the University of Limpopo, laid into Max Price about his response to the protests at UCT. But the critique was not confined to Max. It was directed at all of the historically white universities, even though UCT, the University of Pretoria (UP), Stellenbosch and Wits were singled out. Mahlo succinctly identified his critique, which was shared by many: 'We at the HBUs have confronted protests annually without assistance, and then suddenly when it emerges at Wits and UCT, not only are decisions made that have consequences for institutions in the rest of the system, but both state and society suddenly become responsive to the demands of the students.' Tyrone Pretorius raised the concern of institutional concessions regarding insourcing being made at UCT, and then Wits, Pretoria, UJ and others, and the inevitable pressure on the rest of the universities to follow suit, even though they do not have the financial resources to enable these concessions. There was much truth in all of this, and it was hard for any of us at the historically white institutions to respond to the critique convincingly. Instead, we took it on the chin and eventually agreed to consult more with one another before making firm institutional decisions on matters that affect the collective. This was not entirely effective, and the tension between institutional decisions and systemic consequences continued to rear its head in the coming months and years.

My final – and perhaps most difficult – act of the year was to have an engagement with Beatrys Lacquet about her future. Recall that Beatrys had been involved in an altercation with Kelly Gillespie on the morning of 28 October when the Senate meeting had been disrupted. For a while, there were rumblings in the Wits rumour mill about a charge being laid against Beatrys, and I had indicated in the same rumour mill that, if this were to happen, the investigation would be a comprehensive one that also covered the damage to infrastructure by all individuals, including some of the academics. No charge was ever laid; as an executive, we let bygones be bygones. Beatrys had gone on leave the day after the Senate incident. She had been on the frontline of the protests and had borne the brunt of the student onslaught. She had needed some time off.

The question was whether she should return to her executive post. I had lunch with Beatrys on 12 December to discuss her future. It was one of my more difficult decisions, because Beatrys is one of the strongest people I know. I had always said that, if I were ever to go into battle, she was the person I would love to have next to me. She had also been utterly loyal. But I knew that, if she returned to her executive role, she would again be confronted with the harassment that she had been subjected to. I said this to her; she indicated that she should not be the executive to oversee the insourcing of vulnerable workers. Two months later, I would accept the resignation of Director of Services Theresa Main, who reported to Beatrys, for a similar reason. In the end, we agreed that Beatrys would continue in her executive role until March 2016, after which she would go on long leave that was due to her and return to a position in the Faculty of Engineering and the Built Environment.

The year had taken its toll on all executives, at Wits University and other tertiary institutions across the country. By the end of 2015, we were all utterly exhausted. It is often said that the protests left deep psychological scars on students, academics, and professional and administrative staff. This is indeed true. But it also left deep emotional scars on most of the university executives. Perhaps this was most tragically brought to the fore when Prof. Bongani Mayosi, one of South Africa's most celebrated scientists and the dean of the Faculty of Health Sciences at UCT, committed suicide in July 2018. At his funeral service, his sister, Ncumisa Mayosi, said, 'He was hardly two weeks in his new position and the protests broke out. The vitriolic nature of the students and their do-or-die attitude vandalised his soul and unravelled him.' Bongani's widow, Nonhlanhla Khumalo, stated in a letter to her departed husband, read at the funeral: 'During the protests students sent a list of demands and messages to your private cell phone at all hours. You cared so deeply for people who now treated you as the enemy.' UCT and fellow academics were not spared blame in this tragedy. But what these reflections of Bongani's spouse and sister raise is that what is forgotten in the hurly-burly of political rhetoric is often that there are human beings on the other side of the divide. At a university, those human beings often believe in a higher purpose. While they may differ about how this should be achieved, it is this common belief that brings them together as an institutional community – a community that has to cohere if its broader higher purpose is to be realised. But the institutional community at Wits, and elsewhere, had begun to fracture. It was to be put under even greater strain in the years to come.

3

The turn to racism and violence

THE 2016 academic year began on an ominous note. My first day of work, 11 January, was also the first day of registration for new first-year students, particularly in the Health Sciences faculty. Soon after registration began, at about 09h00, Carol Crosley called to inform me that two small groups of students – about twenty individuals each – were protesting at Hall 29, where the registrations were managed, and at the cashiers' desks on the concourse of Solomon Mahlangu House. The ostensible reason for the protest was academic and financial exclusions.

Immediately, the executive publicly clarified a prior agreement with the SRC that only students who could afford the first fee payment of R9 000 were obliged to pay prior to registration. Those who could not afford it could fill in a form and defer the payment. In addition, as part of the agreement with the state, and as per the presidential an-nouncement on 15 December 2015, all students who had been NSFAS students in 2015 would not be obliged to clear their historical debt before registration, as this debt would be taken care of by the state. The only students who would be obliged to clear their debt before registration were students who did not qualify for NSFAS. We also indicated that we would have loved to extend the concession to all students, but that the total historical debt had already crossed the R100 million threshold – the financial burden of clearing this debt would be unsustainable for the institution.

Soon after clarifying this, it became apparent through engagement with the protesting students that the first fee payment and the historical debt were merely a pretext for reigniting the protest. The protesters believed that, if there was to be no free education, there should be no education at all. After repeated attempts to convince them to allow registration to continue, all of which failed, the executive postponed registration for both 11 and 12 January. Students were encouraged to register online; those without access to computer facilities were assisted through telephone registrations, initiated at 15h00 on the afternoon of 11 January. Fee payments were to be made through banks and the university's banking details were made available to all students.

Our ability to switch quickly to alternative registration processes was in part due to the fact that we had already put backup systems in place at the end of 2015. Nevertheless, despite this, the ones most disadvantaged by the disruption were poor students who did not have Internet access and credit cards. We brought this to the protesters' attention and publicly highlighted the unfairness of this situation, but to no avail. The protesters were adamant that the disruptions would continue for as long as free education was not enacted.

It is also worth noting that these protests were not isolated to Wits University. They were definitely being coordinated – all the institutions in Gauteng were experiencing disruption in one form or another. It was in this context that we immediately activated our comprehensive backup plan, including the private security arrangements we had negotiated and the processes for obtaining an interim court order. In the early hours of 12 January, student protesters who were sleeping on the concourse of Solomon Mahlangu House were evicted. Anticipating the protesters making accusations of sexual harassment, the university filmed all proceedings; when the accusations eventually came a few hours later, not only could we convincingly refute the claims, but we also offered journalists the right to view all the video footage. Within hours, the claims of sexual harassment were no longer being made, or were, at least, being given very little public credence.

By 15 January, we had an interim court order preventing protesters from disrupting our registration and occupying the Solomon Mahlangu concourse. We also brought in a full contingent of private security, with no guns or other dangerous weaponry, to enable registration. Access to the Robert Sobukwe Building and Solomon Mahlangu House, which are interconnected, was restricted to students who were coming to register. Predictably, the measures provoked academics associated with the far left, who cried that the protest was being criminalised and that the campus was being securitised. As usual, they provided no answers as to what should happen to ensure that registration continued.

Some of these colleagues – in particular, Hylton White – sent out an appeal to the global Anthropology community calling for solidarity and asking that letters be sent to my e-mail address protesting our decision to bring in private security. He suggested that the university had been 'militarised', and that this was an attempt to 'pre-empt planned protests'; he dramatically described the resultant institutional environment with the words: 'We now work under occupation'. Ignoring his lack of understanding of what an occupation really means, and the fallacy of his suggesting that the institution had been militarised, without guns or other weaponry, the real concern about this advocacy was its failure to declare that protests had already been underway, that staff and students had been threatened, and that poor students were the constituency who had been prejudiced the most. Given the mobilisation and the deliberate misrepresentation of events at Wits, I responded on behalf of the executive with an open letter to the university community.

The letter essentially explained why we had made our decision. It challenged those who opposed the decision to provide realistic alternatives and castigated them for allowing the rights of so many to be violated, and for being sanguine about violence. It questioned whether, as some of the critics had intimated, the presence of structural violence in the form of inequality and marginalisation can ever justify violence against individuals and arson in a public university. It also reflected on my personal experience of protesters' mistakes at the University of Durban-Westville, where a similar form of political adventurism was attempted in the mid-1990s. The consequence, it suggested, was the decimation of the university

> as its top students and academics … abandoned it. The middle and upper middle class student and academic activists, some with trust funds, slunk away. Some of the academics with second passports simply moved back to their home countries … The real casualties of this experiment were not the activists and academics who had romanticised violence, even though some of them individually suffered. It was the poor black students who had no other alternative but to continue to go to that University.

On the basis of this experience, I urged colleagues to be responsible in their solidarity engagements and not to become complicit in behaviour or support actions that undermined our abilities to retain the university's research-intensive character.

Two sets of reflections are warranted regarding these events and the university's institutional response to them. The first relates to the loss of key staff. It is worth noting that the academic market is a global one, especially for talented staff in particular disciplines. Such staff can easily be recruited to institutions elsewhere in the world, and political instability and threats to their safety are significant factors in encouraging such academic migration. Ironically, one of the cohorts most afflicted by this migration is that of far-left academic critics, quite a few of whom have left in the past 12 to 18 months for academic institutions in Britain, Sweden and other parts of Europe and North America. Many would, of course, argue that their departure was merely a result of academic progression and promotion, and had nothing to do with the political protests at the university, the violence they engendered and the fractured environment they left behind. However, it is difficult not to be cynical about the hypocrisy of it all, since the very academics who were sanguine about the violence, or at least defended the form of the protests, were the first to invoke the privilege of second passports to escape the consequences of these new circumstances. Clearly, it is far easier to write about revolution, neoliberalism and the corporatisation of the university from the comfortable surrounds of the Western academy.

The second relates to the acts of solidarity by colleagues from within the Anthropology community in particular. Some months later – in June 2016, during a lecture to the Scholars at Risk conference at McGill University in Montreal, under the theme Universities in a Dangerous World: Defending Higher Education Security and Values – I lamented this incident, suggesting that these colleagues had abdicated their moral and political responsibilities through the manner in which they had engaged the issue. The problem was not that they had sent letters criticising the university's decision. This was perfectly legitimate. But none of them had bothered to engage with the events on the ground. Instead, they had decided to pronounce on an action thousands of miles away. When they received the executive's open letter to the university community, one or two apologised, but the vast majority simply remained silent. Ultimately, the real problem with these colleagues was not their engagement in an act of solidarity, but the fact that they never took the initiative to investigate the issues and apprise themselves of events on the ground. Essentially, this was solidarity on the cheap, where one does not have to investigate the issues or consider the real challenges in the context where the social action is playing out.

I followed up on the open letter with a visit to all faculties. It soon became clear that the vast majority of academics supported the measures put in place to conclude registration. On 19 January, the SRC and the Wits executive came to a formal agreement in which, among other things, students with a debt of under R10 000 would be allowed to register and their debt would be rolled into their 2016 fees. Those fully funded for 2016, but who had debt, were also allowed to register. The executive and the SRC both committed themselves to raising funds from private and public quarters to assist financially needy students. Regarding the in-sourcing issue, on 26 January, Wits formally announced that, in the interim, while insourcing arrangements were being negotiated, Council had approved the recommendations of the management executive and the

Council ExCo to grant all outsourced workers a top-up allowance, bringing into effect a minimum wage of R4 500, backdated to 1 January 2016.

At the systemic level, initiatives were also underway. On 17 January, the vice-chancellors of Gauteng universities met with Premier David Makhura and the members of his Executive Council to explore provincial support for their institutions. The next day, at a press conference, the vice-chancellors expressed concern about some students and outsourced workers having resorted to violent protests to try to disrupt the registration process. We also called on societal stakeholders to work with us to get the universities back on track. Vice-chancellors also met with Minister Blade Nzimande on 21 January. Each side acknowledged the contributions of the other, and called on students not to engage in violent protest and to allow registration processes to be completed. Collectively, these initiatives stabilised the universities, at least temporarily, enough to allow them to complete their registrations by the end of January 2016.

But the reprieve did not last for very long. A new frontline opened up at Wits University a week later, even though our interim court order had been extended on 2 February. Part of the reason may have had to do with the broader instability in the higher education system. UP had been closed for just over a week following protests by outsourced workers and students associated with the EFF who had forced the institution to bring a halt to face-to-face registration. But no sooner had UP come to an in-principle agreement to insource workers than students from the EFF and SASCO launched another occupation about the university's language policy, prompting Cheryl de la Rey, the vice-chancellor, to object that the protesters were continually shifting the goalposts. UNISA, TUT and UJ were confronting similar outsourcing protests of their own, and Walter Sisulu University in the Eastern Cape had just evicted students from their residences after they had been on boycott for over two weeks, creating a tense standoff. All in all, there seemed to be a general restlessness in the country's universities as students associated with the EFF and Pan Africanist Student Movement of Azania (PASMA), in particular, attempted to launch round two of #FeesMustFall.

In this context, two incidents emerged involving some students spraying graffiti and wearing T-shirts with the slogan 'Fuck Whites' at Wits and 'Kill Whites' at UCT. When some staff and students at Wits first complained to me about a student wearing a T-shirt displaying the offensive slogan, my advice was to ignore it, because any action against the individual would feed the protest. Against this advice, the matter was reported to the Human Rights Commission; that same day, some fifteen students – many of whom were white – started wearing the T-shirt. As the case at the Commission approached, graffiti of the offensive slogan started to reappear all over the campus. We were forced to issue a public communique.

The communique condemned the slogan and the protesters behind it, and questioned their view that they could not be racist because they were black. This nonsensical view gained currency in Fallist and some EFF circles because of a belief that black people have no power. But power is always a relational phenomenon and is evident in the relationship between any two individuals. The communique clarified this fact and made clear our opposition to racialised slogans of any kind. But we also clarified that our legal advice had suggested that the statement did not, on the face of it, constitute hate speech: it did not meet the narrow definition of the intention to commit harm. In addition, the communique criticised the spread of graffiti because it required the university to incur unnecessary expenditure to clean it, when these resources could be far better spent on supporting students. We called on all within the university community to respect one another, even when there was disagreement. A cohesive university community was a requirement for effective learning.

In the days that followed, there were repeated attempts at Wits University to provoke protests. On 10 February, following attempts to incite workers by implying that they would not be paid the top-up allowance agreed on earlier, we had to release a communique clarifying that the allowance for outsourced workers would be paid. Similarly, a day later, we clarified that we were working with the NSFAS to mitigate the consequences of their inept administration in the processing of NSFAS loans, and that we had put arrangements into place to assist with food and accommodation in the absence of the loans being paid. The executive and management thwarted all these attempts to spark protests, even though the broader system had begun to slip into instability.

At UCT, the Shackville protests had begun on 15 February. This involved student activists staying overnight in a shack constructed on the road in front of Jameson Hall to highlight the accommodation crisis. The protest soon degenerated into the burning of artworks, including those of progressive and black artists. The police moved in to demolish the shacks and protesters responded with a number of arson attempts, succeeding in torching a Jammie shuttle and another university vehicle. The language struggle at UP intensified too, culminating in scuffles between AfriForum supporters and activists from the EFF Student Command, SASCO and other student groups. At the University of the Free State, student pro-testers invaded the pitch during a rugby match in an effort to draw the attention of Jonathan Jansen, the vice-chancellor, and were violently assaulted by the student spectators and their guests. The tempo of student protests and political instability had greatly increased across the system in the preceding three weeks, with arson becoming the preferred weapon.

Unsurprisingly in this context, there was a desire among some student groups at Wits University to initiate disruptive protests too. Eventually, at about 11h00 on 17 February, some protesters burnt a bus near the Knockando Residence, which is outside the campus precinct in Parktown. We immediately increased private security personnel numbers, which we had decreased in the relative calm of the preceding weeks. Thus, when 14 student protesters tried to occupy the Solomon Mahlangu concourse on Friday of the same week and set a mattress alight in the Wartenweiler Library, they were not only quickly arrested and removed from campus, but also charged at the Hillbrow Police Station. They were released the next day, but the university had had sufficient time to kick its suspension processes into gear so that a number of the protesters who had violated the court interdict and were suspected of arson were suspended. They were barred from campus until their disciplinary processes were concluded.

In the coming weeks, relative calm returned. But there were sporadic attempts at fostering protest for the rest of the semester. On 17 March, there was an attempt to disrupt the Steve Biko Centre for Bioethics symposium in the School of Public Health, where four vice-chancellors – Dan Kgwadi of NWU, Max Price, Mvuyo Tom and I – were debating the challenges of transformation. The event had to be temporarily halted when protesters disrupted Dan's and Max's contributions. Some of the protesters became abusive to the point where Mvuyo called them to order. When a few protesters, one or two of whom were drunk, started jumping on desks and threatening people, they were physically removed from the building. Thereafter, I engaged the remaining protesters personally. They agreed to let the proceedings continue if they were given the right to pose questions to the speakers in the open discussion that followed. The meeting ended amicably, but the intolerance of some of the protesters left deep emotional scars on the academics, students and alumni who attended it. After the meeting, at about 23h00, Max, Mvuyo and I went to Savernake, had a late meal and mulled over how to allow protests within parameters that did not fracture the university community.

On 4 April, a group of about thirty students attempted a disruption at the Fees Office. This was followed by a bigger group of about one hundred and fifty students and outsourced workers, some from within and many from outside Wits, starting a fire in an empty lecture theatre in the Umthombo Building and disrupting a few classes. The protests, led by Chumani Maxwele from UCT and Vuyani Pambo, resulted in an altercation between Chumani and queer activist Thenjiwe Mswane, who tried to disrupt the protest with a sjambok. In response, not only did we bring in private security once again, but we also requested the police to arrest those acting in violation of the court order. We suspended those individuals and barred Chumani from Wits premises.

As soon as the situation had been brought under control, students at our Education Campus in Parktown embarked on a protest on 7 April, largely because not all were recipients of the Funza Lushaka bursaries provided by the Department of Basic Education and administered by the NSFAS. Again, the situation was quickly stabilised. With Andrew Crouch, Tawana Kupe, Zeblon Vilakazi, Dean of Students Puleng LenkaBula, Humanities dean Ruksana Osman and Karin Brodie, head of the Wits School of Education, I engaged the entire student body on the Education Campus and responded to their complaints. The meeting was chaired by the chair of the Education Students' Council, Jamie-Lee Mnisi. When we decided to conclude the meeting after two hours, there were howls of protest from some of the students who were associated with the political parties. When Jamie-Lee engaged us, I pointedly asked her whether this was going to turn into a hostage situation, as I would then have to get security to act appropriately. She quickly responded that this was not the case. We agreed to give the meeting another 30 minutes, after which we concluded the deliberations.

The meeting did agree that the executive of the Education Students' Council would continue to engage a team from management, including the head of the school, to address the concerns of the students. On 18 April, the executive released a communique that explained the number of applications received for financial aid by education students, and the proportion who received support through the Funza Lushaka programme and general financial aid from the university. We also committed not to deregister students who did not receive Funza Lushaka bursaries, and to give them until November to pay their fees without interest penalties. Finally, we agreed to investigate low-cost meal options for the Education Campus and open a satellite financial aid office there in the 2017 financial year. For a few weeks, the campus settled once again.

The semester's final incident occurred on 25 May, when fifty to eighty workers decided to disrupt operations at the dining hall and at the Matrix, which is the student centre. It was a targeted incident: examinations were about to begin. Workers at retail establishments on campus insisted that they, too, wanted to be considered for insourcing, and threatened to disrupt examinations if they were not. Again, we responded firmly that we would not tolerate attempts at disruption and that anyone involved in such activities would be suspended and barred from the campus. We also agreed that the Insourcing Task Team would address the workers after 10 June, when Council was due to make final decisions about insourcing arrangements. The workers reluctantly agreed to this, and the June examinations kicked off in earnest. The first semester concluded about three weeks later, without any further incident.

Two sets of deliberations about these developments are worth highlighting. The first arose from the constant attempts by a group of student political activists to spark off a new round of protests. Often, it did not matter what the issues were. Some of the activists would deliberately mislead other students and workers about matters affecting them. Students were told that they would be deregistered from the university for not paying fees, and outsourced workers were told that management had reneged on one or another agreement, even though this was not the case. During the April incident, I had to call in Deliwe Mzobe, one of the outsourced workers on the Insourcing Task Team, because she was found to have violated the court interdict and participated in disrupting university operations. I warned her that she risked being suspended and that, if this were to happen, she would not be allowed onto our premises. In the engagement with her, it became apparent that she had been under the misconception that poor students would be deregistered. When I told her that this was just not true, she came clean and informed me that this was essentially what the student activists who were trying to spark off another round of protests had told her.

These continuous attempts to mislead students and workers forced the executive to release regular public communiques reiterating agreements arrived at with the SRC and the Insourcing Task Team. But these regular communiques, and twice-daily reports on incidents during protest cycles, were also prompted by critiques from academics, professional and administrative staff, and students who felt that the executive had not been sufficiently adept in its communications during the 2015 protests. Some members of Council also felt that we were not professional enough in our communication and encouraged me to hire a professional communications company. I demurred, arguing that the kind of communication required in the midst of student protests was very different from that required by a company in the middle of a crisis. I insisted that our internal communications team was far more attuned to the issues and would rise to the challenge. The critiques did force us to up our game, however; we put a new communication plan into play in 2016.

The second set of deliberations relates to the issue of violence and security at universities. In early January, in both a review of the 2015 protests and the open letter to the university community, I explicitly bemoaned the fact that a small group of protesters had resorted to violence and suggested that we had been compelled to bring in private security to guarantee the university community's safety. Of course, the student leadership and a number of the academics on the far left challenged this. Natasha Vally and Sarah Godsell, two doctoral graduates from Wits University, questioned my causal relationship between protester violence and the use of private security. After the normal labelling that has become common to any critical engagement with vice-chancellors in South Africa, they got to the substance of their argument – which was, essentially, that the executive did not sufficiently appreciate the fact that the protesters were confronting the system's structural inequities that resulted in high fees and low wages for workers, and that, instead of bringing in security, we should have sought 'more meaningful approaches and forms of engagement around the underlying issues that [had] given rise to this situation in the first place'. Mia Swart, who was then an academic in the Law faculty at UJ, similarly made some disparaging remarks about the struggle credentials of vice-chancellors, criticised us for bringing in private security, and suggested that we should rather have engaged the students. Much of this also came up in some of the engagements in my meeting with the Faculty of Humanities in the aftermath of my open letter. When I confronted these colleagues about what they would have done when protesters rebuffed a negotiated resolution to the matter, Karl von Holdt was one of the few who responded. He suggested that we should have considered what occurred in California during the student protests in the 1960s: closing the university and allowing for public engagements and learning on the inequities of the global system.

It is perhaps here where the real disjuncture with the far left lies: we simply operate from different contextual realities. In my reality, this was simply not possible. Our students and their families were not California's middle classes. They could neither afford, nor would their families allow them, to be out of class for such long periods. Also concerning is how sanguine these scholars were about violence at the universities. Not one expressed abhorrence about it, and a few implicitly justified it by making reference to structural inequalities, as if this somehow legitimised individual acts of violence. Perhaps most problematic was the refusal to recognise that we had indeed attempted to negotiate with the protesters, but had been rebuffed. In this worldview, protesting communities can never make strategic miscalculations and must, therefore, always be supported. There was no recognition that the call of 'no education if there is no free education' was irresponsible and that, in the 1980s – when there had been a similar call of 'liberation before education' – it was activists such as Neville Alexander from within the liberation movement, regarded by many from the far left as an inspiration, who rose to contest the call.

The essential problem with this worldview was that these academic activists clearly did not 'comprehend the security-freedom conundrum' that Achille Mbembe identified in his reflection on Herbert Marcuse and Theodor Adorno's debate on the prospects and tactics of Germany's student struggles in the late 1960s. Mbembe insisted, in this contribution, that 'not all security arrangements ... are inimical to freedom. Freedom in and of itself does not automatically generate security. Each has to be supplemented, [for which] neither angelism nor callousness will suffice'. Mbembe called for an approach of 'ethical pragmatism – a pragmatism that is open at its ethical core to being constantly contested'. Implied in this call is a critique of reflex responses, and a demand for contextual analysis and conclusions to be drawn from deliberation on a case-by-case basis. This conundrum and debate would return in an even more acute form in the latter part of 2016.

These issues fractured not only the broader university community, but also the grouping that imagined itself as the university's progressive community. This was most pronounced within the Humanities faculty, which often prided itself on having the most politicised and socially conscious academy in not only the institution, but also the country. But within this progressive community resided all kinds of political strands, and these political questions were to accentuate the divides within it. As the far left became more strident, it became more judgemental of others within the progressive community who questioned uncritical support of the #FeesMustFall movement. Scholars such as Achille Mbembe, Shireen Hassim, Lucy Allais, Cathi Albertyn, David Everatt, Sarah Nuttall and Sharon Fonn came under particular attack, sometimes in the most personal of ways, simply because they questioned some of the strategies and tactics adopted, or were seen to be sympathetic to some of the challenges that the executive confronted. Interpersonal relations fractured as the political divides translated into personal animosities that were to become even more accentuated in the months to come.

My personal relations with most academics, including those on the far left, remained cordial throughout this period. I was aware, of course, of the negative depictions and misrepresentations of the executive and of me that some on the far left were party to in closed circles, both physical and on Facebook. Yet I ignored most of this, which meant that some of these academics would continue to engage me, arguing for one or other course of action. In a few cases, I even engaged individuals late into the night, recognising that they were merely a front for communication with a broader group of individuals. The only exception to this emerged when an academic from the far-left cohort, based on a misrepresentation of my remarks in an engagement with the Faculty of Engineering and the Built Environment in February 2017, wrote to Ruksana Osman as the Humanities dean and alleged that I was intending to institute punitive cuts against the faculty to get back at individual academics. I responded angrily and firmly to this conspiratorial allegation, correcting the misrepresentation and then terminating any further direct correspondence with the individual, making it clear to the latter and the dean that all further interaction with me would have to follow the formal line of managerial authority. There had to be an ethical line that I could not allow others to breach without consequences. But beyond this individual incident, relations with academics, even those of the far left, remained cordial and professional.

While protesters and the executive were playing a cat-and-mouse game in round two of #FeesMustFall, the Commission of Inquiry into the Feasibility of Making Higher Education and Training Fee-free in South Africa (the Heher Commission) eventually got off the ground. In the original plans, it was meant to kick off almost immediately and conclude its deliberations by June 2016 so that its recommendations could come in time to address the fees question for the 2017 academic year. This did not happen. Having only been activated in late April or

May, it requested and was granted a year's extension, and would only deliver its report by late August 2017. At the beginning of its public hearings, I was invited to participate and make a presentation to the Commission. We decided, however, that it would be far better to use the opportunity to craft a collective response from the university community.

Tawana was tasked with putting together a committee representing all stakeholders with a mandate to hold internal hearings, gather the collective views of the community and communicate these to the Commission. The team chosen was chaired by Hlonipha Mokoena, a senior academic at the Wits Institute for Social and Economic Research (WISER), and included representatives from all faculties. The team also included David Hornsby, who not only represented the Faculty of Humanities but also served as the chair of the Academic Staff Association of Wits University (ASAWU). The panel hosted four or five internal hearings and received multiple written submissions, all of which were collated in a presentation that Mokoena, some members of the team and I delivered to the Heher Commission on 10 August 2016.

The substance of our message to the Heher Commission was to support the idea of free education and highlight the inclusive benefits that society could derive from it. The team also stressed the importance of thinking through the funding required in comprehensive terms to include tuition, accommodation and subsistence costs. We did not put forward a specific proposal on financing arrangements. Instead, we noted the variety of available financing models and indicated that an eclectic mix of these may ultimately be required to address South Africa's specific challenges. The engagement with the Commission was an amiable and stimulating one, in stark contrast to later ones where vice-chancellors like Max Price were mobbed by student protesters and the hearings degenerated into political spectacles.

As the first semester of 2016 came to a close, ominous political signs loomed on the horizon. The primary reason was that the budgeting season for the 2017 academic year was approaching, and the budget could not be finalised without a decision about the student fee increase. Institutions had not begun consultations with the student leaders as they would normally have, because it had been agreed at a meeting with the

DHET on 3 March that the minister would take the lead in this regard. It was these engagements and their consequences that were to define the politics of the second half of 2016.

By June 2016, vice-chancellors had become particularly concerned about the fee increases for the following year. Part of this had to do with the fact that the DHET had commissioned the CHE to investigate and make proposals about a new fee regime for universities in the country. But its first order of business was to determine a recommendation for the fee increase for 2017. The CHE team had done significant work in this regard and reports emanating from it suggested that it was leaning towards recommending a fee increase in line with the consumer price index (CPI), which was in the region of 6 per cent.

Several vice-chancellors were very concerned about this: a CPI increase would not cover institutional costs, especially at universities such as Wits that were research-intensive and had to contend with library journals and research equipment costs that were priced in dollars and euros. Moreover, the CHE's own investigation into university expenditure concluded that this stood at about 1.7 per cent above CPI. Why, then, would they recommend a fee increase of 6 per cent? When I confronted one of the task team members about this, they acknowledged the phenomenon of higher education inflation (HEI) but indicated that the outcome was a political compromise which the team believed would avoid a student explosion. I contested this, suggesting that it would make no difference – in terms of protests, at least – if the fee increase was set at CPI or HEI. 'By recommending that it be set at CPI,' I challenged, 'not only would it spark the student mobilisation, but it would also set back the universities with a fee increase that would necessitate deep expenditure cuts.'

The issue became the focus of the USAf board meeting on 22 July. The vice-chancellors collectively agreed that their motivation to the minister would be for an increase along the lines of HEI, which should be in the region of 8 per cent. If the state were to go with CPI at 6 per cent, we would not object to this, but would request that the 2 per cent difference be made up by the state. USAf CEO Ahmed Bawa was mandated to deal with the long-term finance challenge by initiating a process to think through a policy for the comprehensive financing of the higher education system. The meeting also agreed that future protests would be managed with a mix of engagement and security protocols, and that students implicated in violence would not be considered for amnesty at any of the universities.

This meeting was ultimately followed with an engagement between vice-chancellors and the minister on 11 August. The consultation began with the minister summarising the CHE recommendation for a CPI increase of 6 per cent. I then responded on behalf of the vice-chancellors, contesting this recommendation and indicating that it would financially compromise two-thirds of the universities in the system. I also recommended that the state make up the 2 per cent deficit and called for the establishment of a multi-stakeholder forum in which we could get business to share the universities' cost burdens. Other vice-chancellors also responded, including Ihron Rensburg, who argued passionately not only for the minister to consider making up the 2 per cent deficit in the short term, but also for the burden of financing the universities to be shifted from the students to the state in the medium term. In the end, the minister proposed that we not make a final decision, but have another consultation towards the end of the month.

The second consultation with the minister occurred on 30 August. At this meeting, the minister suggested that there was no appetite, in either the ruling party or the state, for another round of #FeesMustFall protests. Government therefore wanted to draft principles for a no fee increase. He also suggested that there was broad agreement within the state that NSFAS beneficiaries must not be prejudiced in any way, but that the problem of the 'missing middle' remained. In this regard, the Treasury had agreed to find resources to assist with the fee increase for all students with a family income of less than R600 000. But the minister was not convinced that student leaders would accept this proposal, even though the R600 000 cut-off emanated from student consultations in which it had been argued that a R500 000 limit was too low. Ultimately, this meeting also ended unsatisfactorily, with the minister agreeing to consult with the students further on the proposal – although not many in the meeting were convinced that this would be successful.

The vice-chancellors had hoped that a final recommendation about the 2017 fee increase would be made in July, in time for the beginning of the budgeting process in most institutions. But this did not happen, mainly because the DHET had not concluded its consultations with students and other stakeholders. When the decision was finally announced in the middle of September, all hell broke loose in the higher education system.

4

The struggle over insourcing

OUTSOURCING, especially of vulnerable workers, violates human rights. It is important to state this boldly at the outset for two reasons. First, many do not recognise the exploitation of vulnerable workers, who are paid relatively low wages and denied basic benefits. While this business model may work for selected professionals whose scarce skills give them negotiating power, it is particularly harmful to vulnerable workers' and poor people's working conditions and living standards. Its existence was a political scar, therefore, on the higher education system, whose institutions professed to be committed to the public good.

Second, it is important not to allow some individuals to present the Wits struggle for insourcing as one between advocates for human rights and those against them. No one in the current Wits executive was ever of the view that outsourcing was a humane business arrangement. Indeed, it had been a source of tension at Wits University ever since workers had been outsourced at about the turn of the millennium. In my first Senate meeting at Wits University in 2013, the issue reared its head; I categorically stated that 'I do not need to be convinced that outsourcing exploits vulnerable workers and needs to be changed'. But I also indicated that 'insourcing will come at a significant financial cost which will require multiple trade-offs that will impact on all within the university community'. Advocates of insourcing within the academy never sufficiently appreciated and internalised this latter reality. As Chapter 2 indicated, when Eric Worby was challenged to develop a business proposal for effecting insourcing without compromising the university's finances, he demurred, citing that it was not his responsibility to do so. The battle over insourcing, then, was never about the importance of doing it, but rather about how to do it, what the trade-offs would be, and whether institutional stakeholders were prepared to pay the costs associated with advancing this human rights obligation.

The student and worker protests in 2015 changed the terms of the debate. Whether to insource was no longer the question; the only issue under consideration was how to do it in a way that enabled us to continue to deliver collectively on the university's mandate. In this sense, the student and worker protests were essential for enabling change. They demonstrated the power of social mobilisation in opening up the systemic parameters of what was possible. Political activists and social movement theorists have long spoken of the power of social mobilisation. Progress in society often happens in response to mobilisation of one or multiple sectors, which impose systemic or institutional costs and compel decision-makers to initiate significant reforms. South Africans know this better than most others, given the role of mass mobilisation in bringing the apartheid state to its knees.

But social mobilisation is only the first part of the story. It is also important to understand how the decision to insource was effected within the university setting, how it was paid for, and what the institutional consequences were. For anyone who is interested in advancing social justice, this second part of the story should be as essential as the first. Otherwise, we risk unintended consequences. In the case of insourcing, the reform could have come at the cost of the institution's mandate, or it could have been financially unsustainable and subsequently reversed.

It is this second part of the story, then, that the pages that follow capture. It is a story of the social struggle of protesting students and workers to open the systemic parameters for imagining a different labour regime within the university. But it is also about the messiness of how it was done, how it was paid for, and its institutional consequences. It kicked off the moment the university made the in-principle commitment to insource vulnerable workers, itself only a result of the social mobilisation of the students and the workers. It is a story that is not complete, but rather one that we are still living through. The collective decisions that we make now and how we behave will crucially influence the long-term viability of the university's new labour regime, and determine its institutional consequences.

As Chapter 2 showed, the straggling group of protesters in the 2015 protests had been brought on board by the end of October with an in-principle commitment to insource vulnerable workers in a financially sustainable manner. A multi-stakeholder task team was established to develop an insourcing plan. It was to comprise student representatives from the SRC and the #FeesMustFall activists, worker representatives and academics sympathetic to their agenda. The #FeesMustFall activists initially objected to having the SRC on the committee, but we insisted that they be there as the official representatives of the student body. The Insourcing Task Team also included two representatives of the executive – Linda Jarvis as CFO and Commerce, Law and Management dean Imraan Valodia – and two representatives of the Council – Randall Carolissen as chair and Theunie Lategan as the head of the Finance Committee. Randall was to be replaced by Isaac Shongwe soon after. The choices of the executive and Council representatives were deliberate. Imraan was deployed because of his economist background and his union experience. Isaac was perceived as politically astute and would be able to broker relationships with others on the task team, while Linda and Theunie were meant to guard against the proposals becoming financially unsustainable.

Of course, the numbers on the task team were heavily loaded against executive management and Council, given that the student, worker and academic representatives comprised more than 70 per cent of the committee. Indeed, almost all the stakeholders acted in concert. They caucused before meetings; when proposals were put forward, in most cases from the worker representatives, it was quite apparent that consultations had occurred outside the task team. Moreover, the other stakeholders – including the two academic representatives, Shireen Ally and Noor Nieftagodien – rarely bothered themselves with questions of affordability or whether decisions would compromise the primary mandate of the institution. All of them effectively operated from the assumption that public education should be fully funded by the state; they gave no thought, therefore, to trade-offs between competing priorities. Of course, when they were engaged individually on this issue outside of the meetings, they would acknowledge the systemic constraints on the institution and the need for the reforms to be phased in. But this never seemed to inform the task team's actual deliberations. Issues of affordability and trade-offs were left to the executive and Council representatives, who could easily be outvoted. But the task team's mandate was merely advisory; Council had to consider and approve its recommendations. This served as a check and ensured that, ultimately, there would be a measured approach to insourcing vulnerable workers.

The choice of the chair of the task team was at first controversial. The #FeesMustFall and EFF students had suggested Dali Mpofu, chairperson of the EFF. These activists, to be honest, were far more organised, proactive and adept than the members of the ANC-aligned SRC. In any case, I was opposed to having any politician chair the task team, but all the other representatives, including the SRC and the academics, supported the proposal. Ultimately, we decided to concede on this and allow Dali to chair the task team as a measure of good faith. And while this seemed a questionable strategy at first, in the end it turned out to be a wise choice – Dali's legitimacy with the outsourced workers and the more radical students ensured that the task team could sell the final plan to all the stakeholders.

The first order of task team business was to consider a proposal for the institution to pay a top-up allowance to address the workers' very low salaries. After some deliberation, the task team agreed to recommend to Council a minimum wage, below which no worker employed by a service provider should be paid. It also recommended that the university provide a top-up payment to service providers to ensure that this minimum wage came into immediate effect. Although initially there was a consideration of R6 000, it ultimately came down to two proposals – R4 500 and R5 000. Unsurprisingly, most task team members voted to propose the latter as the minimum wage. The matter was first considered by the Council Executive; on 14 January 2016, Council decided on the grounds of affordability that R4 500 would become the minimum wage from 1 January 2016 and that a top-up allowance would be paid to all service providers to bring this into effect.

With this issue out of the way, the task team got down to real business. It broke itself into work streams, with smaller groups considering different elements of the challenge. But it soon got bogged down in recriminations. Indeed, for a while, management and Council representatives felt beleaguered. The other task team members would often harangue and verbally confront them. It did not help that a number of the activists in the task team were not the most diplomatic or courteous of individuals under normal circumstances, and were not above using racism and the most diabolical language against the executive and Council representatives. Imraan and Isaac were politically savvy, had seen some of this in their previous lives, and were able to distinguish the acts of spectacle from the serious engagement. But Linda really struggled. It did not help that she had worked with Dali at the South African Broadcasting Corporation (SABC), and was not only unimpressed by her experience there, but saw him as complicit in the destruction of the SABC. Theunie also struggled. Instead of being our institutional check on the issue of financial sustainability, he would often make concessions on which we would then collectively have to hold our ground.

Some of the representatives of the other stakeholders recognised these weaknesses and preyed on them cynically. At one point, it got so bad that we seriously contemplated disbanding the task team and staring down the challenge that would inevitably have emerged. Part of the problem, it seemed to us, was that, despite all the bluster and grandstanding, the representatives of the other stakeholders had no idea how to proceed. And neither did the chair. So, we decided to give it one more shot. How to enable insourcing was the primary focus of the executive retreat on 11 and 12 February 2016, and we invited Theresa Main as the Head of Services to make a presentation and take part in the deliberations. The substance of our reflections was what our best-case scenario on insourcing would be, what we could institutionally afford, who the most vulnerable workers were, and how we could square the expenditure with our affordability limits.

Theresa gave a presentation about the potential extra costs involved if we insourced different categories of workers – cleaning, catering, grounds, waste, security – and concluded with separate financial and operational scenarios. Her financial costings and projections were based on work initially done by Letsema Consulting. After long deliberation, we concluded that our envelope would be R100 million for salaries and a further R20 million for associated operational expenditure. We also concluded that this should allow us to bring into the employee fold all of the categories identified above. The mode of insourcing was meant to be a partnership in which the staff would be brought onto the university payroll, but the management and equipment would remain outsourced. If maintenance workers were to be brought in, they would have to be insourced on a cost-neutral basis. This meant that whatever we were currently paying for the purchase of maintenance services could be redeployed to enable these workers' inclusion. Finally, we concluded that workers at retail outlets at the university could not be insourced. By no stretch of the imagination could they be described as employees of the university; any precedent in this regard, we believed, would imperil the institution financially. We were sympathetic, however, to these workers' plight. We agreed that we would facilitate the development of a workers' charter and insist that any retail outlet with a licence to operate on the premises of Wits University would be obliged to abide by its conditions.

Now that we had a plan, we turned our attention to how to pay for it. We considered a number of ideas, including increasing student numbers, a more measured salary increase, creating further efficiencies in the faculties and central divisions, and increasing income from part-time studies. After exploring all these ideas, we decided to put together what came to be known as the Trade-offs Committee under Andrew Crouch. Its primary mandate was to engage all faculties and central divisions with a view to finding R150 million in savings to compensate for the R120 million insourcing cost and another R30 million associated with financial concessions made to students in the preceding months. The retreat then set the stage for how to proceed in the coming months. Two teams were established: the first with the responsibility of engaging the task team and subtly winning over the rest of the representatives to the plan that had been developed, and the second with the mandate to consult and find the R150 million we needed to enable insourcing and the other #FeesMustFall concessions.

In the months that followed, Imraan and Linda, along with Isaac and Theunie, carried the insourcing plans through into the task team. Gradually, engagements became more constructive and progress began to be recorded. By June 2016, the task team was ready to make a recommendation on the insourcing of workers who were involved in catering, cleaning, grounds, waste and security, and those responsible for driving Wits-branded buses. The insourcing was to happen in January 2017, provided that this coincided with concluding contracts with service providers – or that these contracts could be terminated early without cost to the university. The task team also recommended increasing the minimum wage to R6 000 while workers were awaiting insourcing, and to R7 500 when they came on board in January 2017.

Two categories of staff – maintenance and retail – remained outside of the agreement. The task team wanted more time to enable it to address the concerns of these two categories of staff. I was particularly against the idea, fearing the erosion of managerial authority and the consequences this could have. But Imraan motivated the case on the grounds that it would be useful to retain the task team while the matter of the maintenance and retail workers was still outstanding. Eventually, the executive and I agreed, and the task team was given the first of two extensions. Council ultimately adopted all these recommendations in July 2016, and they began to be operationalised.

One source of tension in the second half of the year was the delay in insourcing as a result of existing contracts: we faced having to pay large penalties for early termination of contracts. The task team was of the view that Services management was not sufficiently robust in negotiating the exit from these existing contracts. By this time, Tawana had replaced Linda, who had resigned; his presence in the task team was useful in overcoming the impasse. He not only identified contracts that the university could end without cancellation costs, but he also overrode the Legal Office and gave Dali and the task team's sub-committee on contracts sight of other service level agreements. Eventually, we agreed to initiate a second round of negotiations with the service providers. This time, the management team was supplemented with members of the task team, including the chair. We remained adamant that the university would not be willing to pay large amounts in penalties to exit a contract. This proved to be unnecessary, however, as the inclusion of the task team members helped to convince service providers to allow exits from the contracts, sometimes on the terms that they would be given another contract involving equipment and man-agement services. By the end of the year, we had sufficient agreements to enable the first cohort of workers to be insourced, now at a salary of R7 800 as a result of new remuneration increases for all staff. By mid-2017, almost all the original categories of catering, cleaning, grounds, waste and security staff were insourced. A bit of fanfare accompanied this: workers were officially welcomed into the university community, with new uniforms and a celebration to which the task team members were invited. In total, about one and a half thousand workers were insourced.

While all of this was happening, the issue of maintenance workers preoccupied the task team. It had been agreed that the cost of insourcing should be neutral. So, the debate in the task team then revolved around what the costs would be and the number of workers who could be insourced. The university commissioned a private company to undertake a costing exercise, recommend a model for insourcing maintenance workers and suggest how many workers should be insourced. The com-pany recommended insourcing only a small number of workers, which created tensions in the task team. To resolve these tensions, Imraan convinced the task team to contract a facilitator. He approached the

Commission for Conciliation, Mediation and Arbitration, which suggested Meshack Ravuku, an organiser with the Chemical Workers Industrial Union and formerly of the Congress of South African Trade Unions (COSATU). Letsema Consulting, which Isaac owned and had undertaken the earlier study on insourcing, was contracted to help determine the new costs. Although there was some concern about conflicts of interest, the company agreed to assist the process without charge. To be honest, Letsema Consulting's earlier financial projections had significantly underestimated the costs of insourcing, but the task team was of the view that they were best placed to assist because they had at least thought through the issues. Eventually, the task team concluded with a number of scenarios involving different numbers of workers to be insourced – 48, 65, 95 and 148.

The task team officially recommended insourcing 95 workers at a cost of about R10 million. Recall that the original agreement was that maintenance workers were to be brought in on a cost-neutral basis, which would have involved insourcing only 48 workers. However, Imraan made the case that we should, at least, consider insourcing 65 workers, at a cost of an additional two to three million rand. He motivated this on the grounds that there had been a small saving in the first round of insourcing, and a concession would be interpreted as a measure of good faith on the part of the university. I reluctantly agreed, fearing that we would be forced to make additional concessions in this regard; after endorsement from the executive, we took the proposal to the Council meeting in June 2017.

At the Council meeting, Dali motivated the case for insourcing 95 workers. In the deliberations that followed, it became apparent that the new chief operating officer (COO), Fana Sibanyoni, was not convinced that 65 workers would be enough to meet the university's maintenance needs and was hoping to use some outsourced capacity to supplement his office. Fearing that this may beckon a new front for protest, I proposed that we support the insourcing of the 95 workers at an additional cost of R7.5 million, which would be derived from efficiency savings in the COO's office. We also committed to an annual review of the workload of maintenance workers with a view to rightsizing this part of the workforce as resignations and retirements occurred. Council agreed to the proposal, and 95 maintenance workers were insourced.

The final category of workers who remained excluded were employees of the retail outlets at the university. The executive had left no wiggle room for the task team on the issue of retail workers – we had made it absolutely clear that no insourcing would be considered. Eventually, this was agreed to; after the detailed deliberations that Meshack facilitated, a workers' charter was developed. This charter would govern the minimum wage and labour standards of all employees of retail outlets at Wits University. The only concession the university made was that we would consider concessions on rentals in exchange for retail outlets' meeting the charter's minimum wage and labour obligations. This decision was also formally adopted at the Council meeting in June 2017.

By the middle of 2017, then, the insourcing matter had been finalised. By this time, Linda had resigned and emigrated from South Africa. The task team was disbanded, some twelve months later than originally planned. But despite this, and its initial hiccups, the team had been enormously successful in helping the university to plan for and manage the insourcing process. In appreciation, Council hosted a luncheon to thank its members for their contribution to the insourcing challenge's positive outcome.

While this was playing out, the second initiative – the Trade-offs Committee – had also got underway. Throughout the first semester of 2016, it consulted with all faculties and stakeholders on the trade-offs that could possibly generate the R150 million saving. This created much angst within the institution. Repeatedly, the then president of ASAWU, David Hornsby, raised concerns about institutional deliberations that spoke to the unravelling of our three-year above-inflation wage agreement, or cuts in expenditure to the academic programme. I had spoken about reviewing expenditure to enable trade-offs at all of my engagements with the faculties and at the Senate, promising that the decisions in this regard would be made transparently and would, as far as possible, try to avoid irreparable damage to the academic programme.

Much of the engagement on the trade-offs was robust, yet courteous and thoughtful. But there were also moments when it was cheeky and laced with barbed commentary and innuendo. One such occasion was a meeting with the Faculty of Humanities on 2 February 2016 when, in response to a question by Mehita Iqani, a senior lecturer in Media Studies, about whether variable pay for executives was also to be the subject of financial review, I retorted: 'All remuneration will be under the spotlight, but this must be done thoughtfully for all categories of staff and must be mindful of competitive pressures.' She was to raise this same question in the Senate, and my answer would be the same. The innuendo, of course, was that the vice-chancellor's and executives' salaries were excessive, a matter that had repeatedly come up in the insourcing and #FeesMustFall protests. In many ways, this was a legitimate issue and needed to be raised. But if it was to be truly addressed, it had to be done thoughtfully and strategically, instead of in the insolent and provocative manner in which it had traditionally come to be raised.

My own approach to the issue was predictably conflicted, as I had to grapple with negotiating my own salary with Council as well as the salaries of my colleagues. I also had to do this in a context where I have repeatedly argued, publicly, that we cannot address inequality in our society without a more measured approach to executive remuneration. But herein lies the dilemma: setting non-competitive executive salaries would result in universities losing their best executives. Of course, this is not an issue for some student leaders and the far left, because they do not believe that executives matter or even make a difference. But if one does recognise the importance of executive leadership, and the value of an institution attracting and retaining good executives, then one has to confront the dilemma of remunerating executives competitively.

This is the challenge that I have had to grapple with and address institutionally and personally, and I have done so in three distinct ways. First, executive salaries at Wits University do contain a component of performance-based variable pay, but this is part of the core remuneration package rather than an additional top-up payment. Thus, when my salary and those of my fellow executives are benchmarked against those of our peers, we remain firmly ensconced in the second half of the top ten of university executive salaries. It is worth bearing in mind that this is in a university that has the highest-paid academic and administrative staff. The net effect is that Wits University's remunerative philosophy is one in which its executives' salaries are located in a second-tier band, while those of its academics and administrative staff are on the top end when compared to those of their peers in other institutions. This is a remunerative outcome that we have willingly entered into because it enables us to retain our executives while still affirming our collective belief in the importance of good academic and administrative staff for a research-intensive university.

The second way in which I have grappled with the tension of receiving a generous salary while holding the view that executive remuneration needs to be more measured in our society is to forsake 50 per cent of my variable pay annually. Council has separately and independently made a reciprocal investment in student scholarships and bursaries. I have done this every single year of my tenure at Wits University, except for 2015, when I sacrificed my entire variable pay. Finally, I have continued to call publicly for measured executive remuneration in society, including for vice-chancellors at universities, and have expressed public support for executive salaries at universities to be legislated. In this way, the remunerative field would be significantly equalised, greatly reducing the pressure on executive salaries at universities and allowing us to become even more measured without risking the loss of key executives.

Much of this is known at the university, which has not prevented some student and union leaders and academics on the far left from using executive remuneration as a tool when it suits them. Of course, there may very well be legitimacy in subjecting some of our strategies to critical reflection – and there may even be more effective ways of managing the tension between accelerating institutional inequality and paying our executives a competitive salary. However, as I indicated earlier, a thought-ful conversation about this has not been possible given the grandstanding and spectacle with which the issue has often been raised.

In any case, the proposals of the Trade-offs Committee were taken to the executive retreat at the end of August 2016. The proposals involved income generation and expenditure cuts. With regard to the former, increases in income of R29 million were envisaged from the more efficient management of a tax on all research and donor funds, known as cost recovery or CORY (an institutional charge for infrastructural and administrative costs); a wider selection of short-course provision; and a better investment strategy for administered funds. But a far bigger proportion of income was to be generated from expenditure cuts. This essentially involved a cut in operational expenditure of 6 per cent in faculties and 8 per cent in central departments, totalling an annual saving of R80 million. It was also proposed that the concession to academics on research incentive monies be withdrawn, generating a further R66 million. Further cuts were proposed on scholarships and concessions associated with staff retirements.

Concerned that the cuts in research incentives, scholarships and staff retirements would severely impact staff morale, I proposed that we consider, as an alternative, an interest honeymoon on all research funds within the university, except in cases where existing contracts restricted us from doing so. After all, at most universities in the country, interest on such funds was absorbed as a matter of course by the institutional centre. Mandy Kort, senior manager in Finance, estimated that this would generate some R50 million and, together with the R80 million in cuts from operational expenditure, would give us the vast bulk of the funds we required. The executive endorsed the proposals and it was agreed that I would personally engage all researchers in this regard. In the two weeks that followed, I engaged the senior researchers of each faculty, requesting that they concede the interest on their research funds to the institutional centre for a period of two years as this would avoid more damaging cuts to the university's academic core. All in all, most researchers in every faculty approved the proposals, greatly enhancing our ability to generate the resources we required to insource vulnerable workers and cover the financial concessions we had made in the preceding months.

By the middle of 2016, we had not only developed concrete plans to insource vulnerable workers, but had also established mechanisms for generating the resources to underwrite this reform's implementation. By January 2017, significant numbers of workers had been insourced; by the end of the year, the programme had been fully implemented. In the months that followed, some members of the university community, including students and student leaders, complained that the quality of services had declined. We responded to this challenge by beefing up our management controls. In addition, the vast majority of the insourced workers joined the National Union of Metalworkers of South Africa (NUMSA), partly at the urging of some of the academics. This greatly increased shop-floor rivalry between NUMSA and NEHAWU. This would greatly complicate wage negotiations in late 2017 and would ultimately lead to a strike by both NEHAWU and NUMSA in early 2018. While the strike was quickly resolved, the fact that it happened and the disruptions that were associated with it, including threats to some academic staff, did signal that the institution, like many other universities in the country, was becoming increasingly prone to industrial action.

This prompted me to write an opinion piece in the *Daily Maverick* in which I expressed concern that the universities were under assault by both external and internal stakeholders. My ire here was reserved for internal stakeholders – the unions in particular, who, even after being offered remuneration that was 2 per cent above inflation, decided to strike. The strike itself was undertaken on the back of poorer service workers; academics and senior administrators did not have the appetite to strike, and likely did not support the action of their own union leadership. Eventually, after about a week, we settled with a differential salary increase of 9.2 per cent for grades 16 and 17. Essentially, this meant that many of the workers who had recently been insourced would have had their remuneration tripled in under two years. Academics and senior administrators received a salary increase of 7 per cent, 0.2 per cent higher than what was originally offered. The net increase in our overall salary budget compared to the original proposal was about R10 million, which was easily accommodated with reprioritisation. But my concern was about what the strike portended for the future.

I was concerned that staff who were the highest paid in the sector were prepared to strike, even though their remuneration offer was 2 per cent above inflation. I was concerned that the unions that had previously entered a three-year wage agreement were now reluctant to do so, simply to maximise their negotiating position. This made the university vulnerable to continuous instability. It troubled me that the internal stakeholder leadership was so focused on short-term gains that the institution's long-term sustainability was no longer a factor in their deliberations. And, ultimately, it troubled me that the internal stakeholder leadership refused to recognise that the institution's numbers would not add up for as long as its government subsidy was below inflation, students refused to pay fees, and workers continued to demand above-inflation salary increases.

In my reflections in the *Daily Maverick* I warned that, if internal stakeholders were not measured in their demands, or refused to take a long-term view of their institutional future, they would plunge the university into a financial crisis and run the risk of returning Wits to the early years of the current millennium when, in an effort to save money, the university had been prompted to outsource many of its vulnerable staff and establish an economically conservative labour regime. I argued that, instead of viewing institutional challenges in terms of zero-sum outcomes, we should consider more measured remuneration agreements, the designation of security staff as essential workers so that they could not strike, and prevailing on unions to enter into three-year agreements. These, I argued, would enable us to balance competing priorities, and facilitate a fiscal and political maturity from university leaders and a measuredness from employees and students.

I expressed these same concerns to the national leadership of the union movement, including Sdumo Dlamini from COSATU, Zwelinzima Vavi from the South African Federation of Trade Unions, Irvin Jim from NUMSA, and Michael Makwayiba from NEHAWU. I urged them to be open to engagement so that we could address the challenge proactively. The matter was also placed on the agenda of a USAf meeting, with a view to opening a conversation at national level with government and other stakeholders. But none of this has generated the institutional or systemic partnerships – the social pact, if you like – that Wits University needs to become a financially viable, sustainable, socially inclusive, research-intensive public university. It remains a work in progress; for as long as this is the case, the final chapter on insourcing at Wits has not yet been written.

5

What's in a name?

THE University of the Witwatersrand is a very different place today from what it was in 1994. Black students comprise 82 per cent of the student population, in stark contrast to 1994, when the number stood at 35 per cent. Women students are in the majority, at 55 per cent compared to 41 per cent in 1994. Blacks comprise 90 per cent and Africans 79 per cent of professional and administrative staff, compared to 76 and 55 per cent in 2005. Black staff comprise 49 per cent and Africans 32 per cent of academics, compared to 27 and 17 per cent in 2005. Much still needs to be done. More needs to happen on the academic staffing front and in the senior managerial cohort. Many other elements of transformation – naming, institutional culture, non-racial and cosmopolitan residences, minimum wages and decent living standards for vulnerable workers – have only recently been embarked upon or accelerated. But despite these challenges, Wits University remains a very different place today from what it was two decades ago.

One would not glean this from the political rhetoric of the #FeesMustFall activists and their supporters, however. This rhetoric portrays the university as an untransformed place, one in which nothing substantive has happened in the 24 years since South Africa's first democratic election. When confronted with the reality that black students and black professional and administrative staff are the substantive majority, and approaching our demographic targets, student leaders first reluctantly concede – and then quickly brush off – these facts as obfuscating the real challenges that black students and staff experience daily on campus. Many graduates who imagine the university to be the same place as they remember it from a decade or two ago would share this view. In the rhetorical fervour of the protests, and the bitter experience of yesteryear, nuance and accuracy – elements necessary for thoughtful activism – have been sacrificed at the altar of political spectacle.

Why is there this scepticism about transformation and its gains, limited though they may have been? It has afflicted not only the student leadership, but also many among the progressive staff. Part of the explanation for this, especially for the progressive staff, is that previous transformation initiatives had been accompanied by an attempt to stabilise the university's finances. This resulted in transformation being ensconced in a particular political economy. As the numbers of black students increased, so did class sizes, resulting in an exponential increase in staff–student ratios. There was also the simultaneous closure of academic development and tutorial programmes. These were national trends, of course, but this provided cold comfort to the academics and students at the coalface. The net result was a deep mistrust of the transformation programmes that executive management initiated.

It must be said, however, that the university of old, with small classes and homogeneous communities, is an institution of the past. Too many academics imagine the research university to be the Ivy League of North America – Harvard, Princeton, Stanford and Yale – or the elite, empire-established institutions of the United Kingdom – Cambridge and Oxford. But the former universities are only really possible because of high student fees and massive endowments, and the latter because of large government subsidies, slightly lower student fees and massive college endowments drawn from an empire of the past. Neither model is practical for the research universities of the 21st century, and our model of transformation should not be burdened by it. Of course, academics and executives understand some of this as we experiment, reform by reform, to establish a research university that is contextualised in, and speaks to, the realities of contemporary South Africa.

This explanation of the scepticism about transformation speaks to the experience of the progressive academic and not the student leadership. After all, students are a transient group; much of their leadership was not there to experience earlier transformation initiatives. The students' scepticism arises from the deep anger of exclusion, emanating in part from a lack of resources and a lack of identification with their institutional surroundings. But while their critique is powerful because it emanates from a real experience, the ideas they pose as alternatives are rudimentary at best and dangerous at worst. Some believe that to highlight this is to caricature the student protest, but to remain silent when so many of these ideas are flawed in an epistemological, pedagogical and technical sense would be to compromise the university itself. Empowering and enabling the development of a new generation must never be confused with patronising and romanticising. These ideas must be challenged and replaced with alternative ones drawn from a collective process involving all stakeholders, including academics and students, and ensconced in sound epistemological principles and pedagogical practices.

It is also worth noting that another part of the scepticism of the student leaders emanates from their being located in political parties. They are as much political party actors as they are student activists. Their critique is therefore party politically informed to advance a party political agenda. Too many who romanticise the decolonisation rhetoric ignore this, and do so at their peril, for it is important to distinguish the spectacle of critique from the reality of it – especially if one wants to fashion solutions for the contemporary institutional challenges in higher education.

Transformation is not an immediate outcome. Rather, it is the result of the slow accumulation of structural reforms. It must be imagined as a continuous process. As one set of reforms is initiated, it comes up against structural and institutional constraints, which inform the development of a new round of reforms. The real debate is what characterises a reform as structural. Structural reforms cannot simply be accommodated within existing institutional parameters. Rather, they challenge and extend these parameters to create a never-ending cycle of reforms, constraints and further reforms. This conception of transformation is evident in the pages that follow. Also evident in these pages is how the conceptual ideas for the structural reforms on the gender front were informed by the academic and student activists, while those on the racial front were led – or at least institutionally conceptualised – by executive management. This greatly impacted on the trajectories of the respective reforms, and needs to be deliberated and addressed if we are to record substantive further progress.

Finally, the pages that follow will also identify the challenges and tensions that are emerging on the gender, racial and broader transformation front. Many progressive analysts refuse to highlight these for fear that those opposed to transformation will use them to subvert the transformation agenda. But remaining silent is deeply problematic, for it allows those who are opposed to a transformative agenda to dominate deliberations about it. Far better, I believe, is to highlight the challenges, enable a process for their deliberation, and develop progressive responses. There is an urgent need to understand where progress has been made, where it has not, and why this is the case. We need to understand what the trade-offs have been when transformative advancements have been made, and what their unintended consequences were. This requires a dispassionate analysis of successes, failures and obstacles to transformation, and how these can be overcome. We also need a historical perspective on transformation so that we can learn from past social experiments and not repeat our failures. But most of all, we need honest deliberation, committed to the goal of transformation but unburdened by emotion and labelling so that we can think through how to continue to advance in a way that accords with our institutional mandate and enables the university to contribute to society's inclusive development.

Wits University recorded substantive transformative progress on the student front during the tenure of my predecessor, Loyiso Nongxa. This was largely a result of policy changes that, on one hand, increased student numbers at the university and, on the other, emphasised poverty and distance from home as variables in the allocation of spaces within university residences. This was meant, in part, to address the university's financial crisis; as indicated earlier, it was also preceded by the closure of academic development and tutorial programmes. It not only increased academics' work burden, but also compromised the throughput of many students, especially poor black students. Nevertheless, the number of black students at Wits University dramatically increased within a few years.

Of course, criticisms were still levelled against the admission process by progressive academics and activists, who held that we had not considered class criteria – and that, by taking only race into account, we allowed African and Coloured students from privileged backgrounds equal treatment to those from poor and disadvantaged ones. As a result, soon after I took over as vice-chancellor in 2013, we instituted a review of our admission process for the MBBCh programme in the Faculty of Health Sciences. This is one of our most popular academic programmes; on average, we receive 10 000 applications for 220 academic places. Academic assessments for admissions are based on two examinations: the final Grade 12 examination and the national benchmark tests. Each comprises 50 per cent of the assessment. White and Indian students, who often perform better in these tests as a result of better schooling systems, are required to achieve a higher point score to gain entrance than African and Coloured students. An alternative graduate path to the MBBCh, known as the Graduate Entry Medical Programme (GEMP), is for those students who have completed a full degree and meet certain minimum requirements. Their entry, however, is to the third year of the MBBCh, which means that they can complete this degree with an additional four years. As a result of the review, we revised the admission criteria to introduce both class and rurality as variables in our admission process. Forty per cent of seats in the MBBCh programme are now determined simply on the basis of academic results. The remaining 60 per cent are reserved in three equal allotments for the best-performing students from rural schools, quintile 1 and 2 urban schools, and African and Coloured students from any background. Those too poor to pay for their education were supported financially by a grant arranged with the Department of Health in an agreement with Minister Aaron Motsoaledi. The GEMP admission programme continued largely unchanged, although it was expanded slightly and will be further expanded in the years to come.

The second innovation was the establishment of the Vice-Chancellor's Equality Scholarship programme, with funding from Investec and Kumba. Until 2013, Wits University only had the Vice-Chancellor's Scholarship, which is reserved for the top ten applicants and offers them a full tuition waiver for their entire programme of study. The Vice-Chancellor's Equality Scholarship offers both tuition and accommodation to the top ten applicants from quintile 1 and 2 schools, those servicing the most marginalised of our communities. This means that our assessment of excellence, at least for our most prestigious scholarship, takes into account contextual circumstances and ensures that students are not disproportionally prejudiced on the basis of their class background. By explicitly addressing class variables, both policy innovations, then, have increased the proportion of poor students at the university.

But perhaps the most significant transformative innovations in the early years of my tenure occurred in the arena of gender-based harm. These innovations were largely forced upon us by a series of sexual harassment scandals that erupted soon after I assumed office. There were four cases of serial harassment of women students by staff, which had gone on for years. These involved four senior academics – Last Moyo, Tsepo wa Mamatu, Rupert Taylor and Lord Mawuko-Yevugah – from different schools in the Faculty of Humanities. All the cases had been reported, but our lethargic processes and rigid rules meant that they had dragged on for months, if not years. In late 2012, Tawana Kupe had been involved in a process that resolved to initiate a full-scale enquiry into sexual harassment at Wits University. He was also involved in appointing Bonita Meyersfeld and Joe Mothibi from Norton Rose Fulbright to undertake the enquiry, and in resolving a dispute between Bonita and the Legal Office in which it was decided that the findings and recommendations would be made public. The cases were publicised in early 2013, when activists leaked information about them. Confronted with the scandal, the university accelerated a full-scale enquiry that led to disciplinary proceedings against all four of the staff. These culminated in the dismissal of three of the staff and the resignation of the fourth. Throughout this period, the university community was regularly notified about progress in the hearings, as well as when staff were dismissed or had resigned.

In addition, we instituted a complete overhaul of our investigative and disciplinary codes on sexual harassment and gender-based harm, largely on the basis of recommendations from a task team co-chaired by Bonita, who was then the director of CALS. Many of these recommendations were informed by activists who had long advocated for the institution to change, dramatically, the way it responded to the challenge of gender-based harm. The new infrastructure for addressing sexual harassment involved a gender office that was separate from the transformation office – for a period, at least – and located within it the responsibilities for advocacy, counselling, investigation and prosecution. One of the findings of the task team was that the university was overly concerned with its brand image, to the point of sometimes compromising the demand for justice. It also found that our legal and disciplinary systems had not been sufficiently sensitive to the concerns and needs of victims of gender-based harm; as a result, it recommended establishing a new, victim-centred disciplinary system. This involved, among other measures, the right of victims to be interviewed separately from alleged perpetrators, often in separate rooms, by the disciplinary panel. It would be fair to say that this distinct and separate legal process for cases related to gender-based harm created quite a bit of consternation in the Legal Office and the executive, but after repeated engagements, the new processes were endorsed and implemented.

The new Sexual Harassment Office, later renamed the Gender Equity Office (GEO), was supported by an advisory board of which I was a member. The director of the GEO and the chair of the Advisory Board reported directly to me. To be honest, I was never comfortable with this reporting line, or with my membership of the Advisory Board.

All other divisions, including the social justice offices of Transformation and Disability Rights, reported to other members of the executive. But the Advisory Board and many of the gender activists insisted that this reporting line to me would give the office the seniority and informal power it needed to investigate sexual harassment at any level of the university hierarchy. In the end, we reached an uneasy compromise: matters of administration would be directed to Tawana, to whom the Transformation Office also reports, while the GEO would report directly to me on all matters of substance.

The first director of the GEO was Jackie Dugard, a progressive legal activist who had recently been appointed associate professor in our School of Law and who took a two-year deployment to establish the office. Aside from establishing the organisational infrastructure and redeploying or appointing personnel, the office focused on investigating and prosecuting a number of cases of sexual harassment, on behalf of both staff and students. Several high-profile dismissals for sexual harassment followed in subsequent months and years. The office also undertook two major investigations – the first on gender-based harm experiences in university residences and how to address them, and the second on relationships between staff and students. The latter culminated in the university adopting a new policy prohibiting personal relationships between staff and undergraduate and honours students, and establishing that any violation in this regard could result in dismissal. Exceptions were allowed, but within strict parameters, and only after a full invest-igation by the GEO.

While significant progress was recorded in the first two years of the GEO's operation, significant challenges remained at the end of 2015. First, some students remained sceptical of the GEO's independence. The office was caught up in the politics of #FeesMustFall and the polarisation that subsequently emerged within the university, a matter to which we will return. But perhaps the biggest problem was the disconnect between different arms of the university bureaucracy in addressing rape and other forms of gender-based harm. This situation was aggravated by tensions that emerged between the GEO and Transformation Office as a result of ideological differences and interpersonal rivalry. On all matters before the GEO, different sections of the administration were required to assist in fully addressing the difficulties experienced by the victim. But not all sections of the administration would act in tandem on these matters, or would demonstrate the required amount of empathy. As a result, victims sometimes experienced the university as indecisive and conflicted. In such cases, the matter was to be referred to my office for an appropriate instruction to all divisions in the university. But this did not always happen, creating much consternation all round.

The matter came to a head two years into the life of the GEO and in the midst of the #FeesMustFall protests in 2016. The incident involved two students, a young man and woman from one of our residences who had gone out for the evening. On their return, they decided to spend the night together. In the morning, the woman student accused the man of having raped her. In these circumstances, residence management is meant to separate the alleged perpetrator and alleged victim immediately by moving the former to another residence, and then call in the GEO to investigate the case and provide appropriate counselling and support for the victim. But in this case, after engaging both individuals, Director of Campus Housing and Residence Life Rob Sharman decided against separating them. The GEO asked him to reconsider; he declined. The matter soon blew up in the public domain, with activists accusing the university of being insensitive to the victim's concerns and needs.

I responded by instructing that the implicated students be separated, although by then the matter was moot since both students were off campus: the alleged perpetrator had left as a result of having received threats, and the victim had returned home. I also instituted an urgent enquiry into university management's handling of the matter, to be headed by Nomboniso Gasa, a well-known gender activist. Her report was devastating in that it concluded that residence management had acted inappropriately and violated policy. But it also identified weaknesses in the GEO's management of the incident. When the Director of Campus Housing and Residence Life was found to be uncooperative, the GEO could have elevated the issue to my office, which it did not do in this case. The report culminated in letters of reprimand to selected officials in residence management, some mandatory gender-sensitivity training for individual managers, and the tightening up of protocols at the GEO, especially regarding when matters should be escalated to the vice-chancellor. This event also coincided with Jackie Dugard's departure from the GEO, as her two-year tenure was complete. She had played a phenomenal role in establishing an office and a legal machinery from scratch. Jackie was succeeded by Crystal Dicks, an activist and organiser recruited from the trade union movement. The chair of the Advisory Board also changed hands, with Danai Mupotsa joining Bonita as a co-chair, and then continuing to serve with Charmika Samaradiwakera-Wijesundara from 2018.

Crystal's tenure was distinguished by a greater focus on advocacy, although investigations and prosecutions still remained the mainstay of the office's work. Investigations were initiated in the School of Geography, Archaeology and Environmental Studies, the Wits School of Arts, and the Faculty of Health Sciences, and counselling and support were provided to rape and gender-based harm victims from both university and private residences. It is worth noting, here, that a few of the student cases involved politically high-profile male student leaders who were accused of rape, sexual harassment or both. Some of the cases involving staff and students culminated in disciplinary hearings, dismissals and resignations. But these initiatives were accompanied by a greater focus on advocacy and student engagement, with activists being recruited from the student body, trained, and then mandated to work with groups of other students on sexual harassment awareness, support provision and identifying potential trouble spots. In addition, largely at my insistence, the GEO managed the university's involvement in the United Nations HeForShe programme coordinated by the office of the executive director of UN Women, Phumzile Mlambo-Ngcuka.

Yet tensions remained between the GEO and the university executive, especially about resource allocations to the GEO and how selected cases were to be managed. At the same time, we began to address the criticism that separate offices did not allow the institution to deal with the intersectionality of discriminations. Another task team, this time established internally and comprising Danai, Shireen Hassim and Charmika, investigated the issue in the first half of 2016 and recommended keeping the offices separate, but increasing coordination and resource sharing. In a subsequent discussion with the task team and all the directors of the social justice divisions, it became apparent that, despite the wisdom of bringing together the different strands of social justice provision, existing rivalries prevented this from happening effectively. In an executive meeting on 13 September 2016, it was agreed that the offices would be kept separate for a period of two years, and then brought together in 2019. In February 2018, after a joint review by Tawana and Bonita, it was finally agreed to merge the offices and create a single Social Justice Division. Each of the social justice areas – gender, race and disability – would remain as distinct organisational foci and operate as such, but they would share corporate services and coordinate resources for providing counselling and engaging in advocacy.

In addition, I stood down from the Advisory Board at the beginning of 2018 with the consent of the other members. It had been apparent for some time that the Advisory Board deliberations seemed unduly skewed by my presence, which fostered adversarial interactions between me and others in which I would inevitably have to explain one or other decision that the university had made. It was implicitly assumed that my exclusion would enable the board to deliberate more fully on the strategic and tactical considerations for addressing rape and other forms of gender-based harm. These changes reflected a common recognition that there was no ready-made formula for addressing the scourge of rape and gender-based harm, and that organisational forms and social justice activities and programmes had to be crafted as part of a continuous process of innovation and renewal.

While much of this played out, so too did struggles about issues related to racism and institutional alienation. In November 2014, some months before the #RhodesMustFall incident at UCT, I hosted a dinner at Savernake with senior African and Coloured academic staff to discuss their experiences at the university and their views on our transformation challenge. Tawana joined me at the dinner. Without exception, all the academics believed that we had a racism and transformation challenge at Wits University and needed to develop a programme urgently to address it.

This prompted me to launch a consultation exercise at the beginning of 2015, on how to address the racism challenge and accelerate the implementation of our transformation agenda. In one of my early meetings, with the Faculty of Humanities, I was struck by the fact that not a single African staff member spoke, even though there were many at the meeting. I raised a concern about this. After the meeting, a number of African staff approached me and indicated that they were not comfortable speaking in the open forum and would be willing to engage, but only if there was a meeting of African staff only. I in turn was uncomfortable with this proposal, not wanting to segment staff racially in my consultation exercises. But I also knew that I had very little option. If I wanted to get to hear the widest range of views on how people experienced Wits University, I had to be willing to compromise. Eventually, I conceded to a meeting of only African and Coloured staff. The decision provoked some anger among other staff. A number of progressive academics criticised me for racially segmenting staff, suggesting that I was pandering to racism, while others expressed concern that, by excluding Indian staff from the meeting, I was undermining a definition of black that had long prevailed within the liberation movement. My simple response to all these criticisms was that, while I too was uncomfortable with having meetings with groups defined on a racial basis, a pragmatic response was the most sensible one under the circumstances if I wanted a diverse and honest view of peoples' experiences at the institution.

The consultation with the African and Coloured staff took place at the Wits Theatre. There was a significant turnout at the meeting, which first had to deal with the fact that a staff member of Indian ancestry, Vinodh Jaichand, had insisted on attending on the grounds that he identified as a member of the black community. The matter was soon resolved; most people were comfortable with him remaining. With that, the meeting got underway and staff became quite open and vocal about their experiences. A significant majority indicated that they had experienced implicit, if not explicit, racism at the university. Many of the African and

Coloured staff said that they felt alienated from the institution, and that not enough was being done to transform it. The staff expressed much concern about the low numbers of African academic staff and the dominance of whites among the professoriate. There were some expressions of concern that academics from the rest of the continent were prioritised in appointments, although others contested this view and held that these colleagues should not in any way be prejudiced. There was even the suggestion that there should be a moratorium on the appointment of white staff. I challenged this – not only did I think it was unconstitutional, but it went against the ethos of a research-intensive university.

On balance, the meeting was positive and produced a number of ideas about how transformation could be accelerated. At the end of the meeting, a significant number of participants recommended that a similar one be held with white and Indian staff so that their views on transformation could also be canvassed. This duly happened at the end of May 2015, after I released a document I had crafted from the ideas that emanated from the consultation exercise. The meeting with Indian and white staff was not well attended, as many academics objected on principle to such a meeting. But those who attended expressed broad support for the consultation initiative and the development of a transformation agenda. These meetings were complemented by many others, including multi-stakeholder workshops facilitated by Rejane Williams and Melissa Steyn from the Centre for Diversity Studies. It is worth noting that one of the students who attended these workshops and made valuable contributions to clarifying our collective thinking was Vuyani Pambo, who was then still willing to engage. Overall, the consultation exercise proved fruitful. The document I crafted reflected on the different experiences of Wits University and proposed a concrete plan for accelerating the institution's transformation. It was distributed to the entire university community for comment.

The document, called 'Opening the Conversation: Accelerating Transformation for an Inclusive and Competitive Wits', expressed disquiet about the colour-blindness of the liberal mainstream and the race essentialism of some of the advocates of transformation. The former, it argued, did not sufficiently appreciate that the consequences of racism live long after the formal abandonment of race-based policies; the latter, it held, misrepresented the writings of Fanon and Biko, uncritically applied their lessons from a colonial to a democratic setting, and defended incidents on racial grounds even in cases where this was not warranted. In their stead, I proposed an institutional agenda that would be responsive to transformation and affirm the victims of apartheid without reifying race and resorting to racism and racial chauvinism.

I recommended eight specific initiatives. The first was a programme to diversify the academy through the tenured appointment of African and Coloured staff, and the academic advancement of existing staff, for which R45 million was allocated. The second involved expanding existing curriculum reform initiatives by making it mandatory for each school to host a workshop with all stakeholders to review its curriculum so that it was both responsive to the country's needs and globally competitive. The third programme involved student admissions, with a particular focus on selected schools to ensure that they implemented both diversity and meritocracy in their selection processes. Fourth, residences were to be organised in a manner that reflected diversity and cosmopolitanism. The fifth initiative was directed at establishing and consolidating an inclusive climate where students and staff from diverse backgrounds would feel comfortable. The sixth programme involved renaming buildings and other sites by using both indigenous and Western naming traditions, while the seventh required competencies to be developed in indigenous languages among staff and students. The final programme required the university to partner with civil society to lobby for more resources so that it could wean itself off outsourcing vulnerable employees. Each of these initiatives was allocated to a specific member of the executive, and was written into their performance contracts and the broader institutional scorecard against which individual executives and the collective were annually assessed. Progress was overseen by a Transformation Committee that I would chair. The initiatives' daily management was Tawana's responsibility.

The document was released on 21 May 2015 and provoked widespread deliberation and commentary from students, staff and alumni, and even some academics and executives from other institutions inside and outside the country. A few challenged my critique of essentialism, while others suggested that the ideas in the document were not sufficiently responsive to the concerns of the LGBT+ community. Some responses spoke of the importance of developing new pedagogical practices; others, especially those of alumni, recommended learning from experiences elsewhere in the world. One useful comment from an alumnus was that of the president emeritus of Simon Fraser University, Michael Stevenson, who recommended critically applying lessons from the Canadian experience, especially their Research Chairs and Federal Contractors programmes, which tied the receipt of funds to institutions' achieving employment equity targets. Michael was at pains to indicate that Canada itself had some way to go in achieving its equity goals, however. It is worth noting that most of the responses broadly supported the proposed measures. In the weeks that followed, deliberations were held with the senior executive team, faculty boards, Senate and Council. These culminated in the university's adoption of the eight initiatives for accelerating transformation at Wits.

In the months that followed, each executive took the lead to activate the initiative for which they were responsible. Some, such as diversifying the academy, were easy to activate since specific resources had been allocated to the programme. The initiative to bring about cosmopolitan residences was postponed. The task team investigating how to do this recognised the importance of cosmopolitan residences, but argued that implementing them should be postponed for the time being because it would negatively impact on poor students who had come to the university from other provinces. This is because of an overlap between race and class in South Africa, with the result that an increase in the number of white and Indian students in the residences would come at the cost of places for poorer African students. It was suggested that the initiative be reactivated as soon as there was sufficient availability of residence beds. Student leaders had lobbied for a similar outcome and Council ultimately supported the recommendation. It is worth noting that the task team also recommended prioritising first-year students in allocating residence beds. Council supported this, and duly implemented it in the years that followed.

As Chapter 4 indicated, the recommendations for addressing outsourcing were overtaken by events associated with #FeesMustFall, and insourcing was eventually implemented not with state funds, but by reprioritising the university's internal resources. The impact of #FeesMustFall, however, was not limited to insourcing. It impacted on all elements of the transformation programme, and on the initiatives of both the Transformation and Gender Equity Offices. This compelled a shift in the operations of both offices, and a revision and acceleration of the programmes for advancing institutional transformation and addressing gender-based harm.

The #FeesMustFall activists used the term 'decolonisation' to distinguish their agenda of institutional change. Decolonisation was seen as distinct from transformation, which was deemed a reformist programme reflective of the politics of the 'rainbow nation'. By contrast, decolonisation, the activists maintained, represents a much deeper notion of change – one that forces universities to delink themselves from their apartheid and colonial moorings and re-establish themselves in the postcolonial moment. Yet the distinction remained largely at the polemical and rhetorical level: student leaders struggled to make concrete suggestions about what needed to be done. They would rail against racism or corporatisation or patriarchy, but when confronted with the question of what to do about it, or how to craft a specific set of reforms, they would flounder.

Even regarding their favourite bugbears – decolonising the curriculum, democratising institutional structures and challenging patriarchy – the #FeesMustFall activists were bereft of ideas; when they did make proposals, they were either already in operation in the universities or hopelessly inadequate, divorced from any sensible academic foundation. Of course, they did advance practical proposals for rethinking the curriculum in the humanities and social sciences: broadening reading lists, introducing the writings of black scholars and literary figures, and teaching and researching the histories, social practices, healing traditions and remedies of local communities, all of which are curriculum innovations that need to be considered and implemented. But such curriculum reforms have long been underway in South African universities and could easily have fitted into the rubric of transformation.

Indeed, one of the weaknesses of curriculum reforms is that they are largely limited to the humanities and social sciences. They have not sufficiently impacted on the natural, engineering, medical and commercial sciences. Where ideas have emerged from activists within #FeesMustFall, they have often come off as nonsensical and been subject to caricatures of the worst kind. One example is that, in the midst of the protests at UCT, a student leader confronted with the question of how to decolonise science retorted that it 'was a product of western modernity, and should be scratched out. We would have to restart science from the way we experienced it'. She then proceeded to give the example of a village in KwaZulu-Natal where people believed that witchcraft could cause lightning to strike someone, and she wanted the science curriculum to explain and teach this. When there was sceptical laughter from a member of the audience, the chair forced the person to apologise for disrespecting the speaker, who then went on to suggest that the person's laughter and scepticism had simply arisen because his mind was not yet sufficiently decolonised. You could not have had a more Orwellian moment. A recording of the incident went viral on YouTube, and was subsequently used globally to caricature the thoughts of #FeesMustFall activists on curriculum reform. I raise this incident not so much to bother with critiquing it, but rather to demonstrate how some student leaders misunderstand the very purpose of academic study at a university.

To use another example, in multiple engagements on curriculum reform with student leaders from political parties at Wits University, I was struck by how often they identified our Economics curriculum as a focus for reform. They saw it as advancing mainstream or neoliberal economics; instead, they wanted to be taught Marxist or radical economics. There is something to be said for reforming the Economics curriculum at our universities. But the answer does not lie in the alternatives the student leaders proposed. It is worth noting that they did not advocate teaching a plurality of economic perspectives, or even a heterodox economics. Instead, they advocated an Economics curriculum that accorded with their own narrow ideological and political interests. My concern about this advocacy is the implicit confusion among student leaders about the purpose of university education. In a sense, they have confused the university with the political party school. They expect the university curriculum to accord with their specific ideological and political predispositions. But is university education not meant to encourage understanding from a plurality of perspectives? Is it not meant to disrupt one's thinking – to force one to think in different ways in the hope that doing so would foster a critical consciousness, enabling one continually to reimagine and reinvent possibilities?

None of this is meant to suggest that curriculum reform is not warranted. Indeed, it was identified as an integral component of the university's eight-point transformation plan. As the #FeesMustFall UCT student leader Brian Kamanzi proposed, there is an urgent need to rethink pedagogy in the science and engineering disciplines so that traditional hierarchical modes of learning, where the academic provides and the student imbibes information, are replaced with more collective learning experiences. Classrooms, laboratories, libraries and other infra-structure need to be redesigned to enable these new forms of learning. Technology needs to be more integrated into our teaching so that blended learning experiences come to the fore and assist in addressing the challenges of big classes. As importantly, there is a need to take ser-iously Achille Mbembe's recommendation for new assessment processes that are less quantitatively organised and less oriented to accounting measures, and far more directed towards scientific study and the pursuit of ideas. Some of these proposals are not immediately possible within the framework of the existing configuration of the university, the regulatory framework to which it is subjected and the resources available to it. But to rise to this challenge, these proposals, and many others, need to be deliberated upon, revised, and then introduced into the curriculum through new forms of innovation and design.

There is nothing to suggest that this can only occur under the rubric of decolonisation. Why, then, did so many – including me – so quickly abandon the term 'transformation' in favour of 'decolonisation'? My suspicion is that too many of us simply took the approach, 'What's in a name?' when students introduced the term in the wake of #FeesMustFall. Rather than entertain the debate about terminology, we adopted the term in the hope that it would enable a real conversation about the substance of the issue. But instead, all it did was locate the debate at the highest level of generality, on the level of polemic and the rhetoric, rather than in the specificity of the subject matter and the pedagogy – which is where the conversation needs to be located if we are to make real progress on curriculum reform.

The same can be said of the debate on democratising institutional structures. Again, #FeesMustFall activists have located their advocacy on the level of polemic and rhetoric. They argue that the structures of governance and decision-making are hierarchical and elitist, reflecting the interests of elites, corporatist practices and/or the old order. Moreover, there is scepticism of leadership because of the potential of co-option – the recommendation, therefore, is to reorganise decision-making so that it is located at the level of the mass meeting or the assembly. There is no detailed proposal for how this is to be done, or whether it is even feasible. Nor is there any consideration of how conflicts of interest will be managed, or the implications of the lack of specific expertise that is likely to prevail among general audiences on matters of academic governance and decision-making.

Again, these criticisms should not be interpreted to mean that there is no need for reform of decision-making in this regard. Indeed, there is an urgent need to deliberate on the issue of representation in structures of governance and decision-making. After all, representative structures clearly do not carry the legitimacy that they may once have. The issue, then, is which combination of representation and participation needs to be introduced in structures like the Senate, Council and even the SRC. Yet this is not where the #FeesMustFall activists locate their debate. Indeed, when the issue of reforming the SRC came up at Wits University in late 2017, #FeesMustFall activists and even SRC leaders were almost absent from the debate. The only time they really became activated on the issue was when the reforms started to be implemented, months after Council had adopted proposals. The reason is simple: so focused are student leaders and activists at the level of the political and the rhetorical that they are ill-prepared to engage in the specific reforms required to restructure decision-making. Yet this is where the real stuff of organisational reform happens.

Developments on the gender front were no better. As #FeesMustFall continued, gender and LGBT+ issues emerged at the forefront – within the movement and in the broader institution. At Wits University, there was much consternation among women activists about how women leaders were being forced to concede leadership to their male counterparts. I first observed this on the night on the concourse, when Shaeera and Nompendulo were often forced to hand the microphone over to Mcebo and Vuyani on major issues. These concerns grew in the weeks and months ahead, and became even more pronounced when male political leaders were embroiled in rape and sexual harassment incidents. Similar developments were observed at UCT as women and LGBT+ activists asserted themselves against male leaders and accused Chumani Maxwele of rape. The activists, especially those associated with the Trans Collective, protested their exclusion by shutting down a #RhodesMustFall exhibition in March 2016 by throwing red paint on photographs and lying on the floor with their naked bodies painted with red paint resembling blood. At Wits University, graffiti of the word 'Imbokodo' began to appear around campus, referring to the slogan of the 1956 Women's March: 'Wathint' Abafazi, Wathint' Imbokodo' (you strike a woman, you strike a rock). Some women and LGBT+ activists also held a number of demonstrations outside the Great Hall by appearing topless, while other activists took to wearing the doek in a symbolic assertion of their power. All of this heightened awareness of both gender and LGBT+ struggles, and enabled significant mobilisation, especially in cases that emerged around rape and other forms of gender-based harm.

Even in this environment of heightened awareness, however, not many imaginative proposals were made for addressing patriarchal practices. Both activists and members of the Advisory Board would get exasperated with me when I challenged them to name a single constitutionally compliant request they had made and that the university executive had not acceded to. Regular rotation of wardens, mandatory representation of women on residence committees, and gender sensitivity training in the first-year orientation programme and of all student leaders in residence are all measures that activists and the GEO have requested within the past two years. Every measure has been agreed to and implemented. Although these are sensible measures and create a safe environment, they are not policy reforms that have shifted the institution significantly from its patriarchal roots. To be fair, much of the existing GEO machinery reflects the recommendations of the task team – which was, of course, itself influenced by the proposals of gender activists within the university. Moreover, Crystal would argue that insufficient resources have been made available to address the structural dynamics of patriarchy within the institution comprehensively. But it is also true that, since the 2013 task team, we have not had proposals of a similar scale and character. This is necessary for us to record significant further progress in the struggle against patriarchy at the university.

The decolonisation rhetoric, then, was constructed so firmly on the political and rhetorical level, and was so focused on the critique, that it did not sufficiently empower activists to make imaginative, concrete and specific proposals for improving the institutional environment. But this is not to say that it did not have any value. Indeed, mobilising around these issues and the critique forced the executive to accelerate the initiatives already underway within the university and to publicise them regularly. Each member of the executive had to report regularly to the senior executive team on their initiative's progress, and we began to release regular reports on the transformation plan's overall progress. The net effect is that the university is in a position to provide a detailed transformation report card, reflecting its progress and its failures.

There have been significant successes in four distinct areas. The most significant of these successes is at the level of the appointment and development of African and Coloured staff. Twenty-eight new tenured appointments have been made, 60 per cent of whom are women. This is in addition to normal appointments. Simultaneously, 40 enabling grants were made to existing African and Coloured staff to support their academic development and to ensure that they can meet the requirements for promotion. Second, 13 new buildings and other sites have been renamed, reflecting both the indigenous tradition of naming on the basis of symbolic expression and the Western practice of naming after individuals. The two renaming exercises that received the most attention and coverage were the renaming of Senate House and Central Block to Solomon Mahlangu House and Robert Sobukwe Building respectively. Third, as Chapter 4 demonstrates, the insourcing of vulnerable workers was completed by the end of 2017, with about one and a half thousand vulnerable workers brought onto the university payroll and their salaries more than doubling. In addition, the workers' charter ensures that a minimum wage and conditions of service will come into effect for all employees of retail outlets on university premises. Finally, significant progress has been recorded in establishing an innovative legal and organisational machinery to address rape and gender-based harm, and in adopting new policies to outlaw relations between staff and undergraduate students.

A modicum of success has also been recorded on two other fronts. On the language front, a new board was established in 2017 with representation from multiple stakeholders and with a mandate to create awareness and implement the new language policy. Given the limited institutional resources available, the first step in this plan was to change all letterheads, business cards and signage to reflect three languages: English, isiZulu and Sesotho. Language courses specialising in conversational isiZulu and Sesotho have also been established. These are not mandatory; in a year or two, the university needs to assess take-up. Of course, these reforms are largely accommodative, and cannot by any stretch of the imagination be described as structural or transformative.

There has been more significant progress on the curriculum front. Indeed, the Faculty of Humanities has, in the past two years, implemented 15 new curriculum innovations, through either the introduction of new courses or the revision of existing ones focusing on the histories, politics, philosophies, challenges and cultural practices of African societies. There have also been other forms of curriculum innovation. In the past few years, programmes have been designed on a 3 + 2 model. Students who complete one full degree in one faculty can then proceed to the last two years of study in another programme, earning an additional degree in another faculty. Examples of this are the BA in Digital Arts and the BSc Engineering in Digital Arts, the BSc Biomedical degree as a pathway into the MBBCh, and a BSc Physics as an entry to the BSc Mechanical Engineering degree. New programmes have also been introduced in all faculties. These include undergraduate programmes in film and television, Intermediate Phase education, audiology, speech-language pathology and clinical medical practice; postgraduate diplomas in taxation, specialised accountancy, vocational teaching and leadership development; and finally, postgraduate degree programmes in entrepreneurship, finance and investment, and nuclear technology, and a professional MBA. These are supplemented by external curriculum partnerships like that of our Faculty of Engineering with the University of Venda, in which we assist in the development of their programme in electrical engineering and thereby create a pathway for some of their students to come over into the senior years of our engineering programmes. The net effect will be an erosion of the traditional institutional divides between historically black and historically white universities.

This extensive list of curriculum reform initiatives aside, it is worth highlighting that the initiatives fall into two distinct categories: those of a technical character that respond to demand or the needs of a society or economy, and others that emanate from a more epistemological foundation and challenge the inherent assumptions of our university degree programmes. For instance, Andrew Crouch regularly gets exasperated by students and academics who accuse the university of not reforming its curriculum. He points out the litany of curriculum reforms identified above, but he and the critics are talking at cross purposes. While they imagine curriculum reform to mean innovations that question the epistemological foundation of universities and society, he refers to the technical innovations in course offerings that are responsive to the needs of that same society. Of the litany of the past few years' curriculum reforms, the critics would probably hold that only those in the humanities pass their litmus test.

It is fair to say that we probably require both forms of curriculum innovation: those of a technical character that respond to the needs of the current market and society, and those of a more epistemological character that point us to an alternative future. It is also worth noting that curriculum change will not happen in a single moment, but will result from a process of ongoing reforms of our academic offerings and their related pedagogical innovations. The precise mix of these reforms and their real academic content mean that these initiatives would have to begin at school and departmental level. The university executive's role is merely to create an enabling environment that allows all stakeholders – academics, students, alumni, professional associations and others – to see themselves as active agents who advance ideas and engage collaboratively to create and revise the curriculum so that it is relevant to contemporary needs and is both locally responsive and globally competitive. Curriculum reform, therefore, is underway – but we have only begun to scratch the surface of what is possible.

Perhaps our biggest failures on the transformation front lie in the domain of cosmopolitan residences and institutional culture. As indicated earlier, Council and the executive decided to postpone the initiative to diversify our residences until we had enough beds to meet demand. Immediate implementation of the programme would have significant adverse consequences for the poorest and the most marginalised within the university community. But it is in the arena of institutional culture where our biggest failure lies. Subtle racism is still experienced in the institution; black staff and students continue to feel alienated. White staff and students are feeling increasingly defensive and are unsure of what is required of them. The institutional environment is further complicated by the deep fissures that emerged in the wake of the 2016 protests in particular. Staff increasingly report that some students are particularly rude in the classroom. On occasion, they have felt threatened. This forced me to release a public communique in June 2017 calling on the university community to recognise and respect the values of civility in their daily interactions, and warning that anyone who threatens another member of the university community could be subject to disciplinary action.

However, far more needs to be done on this front. Until now, the Transformation Office has hosted a significant number of dialogues and focus groups across the institution. But these have not had the desired outcome. Part of the problem is the broader political environment, which has been far more fractured in recent years; this has been further aggravated by some political parties and/or party factions that are actively deepening society's divides for short-term political gain. It is also true that the university can do far more to enable deeper deliberations within its community – deliberations that need to go beyond the normal consultancy-oriented institutional conversations that have become the norm in corporate South Africa. We do indeed need honest institutional conversations. But what we need even more is for institutional executives, managers, activists, union and SRC leaders, and other stakeholders to go back to the drawing board and determine more imaginative ways of building a cohesive university community. Only then will we begin to make significant advances on the transformation front.

If there is one truism in the world of social transformation, it has to be that we are the agents of our own liberation. Of course, this agency has to be part of a collective if it is to have systemic effect, but it does require individuals' full and active involvement. Many advocates of transformation do not seem to understand this. Indeed, as I suggested earlier, too many are focused at the level of critique and generality, polemic and rhetoric, divorced from detailed deliberations about specific proposals for transforming institutions. Their role in transformation is limited to protests, and to complaining about executive management, rather than actively contributing ideas about how to transform institutions. This is why there is such limited participation by these student activists and leaders in the forums where the minutiae of reforms are being fashioned and decided.

This circumscribed role is not limited to student activists. It also reflects the attitude of some senior black academics who profess to be committed to the transformation agenda, yet are almost completely divorced from day-to-day interactions about how to transform institutions. I stress that this does not apply to all black staff. Indeed, it does seem as if the burden of transformation – in the form of attending meetings, advancing its agenda and monitoring compliance – often falls on the shoulders of junior black academics to whom heads of schools and departments allocate these responsibilities. This impairs junior black staff members' ability to perform on the research front and compromises their prospects for advancement and promotion.

But it is also true that some of the senior black academics, particularly those of a far-left ideological persuasion and, ironically, those who have benefited the most from the focus on transformation in institutions, are the ones who refuse to get involved in the daily fashioning and structuring of reforms and initiatives to advance this agenda. Their engagement with transformation remains in the sphere of the critique and complaints about what others have done. The response I have so often heard from them – 'Wits has broken me' – provokes a thought I never verbalise – 'Where is your own agency in the transformation struggle?' Transformation cannot be advanced by the university executive alone; all stakeholders have to be involved. (Many other senior black staff do, however, embroil themselves in the structures and deliberations about how to advance transformation.)

Some progressive white staff also need to be challenged. A narrative that has emerged in recent years, from progressive white and black scholars, demands of white citizens to develop a consciousness about the benefits of 'whiteness'. This call is important: coded into the history and evolution of our social structure and the social architecture of our universities is an inherent advantage for those of white ancestry. Recognition of this is necessary for navigating the daily social interactions with all staff and students. It is precisely the absence of this consciousness about whiteness that enables implicit racism and the failure to understand the alienation that black staff and students experience.

But the consciousness of whiteness cannot be unqualified. As Tawana pointed out in a recent executive engagement, it is particularly dangerous if it translates into a white guilt – which has also emerged in recent years, not only in scholarly articles but also in the public discourse where some white scholars and activists have either voluntarily remained silent, or been told to do so, on issues of transformation, oppression and exploit-ation. A consciousness of whiteness does not require silence. Rather, it requires the consciousness to participate in the collective ownership of the transformation agenda, to recognise that reconciliation is not possible without social justice, and to allow these understandings to inform one's behaviour and discourse. This will build the cohesive and inclusive institutional community we need to advance the project of institutional transformation.

Two other sensitive matters need to be addressed if transformation is to be systemically advanced: the manipulation of race by individuals for personal advancement or enrichment, and the ethical and legal parameters within which protest and solidarity need to be expressed. Recent incidents have highlighted the acuteness of the challenges and the urgency of developing collective responses to address them. The first involved a Twitter controversy in late 2017, when some students from our Faculty of Health Sciences claimed that some of our examinations were anti-black. Some irresponsible political activists and legal figures gave them public support – figures who simply lent their weight on the basis of an assertion without any investigation of the issues at hand.

I was able to respond quickly and firmly to the assertion because, only a month earlier, when similar allegations had reared their head, I had commissioned the deputy dean of the Faculty of Humanities, Garth Stevens, to investigate the issue. His report categorically demonstrated that there was nothing untoward about the new assessment processes, although he did indicate that the communications that accompanied their implementation left much to be desired and needed to be urgently addressed. In addition to responding on Twitter, I wrote a public commentary in the *Daily Maverick* in which I raised the concern about some students manipulating race to bypass assessment processes. I indicated that this was untenable for a university, as it risked devaluing our degree. I declared firmly that we would not tolerate such devious and irresponsible behaviour.

A similar anomaly emerged a few months later at a workshop on decolonising the curriculum, hosted in Cape Town, funded by the Mellon Foundation, and involving academics, executives and students. The first session involved a thoughtful deliberation on curriculum reform, while the second reflected on student experiences of the Mellon fellowship. What was striking was that, while students were strident about decolonisation in the first panel, in the second they urged Mellon to consider providing more fellowships to Harvard, Oxford and similar institutions so that they would not have to be confined to institutions in South Africa. None of the students saw any contradiction in demanding decolonisation in the first panel, then asking in the second for decisions that essentially reinforced the colonial structure of higher education. The officials of the Mellon Foundation and many others remained silent, even though they recognised the contradiction; reluctantly, I stood up and pointed it out, stating that we needed an honest discussion about this challenge.

My decision to deal with both issues publicly emanated from a concern that a tension was emerging between a legitimate, programmatic transformation agenda and some individuals' personal ambitions and desires – individuals who used the former to advance the latter. Of course, using transformation policy for personal advancement is perfectly acceptable, as long as it is consistent with academic, ethical and legal principles and practices. But when it violates these precepts, as is happening increasingly, it runs the risk of delegitimising the struggle to challenge racism within our institution. In the last two to three years, I have been privy to a number of cases where this has occurred. Some of these incidents involved promotions, where some black staff who were not successful simply assumed that the outcome was due to racism. In one particular case, the staff member repeatedly challenged the outcome on racial grounds, even though the entire promotions committee comprised black staff. In addition, in multiple cases staff who had been dismissed or were being disciplined for corruption, sexual harassment or other serious violations cynically resorted to playing the race card as their first defence. It has also become common for parents of all races to challenge our admission decisions by alleging racism when their child is not admitted. In many of these cases, we have been threatened with legal action or with being reported to one or other political authority. In all cases, we stood by our decision.

Nevertheless, in late 2017 I appointed a committee comprising three notable figures – Thuli Madonsela, Barney Pityana and Mashadi

Motlana – and a Wits representative, Garth Stevens, to advise the university about whether individual incidents involved racism and warranted full investigation, or could be ignored because racism was being manipulatively alleged for other purposes. But this is merely a holding action; the increasing number of incidents suggests that there is an urgent need to fashion a collectively acceptable response to this manipulation of race. I need to be crystal clear in this regard. The individual acts of manipulation cannot be used as an excuse to unravel the programme of transformation. This programme is essential if we are to correct the historical racial and gender disparities, and the injustices of our past. Reconciliation has to be ensconced in social justice if we are to create the foundations of an equitable future. But it also requires the courage to distinguish between the programmatic and systemic agenda of transformation, and its manipulative use by small groups of individuals to advance their own personal desires. If recent history surrounding state capture teaches us anything at all, it should be that there is an urgent need to deliberate collectively on how to distinguish between real acts of racism and its manipulation for other purposes.

The second incident revolved around a personal interaction with Crystal on a matter at Rhodes University. Sometime between 17 and 20 April 2016, a number of gender and LGBT+ activists at Rhodes University allegedly kidnapped certain male students who appeared on an anonymous list of alleged rapists on social media and then proceeded to assault them. They refused to release the students when requested to do so by Vice-Chancellor Sizwe Mabizela and only complied when the police were called in. Two of the activists, Yolanda Dyantyi and Dominique McFall, were charged, found guilty in a disciplinary hearing of kidnapping and assault, and subsequently expelled. The ruling caused an outcry among gender activists, and a number of people at Wits University, including students and officials in our GEO, demanded through Crystal that I publicly condemn Rhodes University's decision. When I declined to do so, they not only appealed to Thandwa Mthembu and me as the incoming and outgoing chairs of USAf respectively, but also demanded that we initiate an independent investigation into the events and decisions at Rhodes University. After duly consulting with the executive committee of USAf, we again refused to accede to their demands. Crystal and the other activists then threatened to lodge a protest with the Minister of Higher Education and Training, suggesting that we were not sensitive to the scourge of rape and other issues of gender-based harm.

Ignoring the fact that the appeal to the minister happened in a context where universities are autonomous, my bigger concern relates to the insistence of so many gender activists that it was legitimate for Yolanda and Dominique essentially to have taken the law into their own hands, or their treatment of this action as a minor infraction. No one seem to consider the fact that individuals were kidnapped and assaulted, and that they were never found guilty of rape or any form of sexual misconduct despite investigations by both the National Prosecuting Authority (NPA) and Rhodes University. The fact that so many activists are willing to assume guilt on the mere strength of an anonymous list on social media suggests a willingness to sacrifice the rights of some citizens in order to pursue the legitimate cause of challenging rape and gender-based harm. As one activist retorted when I confronted her about the rule of law and the right to be presumed innocent: 'Given the scale of rape in our society, we should assume guilty, until proven innocent.' I suspect that, while many activists would not phrase it as boldly as she did, there is much wider sympathy for this kind of position in the gender activist community.

At one level this is understandable. For too long, South Africa and much of the world have not been sufficiently responsive to issues of rape and other forms of gender-based harm. There has now emerged a visceral response from some women and LGBT+ activists whose communities have borne the brunt of these atrocities. But an understanding of this must not lead to a condoning. Constitutional law scholar Pierre de Vos recently made a persuasive case on his personal blog, Constitutionally Speaking, republished in the *Daily Maverick*, that there is no constitutional requirement for individuals to presume someone innocent until they are proven guilty. If the facts of the case lead one, on a balance of probabilities, to arrive at a view of someone's guilt, one is entitled to do so and even publicly articulate it. But Pierre makes no case for the individuals to take action and impose penalties on the guilty party. Moreover, he explicitly excludes from this privilege of judgment all those who may preside on the case of the guilty party.

The same, it seems to me, would go for an executive in an institution or a leader in society who has a responsibility to treat everyone in the community fairly. Activists who are keen to entrench an anti-rape, gender- and LGBT+-sensitive agenda systemically have to understand and accept this, or risk marginalising the agenda to the confines of an interest group. Moreover, it is worth saying that creating an enabling environment for 'mob rule' may be emotionally satisfying to some activists, but runs the risks of facilitating a backlash from stakeholders with far more power. Ironically, and even though it may not seem like it, a rule-based society and institutions are in the interests of the poorest and most marginalised among us.

This is not to suggest that we should be satisfied with issues as they currently stand. The current legal dispensation, and the disciplinary one in most universities, is not particularly sensitive to victims of rape and gender-based harm. There is a desperate need to reform this legal machinery, as Wits did in 2013. But the continuation of the scourge suggests that we need to go even further. There is an urgent need for a thoughtful deliberation among all stakeholders about how to do this, and how to test the parameters of the legal dispensation, all the while remaining compliant with the rights-based Constitution and our democratic dispensation. Again, this will only happen if activists see themselves as agents of their own liberation, not only at the level of protest, but also in the context of crafting reforms – legal ones, in this case – to push the boundaries to transform our society in the interests of all, and in particular the most marginalised and disadvantaged among us.

The challenge for activists committed to transforming and decolonising society, in racial, gender and class terms, is that we need to scale reforms to enable systemic change. But if systemic change is the goal, the reforms we consider must not only advance gender and racial transformation, but also do this in a way that simultaneously entrenches the rights of all citizens. However emotionally satisfying it may be to some activists to deny the rights of others, or to invoke only the interests of women or the LGBT+ or black communities on the grounds that these persons have been victims throughout history, to pursue these rights to the exclusion of all others would only result in the perpetual postponement of the rights of the victims themselves. Ultimately, the systemic entrenchment of the rights of historic victims lies in the entrenchment of the rights of all.

6

Hell breaks loose

MINISTER Blade Nzimande announced the recommendation of an 8 per cent fee increase for 2017 on 19 September 2016. His announcement was accompanied by a commitment that the state would pay the fee increase for all those with an annual family income of less than R600 000. The ANC government hoped that this decision would avert the reigniting of the #FeesMustFall protests; I was sure that it would not. The political tides had shifted too dramatically. The demand was no longer no fee increase, but the goal of free education. The ANC's legitimacy had begun to erode significantly as a result of the Jacob Zuma presidency's rudderless leadership and corruption scandals. Political parties had begun to smell blood, and some were not above using the protests at universities to ignite and sustain a movement to take Zuma down. They were not alone: factions within the ANC were embroiled in an all-out war, and some were willing to use the university protests to advance their own ends. None of this boded well for the possibility of students meekly accepting the fee increase and the government's concession to pay only for those with a family income of less than R600 000.

I had met with political parties twice since the emergence of #FeesMustFall to try to convince the party leaders to help resolve the challenge, mobilise their supporters to act accordingly, and insulate universities from their plans. The engagement with opposition party leaders was arranged through Mmusi Maimane and Bantu Holomisa, and was fully representative of the opposition parties – with the exception of the EFF, which did not attend either of the meetings. I was accompanied to the second meeting by Ahmed Bawa. At both meetings, all the leaders recognised the importance of universities and the need for stability. They promised to do everything possible to help stabilise the universities and indicated that they would highlight the matter in Parliament and try to mobilise support for resolving the issue. This was also the message in much of my personal engagement with leaders across the political aisle and with the Parliamentary Portfolio Committee on Higher Education and Training.

Yet none of this made any difference. As expected, on the afternoon of the day on which the recommended increase was announced, students at Wits University embarked on a protest. Within 24 hours, it had spread to institutions around the country. As Chapter 3 indicates, we had hoped for the announcement in July: this would not only have coincided with universities' budgeting cycle, but would also have been long before our final examinations. In any case, the timing was out of our hands. The announcement came four weeks before the final examinations at Wits University. It provoked the most intense protests since 1994, forced our institutional hand in ways we would have preferred to avoid, and significantly influenced the national trajectory of #FeesMustFall itself.

I was not on campus for this act of the #FeesMustFall drama. I had left for New York on the preceding Friday for a HeForShe meeting on the sidelines of the heads of state meeting at the UN. When the protests began on the Monday, however, I stayed in continuous contact with the team back home. Tawana Kupe and even Randall Carolissen and I communicated daily during those first days of the protest, thinking through how to respond. Initially, Tawana was of the view that I need not come back and that the team on campus could manage the protest. But by the Thursday, the fourth day of the protest, he had changed his mind and believed it would be better if I returned.

By this time, I was already in Mexico City for an engagement with the National Autonomous University of Mexico (UNAM), where we reached an agreement that UNAM would second academics to Wits University at their cost to teach Spanish. Earlier in the week in New York, I had attended the annual HeForShe event with university presidents and CEOs of partner institutions. The event received some Twitter traffic after Wits students saw a photograph showing university presidents, UN officials and Emma Watson, who had played Hermione in the Harry Potter movies. Shaeera Kalla characteristically released a racist tweet about my engagement with 'white feminists', but I ignored it and things soon calmed down.

I could not get back to Wits from New York: all flights were full as a result of the government delegations at the UN. The logistics were further complicated by President Zuma's entourage having flown South African Airways, given the controversy about the costs of a presidential jet. In the end, I had to fly to Mexico City, which gave me the opportunity to conclude my negotiations with UNAM before getting back to Johannesburg via Frankfurt. The first flight I could get was on Friday evening, which meant I only arrived back home on Sunday morning.

I walked into a political storm. On the day of my return, Gwebs Qonde, as director-general of the DHET, called and asked me to consider closing the campus. We had been arguing about this for days, even while I was in New York. He was of the view that there was a group of student leaders at Wits who were intent on destabilising the whole system. When I asked how long he wanted me to close the university for, he retorted, 'About six months.' I was convinced that he saw the conspiracy as coming from the EFF, although he did not formally mention the party. I refused to accede to his request.

Gwebs had also independently approached Tawana and Randall with this request. While some members of Council were open to the idea, the senior executive team were generally opposed to the closure. The debate got complicated when a worker took ill after being exposed to an environment in which protesters had discharged fire extinguishers. When the worker died a few days later, Minister Nzimande claimed that the death was a result of the protesters' actions. Tawana had to correct him publicly, explaining that the post-mortem had revealed that he had passed on from an underlying respiratory condition unconnected to the incident. In any case, the possibility of closure was explored, but the idea was set aside on my return to South Africa.

I was always sceptical of Gwebs's analysis that the whole national upsurge was a result of a small group of student leaders at Wits University. This was too conspiratorial for my liking. While I was aware that the EFF was involved, I was convinced that they were not formally orchestrating it, but rather trying to jump onto the bandwagon and use the protests for their own purposes. I saw the protests as part of a general political upsurge of students, and its national flavour was far more spontaneous and loosely linked than Gwebs was prepared to acknowledge. In any case, I indicated to Gwebs that I would not sacrifice the futures of so many thousands of students. The conversation was heated, and it ended abruptly when I refused to accede to the demand and we both terminated the call. The next morning, I called Dawn Taylor as the director of our Legal Office to get our lawyers on standby just in case the department tried to force Wits to close. But I need not have worried – Gwebs seemed to have accepted my refusal to accede to his request, and never asked again. Nevertheless, the incident did get me thinking about the need for an alternative political plan to bring the protests to an end, and it was in this context that I cottoned on to the idea of a poll.

The idea cemented itself in my thinking as a result of an engagement I had with the student leaders that evening when I appeared on Dennis Davis's TV show, *You Be the Judge*. Gwebs was also on the programme, as were two student leaders, Fasiha Hassen and Kefentse Mkhari. Fasiha was general secretary of the SRC and would vacate office in late October, whereas Kefentse was the incoming SRC president. I publicly challenged Fasiha on the show, committing to withdraw all security if she and the rest of the leadership committed to no violence and returning to class. Try as I may, she just would not commit, eventually accusing me after the show of trying to set her up. But herein lay the conundrum with much of the leadership: while many of them may not actually have been involved in the violence, they would not formally condemn it and expose those who were involved. They were willing to call publicly for the withdrawal of security, but never had the courage to commit to peaceful protest, except in the rhetorical sense. It is ironic, therefore, that Fasiha was subsequently to receive the Student Peace Prize from Norwegian students in October 2018. In any case, it had become clear to me that we needed a political plan to compel the student leaders not to view this struggle as a zero sum game, and to sensitise them publicly to the fact that they did not carry the mandate of all the students.

But even before we embarked on this plan, I was embroiled in an SMS altercation with Mcebo Dlamini. Just after 09h00 on Monday, Mcebo sent an SMS:

> Students are marching to your house to table internal demands at 12pm, no violence, nothing, just memorandum ... Please come to your gate and receive the memorandum. You can take it behind your gate.

I responded:

> My brother, there are some things that just should not be done. Any attempt to go to the house is effectively a threat to my family. Whether there is a promise that there will be no violence is not the issue – the mere march itself is a threat to my family and this is just not acceptable. It is not fair. I ask you to reconsider and ask you not to do this.

Mcebo replied:

> We need you to receive the memorandum ... advice [sic] how you propose receiving the memorandum. Otherwise the march continues. If the police shoot us then your hand will be dirty with the blood of students.

I responded again:

> Dear Mcebo, don't threaten me with the blood of students. It is irresponsible. I do not control road access. The police and municipality manage this and they do so on their own protocols. You should not be playing with the lives of

students. If you want to give a memorandum, you should do so on campus as is normally done. The protocol as you well know is to go through the Dean of Students.

Mcebo replied again:

See you at the house with the students. Don't make a mistake and not be there. I thought you want to work with me but you are still arrogant.

And again, I responded:

Here we go again when you resort to threatening. You once told me you operate on principle, but what principle is it when you resort to threatening my family by going to the house. Even struggle has rules which I have always respected even in your personal case. You are violating the rules. Building a better society cannot be done by threatening anyone who does not agree with you. Otherwise you repeat the mistakes of history and the existing and past political elites. Learn from our past so that we do not commit the same mistakes. I will not be at the house. I ask you again not to go there.

After a few more messages in which I directed him to Puleng LenkaBula, the Dean of Students, whom he refused to consider, Mcebo ended the interaction with an exasperated 'Haai ke!' The protesting students did not go to the house, even though they would march past it en route to the Medical School.

Later that Monday, we decided to call for a poll. The purpose of the poll was to puncture the student leadership's belief that they spoke for the students. We decided to call their bluff. The question the poll would ask all students and staff was whether they wanted us to open the university and complete the year, even if it required bringing in security. It was boldly and provocatively phrased so that there would be no ambiguity. We set the poll for Thursday, which would give us time to prepare the logistics. The poll would be conducted via SMS for students, assisted by Telkom. Initially, we had hoped that the Independent Electoral Commission (IEC) would verify the results, but they declined, not wanting to get involved given that the student leadership opposed the poll. Frankly, I was appalled by the decision. I cannot think of many places in the world where the IEC would refuse to adjudicate a referendum called by a public institution, when it had the capacity and opportunity to do so. We eventually appointed SizweNtsalubaGobodo, a black-empowered auditing and advisory firm, to confirm the accuracy of the results.

Of course, a debate emerged about the legitimacy of our decision to conduct a poll. Many on the left believed that matters of principle could not simply be arbitrated by a majoritarian decision through a poll. To be honest, I concurred. In a constitutional democracy, issues of principle have to be determined on the basis of the Constitution itself. But we were never making a statement of principle with our poll. Rather, it was a strategic decision to demonstrate publicly that the student leadership, in demanding a permanent shutdown, no longer spoke for the majority of students, black or white. And we admirably succeeded in this regard. Student leaders knew, of course, that this would be the case, so they decided to petition the court to interdict the poll.

On the eve of the poll, we had to go to the courts to defend our right to canvass the views of our students. Fatima went with me to court at about 23h00. Andrew Crouch was also there. A number of student leaders were there as well, but the two figures who stood out were Mcebo and Shaeera, neither of whom was actually on the SRC any longer. They had a formidable legal team, led by Dali Mpofu. Our case was led by Wim Trengove, a senior counsel with equally impressive progressive credentials. Sometime in the evening, I called Mcebo aside and spoke to him about how this decision to contest the poll legally compromised them politically. I also indicated to him that, while we could not allow a permanent shutdown, we would be willing to support them in their demands if they agreed to go back to class. Mcebo listened politely and indicated that he would consult with the others. I knew then that this was not going to happen.

The case was fought on the basis of whether I could use a majority decision of the students to decide to open the university. Wim made the argument that I was not using the poll to determine the decision, but merely to gather the views of the university community, as was my right. At about 02h00, Fatima and I decided to call it a night. Andrew had kindly agreed to stay until the conclusion of the case and promised to call me as soon as there was a decision. At about 04h00, he contacted me to say that we had won. The poll was on.

The poll received quite a bit of coverage in the media. UCT had decided against the idea, so the decision at Wits had national reverberations. Students were polled via SMS, but a technical glitch on Telkom's side meant that some six thousand students did not get the SMS, so they could not vote. Nevertheless, about thirty thousand students did get the SMS and participated in the poll. Staff were polled via e-mail, and we put facilities in place for those who did not have computers. We had to wait for the auditors to determine whether this was a free and fair poll. By Friday, we had the results of the student poll, with the auditors requiring a few more days to conclude the verification of the staff results. The results were unsurprising. Some 77 per cent of the students who participated voted in favour of us opening the campus and resuming the academic programme. When the staff results were announced a few days later, they were even more favourable, with 91 per cent voting in favour of resuming the academic programme. It was a devastating indictment of the student leadership and their supporters, who were advocating a national shutdown against the wishes of the very constituency they purported to represent.

As all this played out, we were also keen on ensuring that societal stakeholders were fully briefed on developments in the universities. One of the more important constituencies was, of course, the religious leaders. Earlier in the week, on Tuesday 27 September, UP's Cheryl de la Rey and I briefed the Anglican bishops on developments on our respective campuses. I informed them about the engagements with the protesters, other students and department officials, and how the decision to poll the university had come about. Both Cheryl and I urged the bishops to try to use their influence to ensure that the protesters acted peacefully and in the interests of the entire student community. I also recall bemoaning, with a little humour, an incident of the previous evening in which a sangoma who had been brought onto the campus, had prayed for the students and cursed both Minister Nzimande and myself. Archbishop Makgoba responded that this was inappropriate and he, and a number of others, promised to pray for us. I remember smiling at the irony of the conversation; I, a Muslim, had been cursed by a sangoma and prayed for by Anglican archbishops. South Africa was truly a society of enormous complexity, immersed in modernity and traditionalism, where anger and hate manifested simultaneously with some of the most amazing forms of tolerance and love.

The results of the poll were announced on Friday. On Saturday, we had a Council meeting to decide how to proceed. The results of the poll reinforced my belief that we should open in the coming week. Those who would be most prejudiced by a long-term shutdown would be the poor and disadvantaged. I also thought that it was untenable for political parties to play games with the futures of young people, and that this could no longer be allowed to continue. Most of the Council agreed, although David Dickinson was unsurprisingly opposed. The representative of the Postgraduate Association, LeeAnn Masilela, was also concerned about opening against the wishes of the student leadership, and she requested us to consider opening without the presence of security and the police. I was concerned about this, but we nevertheless agreed on a compromise involving a phased opening: staff would return on Monday and students only on Tuesday. The police would stay outside the university gates on Monday so that we could determine the feasibility of opening without their presence.

On that same Saturday, some of the student leadership met and decided to continue with the protest and force an indefinite shutdown. Those who had a different view were easily silenced, and the political rivalry between the ANC-aligned organisations and the EFF meant that neither could come across as being measured and reasonable, lest they be criticised or labelled as sellouts by the other. Ironically, it made no difference to any of the leadership what their constituency thought of the shutdown idea. In a sense, they saw themselves as commissars of a revolution who knew what was best for the rest of the student community. Their small group of supporters within the academic community were less interested in the future of the academic programme than in the politics of the moment, whatever the immediate consequences for the vast majority of students. The stage was set for a political showdown at Wits University in the coming week.

We kicked off on Monday 3 October with only the staff returning. The police were moved to the perimeter and we dramatically decreased numbers of private security. I had to spend the day off campus at the Higher Education Multi-Stakeholder Forum hosted by Minister Nzimande. While on the podium with President Zuma, Minister Nzimande and Irvin Phenyane, chairperson of the Higher Education Parents Dialogue, among others, and awaiting the start of proceedings as negotiations were underway to get students to agree to participate in and not disrupt the engagement, I received a call from Shafee Verachia, a former Wits SRC president. He asked if I would be willing to endorse the students' financial model officially, as that would enable them to defuse the crisis and get students back to class. I refused on the grounds that I had never seen the document, but he insisted, saying that he would e-mail it to me immediately. Again I refused, making it clear that I would not endorse a set of proposals I had not read and had not consulted on with the other vice-chancellors. The meeting ended in disarray because student leaders were unhappy that the president had simply read his speech and left. The forum should probably never have happened. It was one of those events where the political mood had been misread by the Minister and Department officials, who had hoped to corral the student leadership into an agreement through an interaction with senior government and ruling party leaders.

The situation on campus was no better. About five hundred protesters had assembled to denounce the reopening of the university and subsequently dispersed into smaller groups. While the biggest group was contained by security, smaller groups made their way into academics' offices, intimidated and threatened them and, in a few cases, forced them to leave. As a result, there was much anger on campus. So serious was the matter that even the ASAWU leadership felt compelled to release a statement condemning the protesters for threatening their members. I also released a communique that evening, apologising to staff, explaining what had happened, and informing them that we would continue with the opening – but this time with the full deployment of private security and police. I also concluded the communique by urging staff to work with me to take back the campus.

But we also needed a backup plan. On Monday evening, I got a call from Sipho Maseko, CEO of Telkom and an alumnus and supporter of the university, who first sympathised about what was happening on campus and then recommended that we think about using Tiego Moseneke as a mediator. Tiego, who had been the president of the Black Students Society in 1985/1986, would, Sipho suggested, be perfect for bridging the divide that had opened up at Wits. Eventually, we agreed that both of them would play the mediation role and I would phone and engage Tiego about this first thing in the morning.

Tuesday 4 October was particularly difficult. The academic pro-gramme opened successfully in the morning and the few sporadic protests were easily contained. By about midday, however, the protesters had grown to about five hundred, in part because a gate between the Holy Trinity Church and the university had been breached, and protesters from outside had been brought in by some of the political parties. The protests were most pronounced outside the Great Hall. Here, protesters broke the nearby concrete bins and dug out the paving to create sizable rocks with which to attack private security and police. Security and the police were preventing them from breaching the blockade into the Sobukwe Building and accessing the Solomon Mahlangu concourse. As the stoning inten-sified, the police tried to disperse the crowd, altercations flared and, in the ensuing clashes, both protesters and police were hurt. Windows and cars were also damaged.

There was one notable incident in the midst of the chaos. A police captain tried to arrest Mcebo as he led the charge to get into the building. A scuffle ensued; Mcebo prevailed and got away with the captain's helmet and shield, and the policeman was injured. The incident would come to haunt Mcebo – he was charged with assaulting a police officer and steal-ing government property. The case would drag on for almost two years.

Mcebo avoided capture, but a number of others were not so lucky and were arrested. At about 14h00 the protesters moved on to the Hillbrow Police Station, where their comrades were being held. Calm returned to the campus. After a long deliberation, the executive decided to proceed with the academic programme the next day. We had always known that it would take a few days before the campus would be fully stabilised, so it was important to persevere. An announcement about the continuation of the academic programme was released to the university community.

On the same afternoon, I visited the newly appointed mayor of Johannesburg, Herman Mashaba, who had asked to meet and was accompanied by some members of his executive team. We discussed the protest, the possibility of it spilling over into Braamfontein, and the importance of the municipal police. The mayor was largely sympathetic to our circumstances on campus, recognising that university executives could not address many of the protesters' demands. On returning to the office, I received two separate visits. The first was by Deputy National Police Commissioner Gary Kruser, who had just been deployed to campus. This was a huge relief. It suggested that the lobbying of ministers, government and top brass in the police was having an effect. Having a senior figure of authority from the police on the campus was absolutely necessary to ensure police action that was firm but contained within established constitutional parameters. The police, it must be noted, follow their own chain of command, and the presence of a senior officer on the campus allowed us potentially to influence their behaviour. Gary also had a reputation that preceded him; he had been involved in the United Democratic Front (UDF) and in protests as a young activist at UCT and in Cape Town more broadly. Having a senior police officer with political sensibility was valuable, and I indicated to Gary when we met that he was not leaving until the matter had been fully resolved. Gary would find himself at the university for just under three weeks, playing a phenomenal role in bringing calm to the institution.

The second visit was just after 16h00 from Tiego, who indicated that they had engaged the student leadership and arrived at a potential political solution. The leaders were willing to go back to class the following week on condition that we closed for the rest of the week and used the space to negotiate an agreement in which the university would publicly voice its support for the goal of free education. I agreed to take the proposal to the rest of the executive and to support it. I was of the view that a political settlement was the best route to achieving stability on campus. There was, of course, the problem that we had just communicated that we would continue with the academic programme the next day. But this slight embarrassment would be a price worth paying if we could get the campus back in operation without security actions like those that had unfolded earlier in the day. We would also apologise for the change in decision and explain the circumstances that led to it. When we discussed the issue in the executive, there was some concern about whether we could trust the student leadership to stay true to their word. But we eventually agreed that we had to take this political opportunity and try to achieve stability through a peaceful negotiated solution.

There were also some concerns emerging about the mediation team. I saw the mediation team as comprising only Tiego and Sipho, both of whom I respected and trusted. However, other actors now appeared on the scene. Some of them I was entirely comfortable with. Firoz Cachalia, who was from our School of Law and a previous Gauteng MEC, could be trusted to do the right thing, as could Kenneth Creamer from our School of Economic and Business Sciences and the president of the SRC in 1991/1992. The team expanded even more in the days to come with Pitika Ntuli, Linda Vilakazi and Terry Tselane, all of whom began to assist in negotiating a solution to the political impasse that had emerged at Wits.

I was concerned, however, about Dali Mpofu, who had suddenly popped up on campus when the protests had begun. I worried that he was trying to take control of the protests on behalf of the EFF. This was the problem with playing multiple roles, one minute as supporter of and activist in the protests, and the next trying to act as mediator between the executive and the student leadership. I was also concerned about Bishop Jo Seoka, who had also appeared when the protests began. He and Pitika, a friend and colleague from my time at the University of Durban-Westville, had come to see me earlier, indicating that they were on campus and hoping to assist. But I was aware that Bishop Seoka was not a formal representative of the South African Council of Churches (SACC), whose leadership had refused to endorse his interventions and actions. I bounced some of these concerns off Tiego, and he indicated that, while he understood, both the bishop and Dali could play a valuable role because they had a line of communication to the student leadership. In the end, I reluctantly agreed. One could not ask for the assistance of a mediator and then not give him the flexibility to engage as he deemed appropriate.

The next few days were a period of shuttle diplomacy in which the mediators moved between us to fashion a political settlement. It was truly astonishing how many senior community leaders, professionals, CEOs and senior executives from private companies and public institutions gave up so much of their time to help the university. We had hoped to get a series of demands from the student leadership, but when this was not forthcoming we wrote a draft pledge in which we committed to the goal of free education. We handed this draft pledge to the mediators, who refined it in engagement with the student leaders. We also indicated to the mediators that we would be open to marching with the students to an appropriate venue in Johannesburg in support of the goal of free education. Eventually, the plan evolved to include the following: a General Assembly, to be convened by the university and chaired by the chancellor, at which all stakeholders at the university, including the Senate and Council, would voice their support for the goal of free education. The students would be represented at the Assembly with speakers from both the SRC and #FeesMustFall. We would then march as a collective to the Constitutional Court, where we would hand over our collective pledge to the chief justice. This, we believed, would greatly enhance the case for free education and dramatically increase the pressure on government and all role players to find a political and policy solution to the crisis.

Yet there were also indications that the student leadership was hopelessly divided along party political grounds. Despite their public pledge that they represented the students, too many of them were taking instructions from their political parties. This ultimately manifested in the fact that there was never a formal meeting between the executive and the student leadership. Instead, the mediators shuttled between us on Wednesday and Thursday and the plan that ultimately evolved did so through the mediators' direct engagements with both sides. We were meant to meet at the Holy Trinity Church on the edge of the campus on Thursday afternoon. The executive team got there in the late afternoon, but after waiting for at least three hours, without any of the student leadership turning up, we decided to call it a night. It was agreed with the mediators that, should the student leadership still want to meet, they could call us and we would come. Otherwise, the plan was to meet on the Friday morning for the General Assembly where we were expecting thousands of students, staff and alumni.

We used the Wednesday and Thursday to prepare for the General Assembly. I had engaged the chancellor, Deputy Chief Justice Dikgang Moseneke, who had agreed to chair the Assembly. I had also engaged both the Senate and Council to sign off on the pledge and to agree not only to come to the Assembly, but also to march with the students to the Constitutional Court in support of the goal of free education. There was some queasiness about the viability of the goal, but eventually the Senate and Council unanimously agreed to support the call and march with the students. For one brief moment, there was a united response from the university community. Even the far left were on board. After all, this was what they had been requesting all along.

But it was not to last. At about 01h00 on Friday 7 October, I got a call from Tiego, who indicated that the mediators wanted to meet urgently to discuss a new hurdle that had emerged. They came to Savernake at about 01h30 and we met for about ninety minutes, during which our conversation was lubricated by whisky or coffee, depending on preferences. The message was simple but devastating: the student leadership had reneged. They would not go back to class on the Monday as promised. And they would give no guarantees that the meeting would not be captured and the chancellor removed from the chair. I asked the mediators for their view, and almost all of them recommended that we proceed with the Assembly. They hoped the students would see sense and not disrupt the event. But I did not have the luxury of ignoring the threat. I had given an implicit guarantee to all stakeholders that they would be safe if they came to the Assembly. Now I could not guarantee this. If something went truly wrong, they would be right to demand why they had not been warned and why I had gone on with the event under the circumstances. The meeting concluded with me indicating that I would consider their recommendation, discuss it with the executive and members of Council, and make a decision first thing in the morning.

I could not go back to bed after the meeting. I immediately wrote to the entire executive and called a meeting for 07h00. I then tried to sleep a little, but to no avail. At about 06h00, I got up, showered and called Randall to brief him on the latest developments. He agreed to come over and be part of the executive deliberations. By now I was leaning in the direction of cancelling the Assembly. I could not risk people being hurt if the meeting was disrupted. As importantly, I was convinced that a line had to be drawn beyond which further capitulation was irresponsible and dangerous.

There was an air of dejection within the executive when I reported the night's events. But there was a unanimous view that we could not proceed. We began to make preparations. Our head of communications, Shirona Patel, began arranging the press conference, while I briefed Gary on developments so that the police and security would be prepared. I also communicated with Dikgang so that he would not be taken by surprise at the turn of events. We decided that, while the executive would be at the media conference, I would take the lead in announcing the cancellation of the Assembly and fielding questions. Randall volunteered to sit with me to symbolise that the executive and Council were united in their response.

We kicked off the media conference at 09h00. As this was happening, a communique was also sent to the entire university community. The same message was delivered. We explained the events of the previous night, how the student leadership had reneged on going back to class, the threats of disruption of the Assembly, and why we could not take the risk of continuing with the event. I fielded a series of questions related to the negotiations and the protests in general, and then Randall responded to a question confirming Council's continued confidence in both me as vice-chancellor and the executive management. With this, we brought the media conference to a close in the hope that the message would carry to the broader public that the Assembly had been cancelled.

The story led the news bulletins for the rest of the day. All the media stationed themselves at Wits to see how the students would respond. One of the immediate challenges that we confronted was that the marquee for the event had already been erected. Taking it down under the heightened political temperature would inflame the situation. Gary recommended that we leave it up for the moment and take it down in the evening once people had left the campus. The problem with leaving it up, however, was that it gave some of the student leadership an opportunity to create a spectacle by continuing with the event without the university. And this is exactly what happened: seeing the cameras, the student leaders jumped at the opportunity. Mcebo and other student leaders presided over the event. There was, of course, the usual grand-standing. Mcebo announced that the university was now being taken over by the protesters and that a new leadership would be elected. He declared himself vice-chancellor; while much of this was jest and spec-tacle, the fact that it played out in front of the cameras gave it the form of a symbolic challenge to the university's authority. This would have been deeply perturbing to many in the broader student community, and to parents and other stakeholders in broader society.

Many participated in this spectacle. Student protesters were there, as were a few parents and church leaders. Bishop Seoka and Pitika par-ticipated, greatly compromising their mediator status. Tiego had phoned me to indicate that one of the mediators would go over to the meeting to speak to the students, because it would be important to keep the doors open for continued engagement. He also informed me that it would not be him, so it fell to Bishop Seoka – who not only pandered to the spectacle and failed to provide an honest representation of why the Assembly had been cancelled, but also never once mentioned the fact that the student leadership had reneged on an agreement. It was a deliberate misrepresentation of developments over the preceding days.

The most notable presence on the podium, however, was that of union leaders and academics from the far left, including Eric Worby, Daisy Matlou and Noor Nieftagodien. It seemed to have escaped them that this event was happening in violation of the decision that they had signed on to at Senate a day before. Indeed, Noor spoke at the event. After reflecting on the systemic challenges confronting higher education, he went on to suggest that academics would not teach under any circumstances while police were on campus – and that they not only disagreed with the decision to cancel the Assembly, but also disagreed that there should be a deadline for students to return to class. The statement was an astonishing abrogation of academic responsibility. All in all, there was no doubt that some academics and union leaders, many of whom had regularly donned the mantle of impartial observers, had become deeply embroiled in the political populism of the moment.

I observed these events on television with many colleagues by my side. As we watched the spectacle, someone reminded me that much of it would be over in a couple of hours, and the details forgotten in a day or two. After a few hours, people began to peel away from the event, which was eventually brought to a close. When the campus quietened, we sent in the service providers to dismantle the marquee and remove the equipment. We also called a Council meeting for the next day to prepare for the week ahead.

Why this turn of events? Why did the student leadership renege on an agreement in which not only the executive management, but also the Senate and Council, were prepared to support their goal of free education in a General Assembly and march with them to the Constitutional Court? We had essentially agreed to the alliance that Noor had recommended in his speech. Why jeopardise the potential creation of an alliance of students and staff across the system, as well as civil society, business and other stakeholders, to drive an advocacy agenda for the progressive realisation of free, fully funded, quality, decolonised higher education? Surely this would have been a great victory for them. The Anthropology department's Hylton White suggested that the student leadership had reneged on the agreement because they rejected the liberal (and respectable) ethos of the traditional university assembly (meaning General Assembly) and preferred a more authentic, decolonised imbizo. Yet this never came up in any of the negotiations. The only request for a change in the assembly provisions was for an additional student representative to speak on behalf of #FeesMustFall, which was acceded to. In a lot of ways, his explanation was a post facto rationalisation, decontextualised from the politics and reality of the negotiations.

In my own reflection on the student protests in late 2016, I suggested that the answer lay in the political factionalising of the movement and the fact that some student leaders were accountable to outside interests. The mediators had assumed that it was in the rational interests of all sides to institutionalise the matter and arrive at a resolution. But this was not the case for small factions among the student leadership. These factions were tied to political parties – the EFF in particular – with an explicit political agenda to mobilise and to bring an end to the Zuma presidency. They saw this as happening through a mass campaign of mobilising the populace, and a continued shutdown of universities would have greatly enhanced their project. Given that, the student factions tied to this political project could not accede to a resolution within the negotiations. So, they insisted on playing a politics of spectacle, where all decisions were made in the mass meeting, and rational and pragmatic voices were silenced by accusing them of selling out. Other student factions were not politically adept enough to manage this challenge, which effectively meant that these advocates of spectacle were capable of paralysing the process to realise a political solution to the university crisis.

Many who associated themselves with these events did not realise that they were playing to the tune of an alternative political agenda. But this agenda could not be allowed to continue to jeopardise the educational future of thousands of students, many of whom were poor and marginalised. The university executive had to act to break the logjam.

A Council meeting was called on Saturday 8 October to discuss how to proceed in the coming week. The executive was of the view that we had to begin the academic programme with the deployment of both the police and private security. Of course, we had given up the whole of the previous week to seeking a political resolution. Not only had we as a collective university community – including the Senate, Council and executive management – agreed to voice support for the goal of free education, but we had also been willing to march with protesting students to the Constitutional Court to express our solidarity in this regard. We had done all this on the implicit assumption that students would return to class the following week. The student leadership had reneged and, as a result, had crossed a line. I was also of the view that we were being played by some political parties and factions for agendas that had nothing to do with the university.

If we did not open now, we would betray not only the mandate of our office, but also the interests of all of our students, especially the poor and the marginalised, who did not have the luxury of resources to waste a year like some from more privileged backgrounds or with access to the largesse of political parties. The executive also believed that we had to open immediately if we were not to lose the academic year. Most of the Council agreed with the executive, but there was the usual opposition from one Council member who advocated the closure of the teaching programme and the posting of all learning material online. The problem with this idea was that it would have seriously compromised our academic programme, especially in the science, technology, engineering and mathematics fields, and constituted the betrayal of our mandate as a university. In any case, the executive management's recommendation to open the university carried the day. After the Council meeting, we made a public announcement about our opening and began preparing for it.

One of the biggest issues concerning us was the deployment of the police. I had a direct link to Major General Dimakatso Ndaba, who was responsible for the operational control of the Hillbrow Police Station. Our big concern was the possibility of students being seriously hurt with the full deployment of police. We knew that we could not open without the police, but we were also concerned that matters could get out of hand, especially given the incitement that was likely from a small group of students associated with some of the political parties and factions. We also knew that once the police were deployed, we would have no control over operations and would be subject to their operational hierarchy. But at least we had Gary on site, and sometimes even Major General Ndaba. I remained concerned; in a melodramatic gesture on Sunday evening, the eve of our reopening, I sent the Minister of Police, Nathi Nhleko, Gary and the entire top police brass the following SMS:

> Dear Deputy National Commissioner, General, Brigadiers and Colonels, I spoke to many of you in the course of the day, and I thank you for taking my call and hearing me out. Tomorrow Wits' future lies in your hands. As I indicated to some of you, many at Wits do not believe that the police will meet their obligation to safely protect Wits' academic programme and its infrastructure. I hope that your professionalism tomorrow re-establishes the Wits community's confidence in the police force.
>
> Today I saw a video clip of police action in managing a protest in Germany. What was notable about the incident was that the police demobilised the protest without the firing of a single shot. They simply had sufficient equipment and discipline not to be provoked and maintained their line. It was an example of police professionalism. I wish for a similar professionalism tomorrow at Wits.
>
> At stake is the future of 36 000 students. Tomorrow is not a day for legal technicalities. I do not mean to be melodramatic, but tomorrow you hold in your hands the future of Wits University, the higher education system and the country as a whole. Please do your best to peacefully keep our campus safe. Best, Adam

Of course, it did not turn out as I had hoped. Monday was truly hard for anybody associated with Wits University. The protesters responded to the opening of the university with a ferocity that exceeded that of the previous week. Small groups of individual protesters went to some of the classes, disrupted them and, in a few cases, even threatened and assaulted students who had decided to proceed with their academic programme. Again, the epicentre of the protests shifted to the Great Hall where, in a repeat of the previous week's events, concrete bins were broken and paving dug up to create sizable rocks used to attack the private security situated at the entrance at the top of the stairs. When the barrage of stoning against the private security became too intense, police used teargas and stun grenades against the protesters. Gary told me later that, had he refrained from acting then, a number of private security personnel would have been seriously injured. The altercations led to a number of arrests, and all of this was captured on live television. About 50 per cent of lectures had been disrupted. But we had also not expected to be fully operational on the first day. We prevailed, and announced that our academic operations would continue the next day.

One of the events that stood out on this first day was the injury to Father Graham Pugin of the Holy Trinity Church, which occurred when part of the conflict spilled over onto the Braamfontein streets. There was a series of altercations between protesters and the police, some of them around the church on the edge of the Wits campus in Jan Smuts Avenue. In one of these altercations, police fired rubber bullets, injuring Father Graham. The pictures of the injured priest covered in blood were beamed live all over the world, bringing even greater prominence and notoriety to the conflict. I would visit him on Thursday 13 October at the Jesuit Institute, on whose advisory board I served. We would use the opportunity to engage him and Father Russell Pollitt to help broker a peaceful engagement with the student leadership.

The protests continued on Tuesday, but fewer classes were disrupted. Attendance remained low. Again, police used teargas and stun grenades to disperse protesting students. Each day, higher numbers of students attended and fewer classes were disrupted. The protesters responded in two disparate ways. First, they complained that management was not prepared to negotiate. When we publicly declared that we were willing to do so, on terms that did not disrupt the academic programme, they stated that they did not believe in negotiations with leaders and would only be willing to engage in a mass meeting. Of course, we were resolute, having witnessed repeatedly how the mass meeting would become an instrument of political spectacle to prevent negotiated outcomes. What the student leadership was also not saying was that some of them were meeting us on the quiet. I had met Kefentse and David Manabile, the incoming SRC president and secretary general, on two occasions at the Hyatt Hotel; they had run up an alcohol bill of close to R2 000. I had also met Fasiha at the same venue. In all these meetings, they claimed that they could bring the protesters back to class if I withdrew the police and stopped lectures for a few days. The student leadership had deceived us before in this regard. In any case, these leaders overestimated their influence on the protesting students. I said this to them and firmly indicated that the closure of the campus and withdrawal of the police prior to the cessation of violence was no longer on the table. Eventually, we agreed with the mediators and the student leadership on a negotiation that would be streamed live to the rest of the university community, as was occurring at UCT. But again, after agreeing the student leadership pulled out at the last moment. By this time, even the mediators had given up.

The student leadership's second response was to up the ante. As lecture attendance improved each day, so their tactics become more desperate. In the evenings, students would stone the police and private security and then run into residences. When the police pursued them into the residences, others would get hurt, provoking an outcry from a much wider range of students. The action was taken precisely to alienate the police and security from the broader student community. Then, on the evening of Thursday 13 October, there was a full-scale assault on university infrastructure and property. After a meeting on the concourse of Solomon Mahlangu House, about twenty students dispersed in small groups and tried to set fire to the lawn near the DJ du Plessis Building, garbage bins near the Matrix, the old Grandstand in the Science Stadium, the Old Mutual Sports Hall, and the Speech and Hearing Clinic. All the fires were quickly extinguished. These actions would demonstrate that the negotiations were never a serious option, because they violated the political agenda of some factions in the student leadership.

On Friday evening, the violence spread to the streets of Braamfontein. By this time, we had brought the protests on campus broadly under control and lecture attendance was increasing. Much of this was a result of controlling access to the campus. Cars were searched and only students or staff were allowed in. Our weakness was the evenings, when there was the cover of darkness. After the attempted arson on Thursday evening, patrols were beefed up dramatically. The increased security on campus forced protesters onto the streets of Braamfontein on Friday evening. An

SABC truck and a bus were torched. There were several altercations with the police, and a number of arrests. As the violence ensued on the streets of Braamfontein, a debate emerged among us about whether there was an explicit plan to draw the police from the campus, and thereby create a space to attack university infrastructure directly. As a result, we held firm; private security and the police remained at their posts on campus. Other police were deployed to bring stability to Braamfontein. When they eventually did, 11 individuals were arrested, of whom only two were Wits University students. This was perhaps the clearest evidence that much of the violence was being orchestrated by people outside the university.

Our response to these developments was twofold. First, we needed to manage the risk of police incursions into the residences, compromising our plan to stabilise the campus and complete the academic year. We made a decision that police could only go into residences when accompanied by Campus Protection Services. This would give us independent verification of what occurred and, we hoped, ensure that the police's responses were measured. Second, we imposed a curfew on campus so that we could not only contain movements and decrease the risk of arson in the late nights and early mornings, but also prevent attacks on the police and fire trucks when they were called in. Not surprisingly, the curfew drew strong condemnation from the student leadership, civil society activists and the far left, but none could provide a better solution to the threat of arson and attacks. We also pledged that, for each night on which there were no attacks, we would slowly reduce the curfew.

The curfew provoked an engagement with Ahmed Veriava, with whom I had last interacted during the 2015 protests. Our opinions had differed then, but our engagements had always been respectful. This time, however, they were far more acrimonious. I received an SMS from him on Friday 14 October, complaining that 'the current strategy of the University is provoking an intensification of violent confrontation … [creating] a virtual state of emergency and ending any possibility of dialogue'. I responded strongly, accusing him of 'being propagandistic', reminding him about the multiple arson attempts, and saying that 'this is criminal activity and your defence of it is bordering on complicity'.

Ahmed wanted me to agree to an imbizo, and felt that I should have attended the Assembly, even without the guarantees of safety and the return to class. I reminded him that the Assembly had always been tied to the resumption of classes and that, unlike him, I had a responsibility to the entire university community – which meant that I could not agree to an event at which there were no guarantees of peaceful engagement. I also asked him to read the communiques that we had sent out, in which we committed to continued negotiations provided that the academic programme was not compromised and security protocols were in place. This I stressed because he had suggested earlier, as Noor had done in the student meeting, that 'the stakes are much higher than saving the academic programme'. I reiterated that I was still open to a negotiated outcome, but that the 'only non-negotiable is the 2016 academic programme must not be compromised which I believe is the desire of the majority of students and their families'. Ahmed signed off, saying that he would try to facilitate negotiations with the student leadership – which I presume they never agreed to, because he never got back to me.

On Monday, we continued with lectures and attendance was normal. There were still sporadic attempts at disruption, mainly by setting off firecrackers in class. But, slowly, we brought even these incidents under control. Increasingly, students were taking the lead in sustaining the academic programme and holding the protesters accountable. When disruptions occurred, students and staff would stand up to the protesters and resume the class once the disruption was over. Slowly but surely, momentum was building in favour of completing the academic pro-gramme.

But two events occurred to reverse the momentum. First, Mcebo was arrested on the morning of Sunday 16 October at the Junction Residence. Rumours had been circulating for a few days that an arrest was imminent. He was to appear in court two days later for a bail hearing, but bail was denied because the court did not trust that he would engage in peaceful protest. Second, ASAWU decided to hold a peace meeting with community leaders at the Holy Trinity Church with the intention of bridging the divide between the protesters and the executive management. Ironically, this involved some of the very individuals who had sat on the stage some days earlier and committed to the agenda of the student leadership. Now, they hoped to play the role of bridge builder. But there were also other individuals who had now become involved in the ASAWU initiative, including Vishwas Satgar and Michelle Williams. I expressed concern to Vishwas that the meeting would be captured and ran the risk of reigniting the protests just as we were stabilising the campus. The ASAWU leadership had also formally invited the executive to the meeting. This put us in a dilemma. On the one hand, we were convinced that the event would be captured and that we would either be evicted or taken hostage. On the other hand, to decline the invitation would result in accusations that we were opposed to a peaceful resolution to the impasse. We were damned, whichever way we responded. Reluctantly, the executive and I agreed to attend, fully realising that the meeting could turn into a debacle.

We took precautions, of course. A security protocol was developed to evacuate executives if necessary. Security personnel were stationed in the audience to provide support in a hostage scenario or if violence was to break out. Fatima and I had a huge argument about the event. She wanted to attend it with some friends as the broader public had been invited. I opposed this, not wanting to be distracted by worrying about her safety. We eventually agreed that she would give the event a miss.

On Wednesday 19 October, Tawana, Zeblon and I arrived a few minutes before the designated time for the peace meeting at the Holy Trinity Church. We were ushered into the offices, where a meeting was clearly underway between one of the students, Anzio Jacobs, and some of the organisers, including Vishwas and David Hornsby. Community leaders like Jay Naidoo were also present. I had met Anzio once before in April 2016. He had requested a meeting in which he had expressed concern about our strategy for containing the protests, and wanted us to align with the student leadership in the struggle for free education. This, of course, was the usual refrain of the #FeesMustFall activists and their supporters, without any reflection on the fact that we had tried that very strategy just over a week before without much success. My own view is that many who suggested this, including Anzio, assumed that they had greater influence than was really the case, and were unaware that they were playing to a political tune that was not of their design. In any case, after a few minutes an EFF student leader, Busisiwe Seabe, walked in. Judging by the look on her face, she was taken aback by my presence. She turned on Anzio accusingly; he protested his innocence. But just then, the organisers of the meeting came in and started to usher us towards the church entrance. By the time we reached the entrance, Vuyani Pambo was there. Clearly, he had been briefed by Busisiwe. He turned on David, accusing him of duplicity because of my presence. I ignored their verbal altercation and walked into the church with a sense of foreboding, realising that very little of the political work had actually been done to make this meeting a success.

I sat down in one of the front pews as cameras swirled around me. I was accompanied by Father Anthony Egan, whom I had known for many years and whom the church seemed to have deployed to my side for the duration of my presence there. Around me were journalists and documentary makers, including Rehad Desai. I had met many of them before, and could even describe some as friends. Clearly, they were anticipating some drama. You could feel it in the air. They were not disappointed. As the meeting began, Vuyani muscled his way to the front and took over the podium. In his usual flamboyant language and with his penchant for dramatic spectacle, he called me a sinner in the church, blamed me for Mcebo's arrest, and said that the students would not be ambushed into engaging with me. Within minutes, I was surrounded by a mob hurling abuse and insults. Father Pugin tried to calm the crowd, calling on his status as both a leader in the church and a victim of the police, but there was now no pulling back. The church leaders had been outmanoeuvred.

The ASAWU leadership, ashen-faced and also outmanoeuvred, scrambled out of the way. Vishwas tried to calm the crowd. Three people came over and stood by me throughout the period. Father Anthony was there, as was Sello Hatang from the Nelson Mandela Foundation, and Michelle, who reassuringly put her hand on my shoulder. By this time, a mask had descended on my face. I had long ago learnt that, in moments like these, you neither flinch nor react. You remain calm and gaze directly at the individuals hurling the abuse. After a few minutes of standing there, without a response, in the glare of the cameras, Vuyani said that he wanted no violence and that he and the other students would leave the church and give me an opportunity to exit. Thereafter, they would return. When he left, taking with him the most aggressive of the students, I exited through the back of the stage and made my way to a kitchen hall next to the chapel. Tawana and Zeblon left with me. Together, we waited for the director of Campus Protection Services, Mokgawa Kobe, and the security team that had been called.

After a short while, Mokgawa and the security officers came to escort us. As we left the premises through the gate between the church and the university, a student associated with medical support, accompanied by Kezia Lewins from the Department of Sociology, asked me to instruct security to leave the gate open. I declined, aware that it had been the site of a security breach on multiple occasions, allowing people from outside to come in and commit crime and violence. To a torrent of abuse from the student we calmly walked away, locked the gate and returned to our offices. There was no time to feel sorry for myself; we had to prepare for the next day. I worked with Shirona on a media release, expressing regret that I was forced out even though I had been invited and reiterating our commitment to negotiations. After this, we sat down with Mokgawa to go through the next day's security protocols. These had to be strengthened: there would definitely be an attempt to reignite the protests.

A short while later, I got a call from Tiego asking me to allow the meeting to move to the Solomon Mahlangu concourse. I agreed, since it was now past 17h00 and there were no lectures. But I also insisted that there be no occupation, and that the concourse be vacated by the end of the evening. I watched the rest of the meeting on television and on our security cameras. A number of community leaders from churches and civil society, including Zwelinzima Vavi, Thuli Madonsela and Jay Naidoo, addressed it. Of these, only Thuli phoned to ask whether it was appropriate for her to come onto campus and address the students. I readily agreed. Later, I received an SMS from Jay expressing regret about how I had been treated by the student leadership. But none of the leaders publicly condemned what had happened – except Thuli, who did so in the mildest of terms. Essentially, the leaders hoped to win the confidence of the student protesters and then slowly influence their behaviour. It was a mistake that they would continue to make, having forgotten that silence in the face of spectacle simply reinforced the politics of populism that had come to dominate #FeesMustFall.

In the days that followed, I received much sympathy and support. Father Pollitt from the Jesuits closed the Holy Trinity Church, citing that its role as a sanctuary had been violated when I had been evicted. Over four hundred academics signed a petition that was started in the School of Law, also expressing regret about how I had been treated and asserting support for me. Numerous alumni, business and government leaders, and diplomats wrote personal notes of support and solidarity. These little acts of generosity played an important role in stiffening my resolve to complete the academic year.

The next day, as was anticipated, there were attempts to disrupt lectures and tests. Shaeera led a small group, disrupting a chemical engineering test in its final minutes, and was said to have personally torn the script of a student. After disrupting another lecture, they were confronted by a group of police. In the ensuing standoff, police opened fire with rubber bullets and teargas; Shaeera, Busisiwe and a few protesters were injured. They were all treated in the campus clinic, then Shaeera's father took her to Milpark Hospital. When we got the news, I asked for the footage of the incident from both the public domain and our cameras. I was furious. There was no doubt that Shaeera deserved to be arrested, having repeatedly violated the rights of others. But there was no reason for the police to open fire with rubber bullets. She constituted no threat and was directly within their reach. In these circumstances, an arrest was perfectly possible and legitimate. I confronted Gary angrily, who responded by saying that an investigation would be undertaken. A few hours later, senior police officers went to the hospital, took Shaeera's statement, and handed the matter to the Independent Police Investigative Directorate, the branch responsible for investigating police misconduct.

In the days that followed, we had a few sporadic acts of protest. A bus was set alight from inside while students were being transported between campuses. But overall, calm was returning to the university. We announced the examinations, and classes concluded in early November. The examinations were to be conducted with police protection and security personnel were to be stationed in the venues so that they could easily remove individuals who were intent on disruption. We warned that anyone who disrupted examinations would immediately be suspended. These were not ideal conditions under which to write examinations, but we believed that they were necessary for us to complete the academic year.

Some of the student leaders decided to interdict the examinations and were legally assisted by the Socio-Economic Rights Institute (SERI), on whose board I had served for many years. I called its director, Stuart Wilson, and he and Nomzamo Zondo, the director of litigation, came to see me. I expressed concern that they were representing the students in such a frivolous action and argued that the consequences of stopping the examinations would be devastating for poor students and for the country as a whole. I also indicated that we had already made concessions for students who felt traumatised to apply for their examinations to be deferred. Their simple response was that they were merely representing the students and it was not for them to take a political position on the matter. When I asked Stuart what he would do in my position, he replied, 'I would hate to have your job.'

We would go on to have a much more serious altercation a year later when SERI released a report on police action and university conduct during the protests. Not only did the report allege that the police had violated their constitutional duty, but it also made all kinds of allegations about the university's provision of healthcare services during the protests. Yet the authors of the report had not once interviewed or engaged with managers or executives at the institution. The result was that it was riddled with inaccuracies, innuendos and rumours. When Stuart approached me to distribute the report and engage them on it, I refused, arguing that we saw it as seriously flawed and SERI as partisan against the institution, given its role over the life of the protests. Stuart protested, explaining that their role was simply to provide legal services where they were not available and claiming that he was agnostic on the issues. He copied members of his board on his response, including Dumisa Ntsebeza and Zak Yacoob. A flurry of e-mails followed in which I held that, while the right to representation was a principle we are supportive of and believe is necessary for the sustainability of any democratic society ... I also believe that we must carefully differentiate how these principles impose a differential set of responsibilities on various actors in society. I am of the view that while this right must be made available to all (and we know that in reality it is not), the obligation it imposes on different actors in society may indeed be different. These obligations are influenced by whether they are individual or collective actors, the mandates and rules of their professions, and the essential purposes of the organisations. In this regard I believe the obligations on a human rights organisation would be different to that of another which is responsible for providing legal aid, and the obligations would be different to obligations on individual advocates or attorneys. Obviously, all need to represent their clients to the best of their ability, but who they take on as clients and what issues they seek to advise in law, reveals their intentions/biases/political preferences. This is especially true of human rights organisations. This is after all what I see as the conceptual and foundational basis of public interest law. To argue a political neutrality or agnosticism ... is I believe neither realistic nor valid.

The issue was eventually resolved when Zak asked for a telephonic engagement in which we agreed that Tawana and Shirona would engage a team from SERI on the report and correct what we saw as the factual inaccuracies. But the incident and, in particular, Stuart's claim of agnosticism reinforced my concern about progressives with a far-left orientation who were misreading the political moment and acting in a manner that seriously jeopardised the public universities in South Africa.

In any case, the attempt to interdict the examinations was dismissed. They proceeded as planned and without incident. On 9 November, Mcebo was released. We had repeatedly engaged with Tiego on Mcebo's incarceration and had, on one occasion, indicated that we would be willing to approach the courts and ask for his release into our custody. We had even contemplated housing him at my official residence, and Fatima had agreed, but other members of the executive felt that this was excessive. In the end, we made an arrangement with the Jesuit Institute to provide housing for him in the city centre. Tiego communicated this offer to Mcebo, but nothing came of it. He was released as a result of his own legal actions and applied for a deferment of his examinations, which he was granted.

The SRC and other student leaders approached us about a reconciliation process. While we were willing, we insisted that it would have to be accompanied by full disclosure. They agreed to consider the matter, but never returned, so it fell by the wayside. On 1 December, we brought the examinations to a close. The academic year had been concluded as promised. But it had come at a huge institutional cost; Wits University had gone through what was perhaps its most difficult period since the dawn of democracy.

Was it worth it? Were we right to force the completion of the academic year with police presence and security activation? There is debate about this, of course. It was not the only option. The entire higher education system was in turmoil in October 2016, and institutions adopted a variety of responses to the crisis. At the one end of the spectrum were institutions like UJ, which activated quite stringent security measures very early on to complete the year. At the other end, institutions like UCT went out of their way to avoid a security response, closed their academic programmes early, and even postponed some of their teaching and examinations to the new year. Wits University had always been somewhere in between; at the end of 2016, we shifted towards the UJ end of the spectrum. I had always publicly argued that we required a mix of political and security interventions, the precise balance of which was to be determined by the specific circumstances that confronted one.

It is worth noting that Max Price and I consulted closely throughout the late-2016 protests. For a short while we spoke every night, mostly after 22h00 or 23h00, when he would brief me about developments at UCT and I would do the same for Wits University. We compared strategies and spoke through the advantages and disadvantages of our different responses. Our strategies were in part informed by our different geographies and circumstances. UCT is on a mountain and has quite a porous perimeter. It has no fence, no gates and no access control. Each building has to be individually protected. Wits, by contrast, is a much more urban campus, with well-defined boundaries, and is much more easily containable. Our political context was also very different. Wits was more in the limelight, more engaged with church leaders, political parties and civic actors, and more the focus of political parties. It also seems, on the basis of the conversations with Max, that there were far more attempts at arson at Wits than UCT. These circumstances greatly influenced the institutions' responses.

But it would also be fair to say that our differential institutional responses were also partly determined by our own confidence and willingness to initiate security measures. This may have had to do with the fact that the Wits executive was far more united and cohesive than its UCT counterpart. In any case, for the first part of the protest wave in late 2016, we mirrored each other's strategies. UCT engaged in institutional reconciliation negotiations with the Cape Bar as mediators, while we embarked on our negotiations through Tiego and his team. Neither of our political initiatives achieved the desired outcome. But once the negotiated political line had been crossed by our respective student leaderships, the institutional responses of the two universities diverged. At Wits, we activated our security protocols, called in the police, and decided to complete the academic year in 2016. UCT decided to defer at least part of the academic programme and examinations until the new year. Max disputes this. He holds that their negotiations culminated in an agreement with the protest leaders that resulted in

> our being able to run the exams in November entirely without disturbance and minimal security … The extensive exam sessions the following January were because we allowed all students to defer any or all of their exams if they felt the lack of classes or general stress of disturbances prevented them from performing to their best. Many students split their exams across both sessions. Thus many thousands also wrote in January and in order to

accommodate so many, we needed the full three weeks for the deferred exams, which normally are written in one week. For this reason we also delayed the start of the 2017 academic year by a month. There were some selected degrees (pre-clinical medicine, engineering and a few other courses) where the amount of practical time lost during the weeks of suspended classes would have compromised the quality of the curriculum and these courses brought students back in January before the deferred exams to do the practical work that had been missed. This was the only formal teaching that carried over to the new year.

Yet while Max might interpret this as having completed the 2016 academic year, that is not how many others saw it. Many interpreted the decision as UCT not having completed the academic year.

Both of us were criticised by different stakeholders. Whereas most academic staff and students supported our plans to finish the year, we were heavily criticised by both #FeesMustFall activists and members of the far left within the academic community. The latter had recommended the course of action that UCT had adopted. But at UCT, Max also came under severe criticism from many staff, students and especially alumni. Many felt that the executives there had sacrificed the rights of the vast majority for the political preferences of a small, non-representative group of student leaders. Ultimately, only time will tell which course of action was appropriate, under the circumstances. But if compelled to make a preliminary judgement while the memories of 2016 are still fresh, I would suggest that the executive at Wits called it right at the end of 2016. In 2017, Wits University had a far more placid year, with no serious disruptions of the academic programme. The same cannot be said of UCT, which unfortunately had to conclude the year with stringent security protocols and police and dog patrols in the evenings around examination venues. In many ways, UCT had to undertake the kind of security measures in 2017 that it had avoided taking in 2016.

Yet, however differently our 2016 year ended, the problems remained. Neither of us, nor any other university in the country, can continue to be plagued by protests if we want to retain and enhance the quality of our academic and research offerings. If we do not find a systemic solution, it will not only weaken our universities but also compromise economic inclusion and inclusive development in South Africa. A systemic solution to the challenges of universities is the *sine qua non* for South Africa's prosperity and its ability to address its historical disparities.

7

The quest for a political solution

2016 was a difficult year. We completed the academic programme only because, after mediation attempts failed, we did what we thought we needed to do and invoked a range of unprecedented security protocols. While these security protocols, including the deployment of police and private security, got us through the academic year, we knew that a security solution was not sustainable in the medium to long term. We needed a political solution for the crisis in higher education. Given the systemic character of the crisis, it required intervention at national level. But we knew that the national leadership we needed was not going to come from the minister or the president. Whether fair or not, a wide range of the student leadership no longer deemed the minister an honest broker; and the president had lost credibility given the scandal-prone character of his administration. In this context, we began to cast around for alternative leadership to assist in finding a political solution to the crisis.

Earlier in the year, I had approached Archbishop Desmond Tutu to play this role. Randall Carolissen and I had even formally met with him at his office at the Cape Town Waterfront. It was a heart-wrenching meeting. He sympathised with us and understood the problem, but his frailty would just not allow him to play the onerous role required to bridge the divides that had emerged in higher education. The next name to come up was that of Deputy Chief Justice Dikgang Moseneke. Dikgang was an attractive idea: he was the chancellor of Wits University and had, in a previous life, been the deputy president of the Pan Africanist Congress. He had also been passed over by President Zuma for the top job of chief justice, which gave him enormous credibility among the EFF and factions within the ANC that were opposed to the Zuma presidency. Dikgang also came from the Constitutional Court which, having stood up to state officials and politicians in a number of cases, had now earned itself enormous respect among a cross-section of South Africa's populace. From my narrow perspective, I trusted Dikgang to do the right thing as he saw it. Finally, it did not hurt that he was enormously erudite and politically astute, characteristics that would serve him well in bridging the divide in what had become an increasingly polarised political environment.

When I broached the idea with Dikgang in October 2016, we were still deep inside the conflict that was playing out at Wits University. He indicated that he had received similar requests from other stakeholders. He also said that he wished to get President Zuma's views on his intervening in the crisis at universities. He wanted to gather a team to assist in this regard. We discussed some potential names, as well as some of the initiatives that were currently underway at institutions such as the SACC, the Higher Education Parents Dialogue and the Nelson Mandela Foundation. We concluded the conversation with Dikgang promising to consider the idea, talk to others, and come back to me. In the next month, we had multiple conversations; Dikgang reported that President Zuma was very open to him playing this role. He also assembled an impressive range of individuals – Jabu Mabuza, Yvonne Mokgoro, Sello Hatang, Santie Botha, Mary Metcalfe, Malusi Mpumlwana, Jay Naidoo, Thabo Makgoba, Mojanku Gumbi and Pitika Ntuli – and encouraged other peace-building initiatives already underway. For a short while, towards the end of 2016, optimism returned about the possibility of a political solution.

Throughout the conflict in September and October, I was involved in a range of mediation initiatives, in my capacity as both USAf chair and Wits vice-chancellor. Three of these in particular stand out: first, a meeting at the Public Protector's office in Pretoria during the tenure of Thuli Madonsela, in which Ahmed Bawa and I met with a group of student leaders; second, a series of engagements under the auspices of the National Economic Development and Labour Council (NEDLAC); and finally, a series of meetings in October under the auspices of the SACC and chaired by Malusi Mpumlwana. Ahmed and I attended the first meeting. After waiting for an hour or two for all the student participants to turn up, I had to leave. Ahmed stayed behind, however, and eventually did engage the remaining students, who turned out to be from the EFF and PASMA. In his subsequent report, he noted that the students were loud and rude, that they were not in the mood for concessions, and that nothing had come of the initiative.

The NEDLAC meetings were more substantive. They began with a call by COSATU to invoke Section 77 of the Labour Relations Act, which essentially provides for a national strike on a socioeconomic issue. In this case, the issue was free education. I attended a few of the meetings with Ahmed and was struck by how little the representatives of labour and business understood the university system. In the main, their proposals tended to be generic and rhetorical. To be fair, why should these representatives be expected to have a detailed understanding of the university system? Not many of us would have a detailed understanding of the NEDLAC process. But it is worth noting that this engagement was as political as it was solution-oriented. It was about different actors in the conflict at universities mobilising political support from outside the sector for their particular action. In any case, after multiple meetings, COSATU withdrew its Section 77 proposal in favour of a joint statement by all stakeholders supporting free education, transformation of the universities and decolonisation of the curriculum.

The last of these preliminary initiatives was facilitated by Malusi on behalf of the SACC. The meetings were useful in the sense that they brought us face to face with student leaders. One memorable student leader often wore a green blanket, a symbolic identification with Mgcineni Noki, the worker leader who was killed in the massacre at the koppies in Marikana. The striking feature of these engagements was that, while we had honest conversations with the student leaders, we left as distant from one another as we had been when we arrived. Whatever the student leadership's public articulations, in these conversations with this particular leadership, they demanded and expected the immediate realisation of free education and were prepared to shut the universities down until this was achieved. We, on the other hand, saw free education as a goal that could be worked towards, but believed that universities must be allowed to continue with their teaching and research. In that sense, this student leadership reflected the behaviour of protesters within our institutions. While we had temporarily succeeded in getting our academic programme back on track and completing the year, there was an urgent need to develop a political solution to the ongoing challenge at universities.

This is why Dikgang's initiative, which came to be known as the National Education Crisis Forum (NECF), was so important. It was meant to be a process rather than a single event, a build-up of multiple conversations, culminating in a collective conversation about the future of universities and how to transform or decolonise them. The NECF succeeded in mobilising significant resources from corporate South Africa and foundations, which enabled it to host these multiple conversations. Vice-chancellors were invited to only a few of these engagements. On 28 October 2016, Ahmed Bawa and I engaged Business Leadership South Africa for financial support for universities that were obliged to remain open for additional weeks to complete the academic year. We also used the opportunity to brief them on initiatives associated with the NECF.

In November and December 2016, vice-chancellors were involved in a flurry of meetings with the NECF. On 19 November, we were briefed by Malusi and Irvin Phenyane from the Higher Education Parents Dialogue. They informed us that the Fallists had organised themselves in national and regional structures and that Pitika Ntuli, Jay Naidoo and Zwelinzima Vavi were engaging them at a meeting in Durban that same weekend. They also reported to us on the engagements that they were having with the inter-ministerial committee chaired by Jeff Radebe. We expressed concern about the statements of some of the eminent persons, especially those that called for security to be removed from universities without making a concomitant demand for an end to violence. In the end, we agreed to convene a special meeting in which experts would be invited to present on potential solutions that they were advancing to address the fees crisis.

This meeting of experts took place on 3 December 2016. Four distinct presentations were made. One of these was by Statistician-General Pali Lehohla, who made the case that South Africa was failing its younger generations; too few were getting into universities and too many of these were not graduating. He concluded by suggesting that we had too few higher education institutions, and that we needed to provide far more post-secondary access to all students who qualified so that we could create the conditions for the realisation of the demographic dividend for African people. This was accompanied by three solution-oriented presentations by Sizwe Nxasana, Khaya Sithole and Daniel Barlow. In the first of these, Sizwe proposed what came to be known as the Ikusasa financial model, an income-contingent loan scheme funded by investors and guaranteed by government. Next, Khaya, a former Wits University staff member, brought together a group of students to investigate and advance a set of proposals for how free education could be financed. This proposal, described as the Lesedi model, won the support of the majority of the student leadership. The final presentation was by Daniel, who proposed the use of perpetual bonds to finance higher education in South Africa. Many of these financial models, discussed in detail in Chapter 8, focused on immediately addressing the access challenge in South African universities.

The most important of the NECF meetings, however, was the one on 10 and 11 December 2016. Dikgang chaired it personally, and students across the party ideological divide, as well as many vice-chancellors, attended it. The presentations discussed earlier served as a backdrop to a direct engagement between the diverse student leadership and the vice-chancellors, mediated by the eminent persons. In these engagements,

Dikgang constantly had to intervene, indicate that he shared the students concerns, invoke his own radical political credentials, and generally keep the student leadership on board. As vice-chancellors, we had decided to keep our individual engagements to a minimum. Ahmed was to speak on our behalf and respond to questions from the students.

A number of the student leaders, however, would have none of it. They insisted that vice-chancellors be heard individually, and pointedly asked Sizwe Mabizela about disciplinary actions that he had instituted against women student activists. Sizwe did respond, explaining that we could not allow student activists to violate others' rights. Some of the leaders did not appreciate his response, as one of the students concerned was in the room and left in a distressed state. After this, Vuyani Pambo expressed a concern about engaging vice-chancellors like me since I had written a *Daily Maverick* article reflecting on the student protests and criticising student leaders for their behaviour. When Ahmed rose to respond, teasing Vuyani that he sounded like a younger version of me, the student leaders protested and demanded that I respond directly. Eventually I did, summarising my support for the goal of free university education and indicating that this would have to be built over years – even decades. More importantly, I indicated that while we were open to an alliance with students in their struggle, this was not unconditional. Our mandate was to complete the academic year, and this remained non-negotiable.

The two days proceeded very much like this. Every now and then, I would bump into one group or another of student leaders outside of the formal sessions, who would flaunt the fact that they were smoking marijuana on the hotel premises. I teased them that if they really wanted to be revolutionaries, they needed to learn about discipline, to which they responded that their generation would not acquiesce to bourgeois sensibilities and this was their manifestation of decolonisation. None of this banter was belligerent; it was all generally good-natured. In the formal sessions, student leaders pressed both the eminent persons and the vice-chancellors to intervene in securing the release of imprisoned student leaders. Dikgang and other members of the NECF agreed to engage government and the National Director of Public Prosecutions to grant bail. When vice-chancellors were asked about our position in this regard, we responded by suggesting that we had no power on the matter but would not stand in the way of student leaders being released. The meeting ended with student leaders extracting a commitment from the NECF to intervene in this regard. The NECF did try, particularly with regard to Bonginkosi Khanyile, a student leader from Durban University of Technology (DUT) who had been arrested, but with very little success. Bonginkosi would remain in prison throughout December and January, and would only be released on 3 March 2017 after the EFF highlighted the case nationally and his lawyers petitioned the Constitutional Court. All in all, Bonginkosi spent over one hundred and fifty days in jail.

When we returned in the new year, we were able to avoid a repeat of the kind of protest we experienced at the beginning of 2016. The big political moment in early 2017 was the NECF summit on 18 and 19 March 2017. Prior to this, I attended a deliberation involving unions and academic staff associations in universities across the country, as an observer. I also convened a discreet dinner engagement between a select group of vice-chancellors, Dikgang and Malusi. The rationale for the meeting was that a number of vice-chancellors had begun to express concern about whether some of the eminent persons of the NECF had sufficient appreciation of the challenges confronting the universities. There was also the concern that one or two of them had used what was seen as inflammatory rhetoric to describe the situation at some of the institutions. There is no doubt that some of the eminent persons believed that the vice-chancellors were not politically adept enough in managing the tensions at the universities. This was particularly evident at a meeting between vice-chancellors and the eminent persons at the Nelson Mandela Foundation on 13 January 2017. The response of the vice-chancellors was, of course, that the eminent persons did not fully appreciate the complexity of the issues and were misreading the political situation. The vice-chancellors were particularly concerned that too many eminent persons were demanding the withdrawal of the police without any guarantees from the student leadership that students would refrain from violence. Some of this may simply have been tactical, aimed at winning the students over. But some of it did, in fact, reflect the views of certain eminent persons. The result was a growing unease among vice-chancellors that some of the eminent persons were displaying political naïveté, making demands on university executives that we simply could not accede to.

To avoid a rupture between the NECF and vice-chancellors, we agreed in the USAf executive that I would host a dinner with Dikgang and Malusi. The dinner was held a month before the summit, on 20 February, and involved, from our side, Derrick Swartz, Ahmed Bawa, Cheryl de la Rey, Sizwe Mabizela, Sol Plaatje University vice-chancellor Yunus Ballim and me. The conversations were quite frank. Derrick kicked off, airing the vice-chancellors' concerns and indicating that much of the political engagement that the NECF was attempting had already been tried before in multiple institutions. He remarked that the vice chancellors as a collective were committed to a more equitable, inclusive and transformed higher education system. He pleaded for the eminent persons 'to create the broadest inclusive base for political dialogue, cautioning [them] against assuming that a narrow and small militant faction of the student movement is representative of the student voice'. Derrick then expressed concern about 'the unproblematic way in which violence by sections of the student movement is rationalised as a defence against "structural violence", leaving its unintended consequences uninterrogated', and finally cautioned against some of the eminent persons 'adopting belligerent and contestable views whilst wanting to act as honest brokers in a highly inflammable and toxic political en-vironment'. Dikgang and Malusi both responded, recognising the concerns but adding that vice-chancellors should not interpret their face-to-face and tactical engagements as being the sum total of their views on the crisis of higher education. They both also indicated that the eminent persons of the NECF were a diverse group, each with their own strengths and weaknesses. Both did, however, underscore the fact that they were very aware that individual vice-chancellors could not resolve most of the challenges at universities, and that government had to tackle these at a systemic level. The dinner meeting eventually concluded positively, with all of us agreeing to participate and assist in making the event a success.

On the day of the summit, a number of vice-chancellors made their way to the Eskom Academy of Learning. We had agreed that Ahmed would speak on behalf of all of the vice-chancellors. This would deny protesters at institutional level the opportunity to heckle their individual vice-chancellor. The other challenge was that Thandwa Mthembu was being inaugurated as vice-chancellor of the DUT on the same day. Ahmed was to represent USAf at that event. It was agreed that the different stakeholder representatives would simply speak for five minutes at the beginning of the programme, voicing their support for the initiative. If all went well, Ahmed could fulfil this responsibility and still make his flight to Durban for the inauguration. We had also released a public communique about the summit, supporting it and committing to affordable education and working with all of the role players to find solutions to problems like housing and insourcing.

But as soon as we reached the plenary tent where the summit was to be held, it was apparent that the proceedings were not going to remain on schedule. First, many disparate groups of students from a variety of party backgrounds were all congregated at the same place. The political rivalry between them created a dynamic of its own. Each group wanted to demonstrate that it was more radical than the other; the net effect was the sacrifice of the collective agenda to find a solution to the crisis. Also, some of the student groups were refusing to come into the plenary tent and play by the rules that had been agreed. In the end, the proceedings got underway – two hours later than scheduled and only after Malusi, Dikgang, Pitika and the others had engaged the students and convinced them to give the proceedings a chance. It was an inauspicious start.

Dikgang was the first to speak formally. He was able to complete his speech – but judging by the commentary from the EFF and PASMA group of students while Dikgang was speaking, it was clear that disruption was imminent. In any case, the next group of speakers were the students. But the proceedings came to an immediate halt when AfriForum Youth was the first group to be called to the podium. PASMA protested, as did some others. They argued that, as AfriForum was a conservative organisation, the programme should not prioritise it – or even accommodate it. The tensions led to a fracas. Chairs were thrown; Lindsay

Maasdorp, Black First Land First spokesperson, assaulted some of the AfriForum Youth members. The organisers should have anticipated this and had AfriForum Youth speak further down the programme. But now that AfriForum Youth had been called, the organisers should never have capitulated. Moreover, by not taking action against Lindsay they emboldened the disruptive elements in the summit and allowed the intolerance to grow. After another round of negotiations with the student leadership, while everyone else hung around, we got back on track. The representatives from the remaining student parties spoke. Despite some sporadic heckling, all speakers were allowed to complete their speeches.

Then it was Ahmed's turn to represent the vice-chancellors. But given the delays in the programme, he was no longer around – he had had to leave to catch his flight to Durban. One of us had to speak. No one wanted to. As USAf chair, I got stuck with the responsibility. I went to the podium knowing that it was not going to go well. I could not get more than a few words in before the heckling started. When I looked at Malusi, he indicated that I should continue. So, I spoke above the heckling. Before long, a group of EFF students tried to storm the stage, some of whom were from Wits and quite a few of whom had been suspended for one violation or another. At this point, Malusi intervened, asking me to sit, and a new round of negotiations started with this group of student leaders. Again, the mask descended; I looked calmly and unflinchingly at the protesting students. After a while, as the negotiations continued, I came to the realisation that we could not go on like this. I left the stage and signalled to some of the other vice-chancellors; we all walked outside to caucus.

We found a small tent just outside the main venue. Here, UKZN vice-chancellor Albert van Jaarsveld, Cheryl, Ihron, Derrick, Yunus and I discussed what to do. We were all convinced that this would end in disaster, and that it should be called off now before things got out of hand. During our discussion, two students, both drunk, approached us and demanded to speak to Cheryl. They had been expelled from UP and wanted to engage her. Ihron indicated that this would not happen as we were busy having a meeting. The students became abusive to Ihron, who snapped and turned to confront them. Recognising that this could turn nasty, Derrick and I intervened and separated them. The students moved off; we decided it was better to leave. Ihron and I walked to our cars, and Derrick also prepared to leave. But we had forgotten about Cheryl, who was clearly the target of the two students. Luckily, Albert was still there. When the two students, accompanied by others, again approached and verbally threatened her, he escorted her to her car.

While all of this was playing out, the organisers were getting the students back into the tent and trying to get the summit back on track. Now it was Minister Nzimande who was meant to speak. Again, he was not long into his speech when the heckling started from the EFF and some of the others. The YCL rose to the minister's defence, given that Minister Nzimande is also the general secretary of the South African Communist Party. Within seconds, there was an altercation. Again, the conference was brought to a halt. By this time, it was clear that the summit could not continue. Too many of the student groups were focused on spectacle; too few were interested in deliberating the issues. There was no doubt that some had come with a political instruction and intention to disrupt. Coupled with the consumption of alcohol and drugs, the situation was unpredictable and dangerous. Under these circumstances, it was best to cancel the summit.

By the time Ihron and I had reached our cars, it was clear that the summit had been called off. Ihron rejoined his bodyguards, but I had come alone. As more and more people began to leave the venue, I followed Ihron's car as we snaked to the entrance. Suddenly, it seemed that some students had cottoned on to our departure. They started running towards the entrance. The venue's guards wanted to search our cars, as was protocol. At this point, the bodyguards in Ihron's car got out, ignored the other guards, opened the gates, and directed our cars and a few others out of the venue. I had never been as glad to have Ihron's bodyguards present. We drove off, leaving a summit in tatters because the vast majority of us had once again allowed the few focused on political spectacle to disrupt and destroy a process in which we could have negotiated a political resolution to our crisis.

As we sped away, the organisers formally cancelled the summit. Students who were staying at the venue were requested to leave immediately; transport was called to take everyone back. The organisers recognised that leaving the disparate student groups, many politically aligned, in a single venue under these circumstances could be dangerous.

The summit collapsed in a sea of recriminations. The eminent persons were criticised for being politically naive and believing that they could control the diverse student groups when so many others had tried and failed. But it is unfair to blame the eminent persons of the NECF. They had tried to intervene and assist in very difficult circumstances when the official political leadership had been found wanting. The country owed them a collective debt of gratitude for the attempt. What happened at the summit was no different from what had happened at the Wits General Assembly in October, five months earlier. Intolerant rival student groups who could not develop a collective agenda resorted to disrupting the plans that were in play. The single biggest curse of this social struggle had become the political and party rivalry that was eating the movement from within.

I spoke to some of the organisers a few hours later. Mary Metcalfe came over to the house after she had left the venue. We sat in the garden, had something to eat, and reviewed the developments of the day and the preceding weeks. We discussed whether the eminent persons had been too trusting, and perhaps slightly politically naive. I suggested that they had too easily bought into the idea that none of the vice-chancellors was politically astute enough to manage the political aspect of the protests. What they had experienced earlier in the day, I argued, was what vice-chancellors had been confronting for about eighteen months.

Malusi sent an SMS to a number of vice-chancellors expressing his regret at the failure of the summit and his appreciation of our conduct throughout the event. The NECF also released a statement expressing this regret and indicating that, while the vast majority wanted to proceed, it was disrupted by the few who did not want the vice-chancellors and minister to speak. Pitika would subsequently be interviewed by eNCA television news and further alienate the vice-chancellors, who interpreted him as saying that the event could not go on because the minister and vice-chancellors were so unpopular. There was no appreciation of accountability in the interview. While Dikgang indicated in an interview the following day that the eminent persons would persevere in their attempts, most informed observers recognised that this was the end of that project. Student groups had collapsed one of the more promising initiatives to find a political solution as a result of their political rivalry, anarchist behaviour and focus on political spectacle.

In the months ahead, I would approach Winnie Mandela to explore whether she could serve as a mediator with some of the student leadership. Her office did respond, indicating that she would be in touch for a meeting as soon as her health improved. But regrettably this did not happen, and the opportunity did not present itself.

A protest at our Education Campus in April 2017 signalled the dangers of not resolving the systemic weaknesses. We were able to bring the protest quickly to an end, through negotiations and a firm private security response. This time around, we had received very little police support – the police had had to deploy all their forces to Eldorado Park, where there had been massive and violent community protests. Two students would ultimately be expelled for violent behaviour in the protests on the Education Campus. In the months ahead, we managed to stay one step ahead of those who wanted to repeat the events of 2016. Wits University remained relatively stable, but we were continuously on tenterhooks given the broader political instability within the country.

At the end of August 2017, the Heher Commission finally handed its report to the president. Rumour had it, correctly, that the Commission was proposing an income-contingent loan scheme financed by the banks and underwritten by government. This scheme, discussed in detail in Chapter 8, meant that once students started earning an income, and when this reached a particular threshold, payment would automatically come into effect through the tax system. For three months, the country heard nothing from the president. On 30 October, the Presidency informed the nation that the report was at an advanced stage of processing and that an announcement would soon be made. Then, on 13 November, the report was released without the president's response, although the communique did indicate that a response was being developed by an inter-ministerial task team led by Jeff Radebe and the chair of the Financial and Fiscal Commission, which was under the oversight of the Minister of Finance, Malusi Gigaba.

The delayed response from the president created tensions on campuses. On the one hand, we were not keen on a major statement that could spark protests just before the final examinations. On the other hand, the uncertainty provoked unease among student leaders, many of whom correctly assumed that the delay was a political strategy to prevent a new round of protests. Some student leaders approached Max Price and asked him to make a statement condemning the president's failure to respond to the Heher Commission's recommendations. When Max discussed it with the vice-chancellors on 21 October, I objected, fearing that it would be used as a pretext to spark another round of protests. Max did eventually make a statement, and the student leaders embarked on a protest at UCT two weeks later. This, in part, had to do with the fact that DASO had won the SRC elections and the EFF/PASMA students hoped to demonstrate that they still had the capacity to bring the campus to a standstill. These protests would spiral to a point where UCT completed its 2017 examinations in a tent on the rugby field, surrounded by security. Dog units patrolled the tent in the evenings to ensure security from intruders and prevent petrol bombs being thrown onto it from outside the fence on the periphery. CPUT also experienced widespread protests on some campuses, which required a firm security response. All in all, Gauteng universities were far quieter in 2017 than their Western Cape counterparts.

The chance of a protest emerging at Wits in late 2017 was averted by the farsightedness of the EFF-aligned SRC leaders. The EFF had won the 2017 SRC elections decisively, despite a low turnout. During the week before the examinations, on 26 October, the SRC had called a solidarity meeting with the protests at UCT. This was not allowed: university policy excludes meetings being called on campus in the two weeks preceding examinations. The SRC president, Orediretse Masebe, requested permission to go and inform those who had gathered that the meeting could not go on. I granted it, fearing that it would spin out of control if there was no leadership there. Of course, when Orediretse and his fellow SRC leaders arrived at the meeting, they found a number of activists, some of whom were no longer students and not allowed on campus, pushing for a protest. When I came out of a Senate meeting that same afternoon, I was told that a decision had been made to embark on a protest the following day. We quickly scrambled to activate our full security protocols. We were not going to allow another disruption of the academic year this close to the examinations.

At 22h00 that evening, the SRC released a communique calling off the protest. It said that, after the meeting, a number of students – particularly those in off-campus residences – had contacted them to oppose the decision: they did not have the means to pay for additional accommodation if the examinations were delayed. Arguing that the audience at the meeting did not reflect the student community, and declaring the importance of an SRC being responsive to its own constituency, it suggested that it 'won't be careless and excited by instigators who want a shutdown for their own motives'. The SRC concluded: 'The decision is final. Students should continue studying in the libraries and computer labs in order to fully prepare for exams. Exams will continue as planned.' This was perhaps one of the bravest political actions I had ever observed from a group of student leaders in my tenure at Wits University. They resisted activists within their own party and irresponsible baiting by other parties to make a political call in defence of the examinations and the completion of the academic programme. Through this single act of political leadership, Wits University was able to complete the academic year without any protests in 2017.

As these battles, both real and figurative, played out on our campuses, a different kind of battle was underway in the inter-ministerial task team, the Presidency and Treasury, and other structures of government. A new actor – Mukovhe Morris Masutha – had come to the fore. Morris had been SRC president at Wits University in 2010/2011 and had a close relationship with President Zuma, particularly because he had previously dated his daughter Thuthukile. He had also established the Thusanani Foundation to support poor students with scholarships for universities. The foundation had been launched at Wits University in November 2014, in a function at which I had spoken – as had President Zuma.

Morris had begun his doctorate at the University of Bath, but regularly returned to South Africa for significant periods. In both 2015 and 2016, he was present at some of the protests and would regularly engage me on the challenges that existed and what to do about them.

Soon after the Presidency released the Heher Commission report for public comment on 13 November, it leaked into the public domain that Morris was on the advisory committee assisting the process and had become particularly influential, given his proximity to Zuma. It also became publicly known that Morris believed that free comprehensive education should be declared for all students with a family income of less than R350 000 per annum. His motivation for this was, on one level, entirely legitimate, since the R122 000 criterion for qualification for the NSFAS loan had not been adjusted for inflation in more than fifteen years. The proposal was heavily contested within the committee, largely on the grounds of affordability, but Morris's proximity to the president gave his views a prominence that was difficult to contain.

By the second half of November 2017, it was publicly apparent that there was a major policy tussle within the committee. After significant pushback from both Treasury officials and others in the ANC leadership, particularly those associated with the Ramaphosa camp, it seemed as if the decision would be postponed until the Minister of Finance's budget speech in February 2018. But suddenly, rumours began surfacing in the days preceding the ANC conference that the president was contemplating a major policy statement on free higher education in order to tilt the scales at the conference in favour of his preferred candidate, Nkosazana Dlamini-Zuma. In the early hours of 16 December, on the very eve of the conference, President Zuma proclaimed comprehensive free education for all students in universities and technical vocational education and training (TVET) colleges with a family income of less than R350 000 per annum. The plan was to be implemented over five years and would commence with new first-year students in the 2018 academic year.

I had engaged Morris on this plan some weeks earlier when he had requested a meeting with me. He was critical of the Heher Commission's income-contingent loan scheme, having seen how toxic it had become to the broader social fabric in the United Kingdom – not only because it was unsustainable, but also for the financial and emotional burden it imposed on so many young people. He motivated the case for the R350 000 cut-off on the grounds that it would impact positively on more than 90 per cent of the country's households. He also suggested that it would not be as expensive as was being suggested by Treasury and DHET officials, and would nevertheless make a dramatic impact on addressing the skills deficit, thereby contributing to both growth in the economy and inclusive development in the wider society.

Of course, what Morris was not saying was that, while 90 per cent of households in the broader society did earn below R350 000, they were not evenly represented in the higher education system. As indicated earlier, estimates by the DHET and Treasury suggested that only 40 per cent of the students in the system would qualify for the 'free education' concession. Herein lies the dilemma of the proposal Morris advocated: given that it would only cover 40 per cent of students in the system, it did not address the problem of the 'missing middle' – students whose family income was above the cut-off point, but who could still not afford the cost of higher education. It is worth noting that this category constituted the vast majority of students at universities like Wits and UCT, which were ground zero for the #FeesMustFall protests. President Zuma's concession only addressed part of the problem, at a huge cost, and the fear was that it may not have left sufficient resources available for dealing comprehensively with the systemic challenge of access to higher education.

President Zuma's concession was seen for what it really was: an attempt to tilt the electoral balance within the party in favour of Dlamini-Zuma. It did not succeed, and Cyril Ramaphosa won the election. But the new ANC leadership could not backtrack on the concession – this would be political suicide. The official response from the ANC was perhaps most cogently expressed by Minister Naledi Pandor, Ramaphosa's new Minister of Higher Education and Training. In an interview with Eusebius McKaiser on Radio 702 on 8 March 2018, when asked whether she thought President Zuma's announcement was a mistake, she replied:

> No, because the announcement had emerged from deliberations
> we had been having following the Heher Commission report and

recommendations. So these had been looked at in an inter-ministerial task team that I had been a part of. The timing of the announcement was a surprise, but as to its content, we had gone into the issues in some detail.

There could not have been a more categorical statement that President Zuma's proclamation of 16 December 2017 was to remain official policy of the new administration. Our response to the proclamation was cautiously supportive. In a series of tweets, I said:

> Announcement of free education for poor and working class cannot but be positive. Issue is how is it to be paid for? Urgent clarity needed.

> We need to clarify how the financing of free education would work. Urgent need for govt. to clarify with university stakeholders.

> DHET did meet VCs with regard to 2018 fee increase for those with family income of less than R600k. We had no discussion of free education for poor and working class.

I made this final remark to counter the deliberate misrepresentation that vice-chancellors had been consulted about the decision. This was patently untrue; the official USAf statement and my remarks both underscored this fact. The official statement also indicated cautious support for the decision and, like my remarks, expressed the importance of clarifying how the measure would be paid for. What we truly feared was government declaring free education but not underwriting the costs. However, to be fair, all government officials and ruling party leaders committed to the principle of funding the universities and TVET colleges appropriately.

In the wake of Zuma's announcement, the EFF and Julius Malema in particular called on students to flood the universities and claim their place. This was both politically opportunistic and adventurist in the extreme. Not only did it violate the admission requirements and enrolment plans of individual institutions, all of which are determined months and even years in advance, but it was also risking lives by creating the possibility of stampedes, as had occurred some years before at UJ. Both USAf and I made public statements condemning this political opportunism, and publicly called for universities not to be used as a political football by parties and politicians. Wits University, like many institutions, had always had mechanisms to advise walk-in students where to apply and how to do so, and we beefed up our capacities in this regard. In the end, the registration processes at all universities proceeded in an orderly fashion and without significant disruption.

By early 2018, we had had just over three years of sustained political instability at South Africa's universities. Almost all stakeholders were battle weary and had begun to show the scars of the prolonged struggle. The protests had left a polarised environment in their wake, manifesting in fractured relations between staff and students. Staff, both academic and professional and administrative, reported that the increasingly tense environment was not pleasant to work in. This was perhaps most dramatically brought home to me by separate incidents with two senior academics: Mary Scholes and Roger Gibson. Mary, a senior professor in the Faculty of Science and a Senate representative to Council, telephoned me in the closing days of 2016 simply to express support. In the course of the conversation, she broke down, and I realised how deeply the difficult events of 2016 had impacted on her. In a similar incident a few weeks earlier, Roger Gibson, the head of the School of Geosciences, choked up in a Senate meeting while he was reflecting on the deep fissures that had emerged within the university community. Both incidents highlighted the impact of the protests on staff, many of whom had dedicated most of their professional lives to the institution so that Wits University could play the role it was meant to play in addressing some of South Africa's greatest challenges.

But these scars were also evident on other stakeholders. Vice-chancellors and executives were exhausted by the protests' continuous political tension. The students showed the deepest scars, perhaps: many failed, and pass rates plateaued. Some students, and even staff, manifested symptoms of post-traumatic stress. In this context, some of South

Africa's most talented students began to seek pastures outside the country for their higher education options. It became increasingly urgent to turn this situation around. We needed a political solution – or we risked permanently fracturing our universities and forever compromising the possibility of an inclusive developmental future for our society.

8

Making the numbers work

IS free higher education legitimate and affordable in South Africa? And, if so, which financial model should enable its implementation? These distinct questions are often conflated; as a result, neither is answered satisfactorily. Yet they lie at the very heart of South Africa's university crisis.

The legitimacy of the demand for free higher education is, of course, contested. If the question were posed to the protesting students, their leadership, and even many of those in solidarity with the movement, the answer would be a categorical yes. They would hold, at least implicitly, that universities and higher education institutions more generally should be instruments for addressing inequality. But this is only possible if these institutions enable access for students from marginalised communities, and provide support to and graduate such students, thereby facilitating class mobility. If, however, these institutions only enrol the children of the rich and the upper middle classes because of their high fees, they effectively serve to reinforce or even increase the very inequalities that prevail in, or were inherited by, the society. The protesting students and their leaders and supporters would thus argue that universities in particular and the post-secondary education system more generally must be deliberately refashioned with free education as their core principle, so that these institutions generate the inclusive developmental benefits necessary to transform South African society.

There are many stakeholders in society who would sympathise with this view, even if they have questions about its affordability. But there are also discordant voices that grapple with how best to address the challenges of higher education. Nico Cloete, director of the Centre for Higher Education Trust and extraordinary professor at Stellenbosch University and UWC, has argued that free higher education is both 'financially impossible and morally wrong, as [it] privileges the rich'. He is supported in this view by some vice-chancellors – Max Price and Sizwe Mabizela, for instance – who hold that free higher education for all is morally unacceptable in a highly unequal society like South Africa because it subsidises higher education for the rich and lets them off the hook from paying higher fees, which could have been used to cross-subsidise poor students. Again, while I am sympathetic to their concern from a managerial point of view, I do not believe that this thesis is intellectually sound because it ignores the fact that there is no such thing as free education. Someone always has to pay; if we were to declare free education in South Africa, the rich would simply be paying through another mechanism, namely taxes. If one recognises this, then there is no legitimacy to the immorality argument.

Assuming for a moment that there is legitimacy to the demand for free education, is it feasible or affordable? Again, if you were to put this question to the student protesters or their supporters, there would a resounding yes. The affordability of free higher education was most coherently summarised by Salim Vally, Enver Motala, Leigh-Ann Naidoo, Mondli Hlatshwayo, Rasigan Maharajh and Zolisa Marawu in the online journal *The Conversation*, and in their submission to the presidential commission on free education. Essentially, they argued that the costs of free higher education should be underwritten by a tax on the super-rich, what they interpret as the top 10 per cent of income earners in society. But other than articulating a fair critique of government and other policy advocates who limit their policy options to what is feasible within the current fiscal framework, their arguments in this public intervention and in Enver, Salim and Rasigan's subsequent, more academic, contribution in the *New South African Review* do not persuasively demonstrate the proposal's political or economic feasibility. There is no detailed costing of the proposal, nor are there detailed recommendations on the level of tax required to generate the resources for financing the reform. There is also no substantive reflection on how to create the political will for their reform to be considered or how to mitigate the economic backlash that would likely emerge from a dramatic tax increase for the top 10 per cent of income earners. At one level, none of this is surprising: the authors do display contempt for 'pragmatism', as if pragmatism and a radical agenda are somehow mutually exclusive. In the end, the contribution does indeed suffer from a naïveté, a description that the authors chafe at. But they take refuge in the view themselves that they will be subjected 'to derisive criticisms about left wing ideas' because it seems easier and saves them from having to confront real criticisms about the implementation of their proposals.

Yet there are as many questions to be asked of the ANC and government's view on free higher education. The ruling party has never formally committed to comprehensive free higher education, instead preferring to qualify the right, on the grounds of affordability, with the phrase 'for the poor and working class'. A number of its senior leaders – Minister Blade Nzimande in particular – have questioned the moral legitimacy of government investing so much in a university system comprising just over one million students, when more than four times that number are outside the system and/or unemployed. The ANC also relies on the Constitution to support its position since the Bill of Rights obliges government to provide free 'basic education', but categorically stipulates that 'further education' should be realised in a 'progressive' manner based on 'available resources'. Yet one has to say that not even this limited goal has ever been achieved. After all, since the turn of the millennium, the per capita subsidy to universities has declined annually, essentially compelling institutional executives to increase their fees in order to retain the quality of their academic programmes.

But apart from this criticism, is there legitimacy to the ruling party's position that free higher education for all is not immediately feasible in South Africa? Of course, it depends on what one means by free higher education; should it simply involve tuition, as in Germany and Mexico, or should it take a comprehensive form and cover accommodation and subsistence as well, as in Scandinavia? Ironically, here there is substantive agreement among all role players. Everyone recognises that free tuition would not be sufficient as there are too many students without the financial means to cover the costs of accommodation and subsistence. The net result would be wasted resources, as these students would be unable to progress through the system in any case.

Comprehensive, free higher education would come at an astronomical cost. Officials from the DHET and Treasury estimate that Jacob Zuma's proclamation of comprehensive, free higher education for all students in universities and TVET colleges with a family income of less than R350 000 per annum would cover 40 per cent of the system and, once fully implemented, would cost an additional R57 billion per annum, or 4.3 per cent of government expenditure. Extrapolating from this for the whole system, one can assume that fully comprehensive, free higher education for all students would be in the region of an extra R143 billion per annum. And this is a conservative figure since it is now known that the original estimate of R57 billion was hopelessly inadequate and the true cost may be higher than R90 billion. South Africa simply does not have sufficient resources in state coffers to implement comprehensive, free higher education for both universities and TVET colleges.

But the protesters' counterargument cannot be ignored. The vast majority of students who gain access to universities are from the richest 10 per cent of the population, although it is worth noting that, because of South Africa's skewed distribution of income, this represents largely the middle class. Nevertheless, the vast majority of the poor are concentrated in historically black universities. The net effect of this demographic configuration in higher education is that we are reinforcing the very inequalities that were inherited by the post-apartheid state. Any agenda for addressing inequality in South Africa must think through how to refinance universities so that they are capable of educating the children of marginalised communities and thereby enabling class mobility. This is especially true of a society like South Africa, where university education has the highest return for individuals in comparison to any other part of the world. Given this need to use universities to address the challenge of inequality and the problem of affordability, we have to explore the probability of establishing a multi-year, perhaps even multi-decade, programme that gradually shifts us to enabling access for poor and 'missing middle' students to higher education and ensuring that the costs of doing this are no longer a barrier.

A number of proposals have emerged in the wake of #FeesMustFall that purport to address this challenge. Before reviewing the efficacy of each, it may be prudent to identify the principal systemic characteristics that need to accompany university refinancing if these institutions are to address inequality. First, universities depend on other sectors fulfilling their own obligations. In this regard, universities' ability to meet their obligations is significantly constrained by the Department of Basic Education's failure to provide quality education to all South Africa's children. This has to be fixed urgently if inequality is to be addressed.

Second, there is an urgent need to correct the pyramid of post-secondary education. This primarily means that the TVET sector has to be dramatically expanded to become the largest platform in the post-schooling training arena. Moreover, the TVETs have to be transformed. They are not working: their pass rates are dismal and their skill sets are inadequate for the needs of the economy. We need to close many of them and establish new ones that are linked to corporates that have a track record in training. These corporates must produce not only for them-selves, but for their economic sector as a whole. They must be incentivised to do so through the skills levy and the use of tax credits. Such a strategy would be akin to the one in Germany, where there is an integrated economic and vocational plan. Our TVET sector must not only address past injustices, but also train for a new world of robotics, artificial intelligence and mechanisation – what we have come to term the Fourth Industrial Revolution.

Finally, in addition to a well-functioning TVET sector, South Africa needs a diverse university system where different institutions fulfil distinct mandates. Some of these universities need to be distinctly teaching-oriented, where the primary focus is the production of high-quality undergraduates, while others need to be primarily research-intensive institutions, with a focus on research, innovation and the development of postgraduate students. Others still should perform a complex mix of these two functions, depending on their mandate, location and historical evolution. We need to imagine a higher education continuum, with each institution occupying a different place on the continuum of teaching, research and innovation responsibilities. Obviously, there must be mobility within this system so that students beginning at one end of the continuum are theoretically able to move through other institutions to other parts of the continuum. And it must be possible for institutions to evolve and adopt different mandates, should circumstances and needs require them to do so. Our educational institutions must, therefore, be differentiated, each with different mandates and responsibilities, independent and yet connected to one another, creating a seamless system that is both nationally responsive and globally competitive. Such a diverse university system is not only necessary for fulfilling the economy's and broader society's multiple, diverse needs, but would also establish one of the foundational prerequisites for competing effectively in the digitised global economy of the 21st century.

With these foundational characteristics, an appropriately funded university system could help to address inequality and enable the development of an inclusive society. How, then, could this be financed? There are many individual proposals, each with one or another variant of institutional design. This review, however, will focus on the three distinct financial models that have emerged.

Three financial models were developed in the course of the #FeesMustFall protests and were subject to deliberations in the collective forums that emerged to address the crisis. The first of these, entitled Thuto ke Lesedi (Education Is the Light), was a response by the leadership of the student protesters to the charge that their demands were unrealistic and financially unviable. It is said that Shafee Verachia approached a young academic, Khaya Sithole, in the Wits School of Accountancy to investigate a financing model that they could advance in the national debate. Sithole brought together a group of honours students to develop such a model. None were in the formal political leadership of the student political parties, so they were relatively autonomous and insulated from the political hyperbole that normally accompanied the overtly political engagement with the protests. The proposals were thus refreshingly thoughtful and practical, and while they took as their starting point the principle of free higher education and pushed the boundaries of what was possible, they were nevertheless grounded in the fiscal realities of contemporary South Africa.

My first interaction with the proposal, as indicated in Chapter 6, was when I attended Minister Nzimande's Higher Education Multi-Stakeholder Imbizo at Emperors Palace on 3 October 2016. Shafee had asked whether I would be willing to endorse the proposal officially, and I had refused on the basis that I had not seen it or had the opportunity to consult with the other vice-chancellors about it. Shafee sent me the documents in any event, and I did read them in the days that followed. An initial version of their proposal basically made the case for financing free education through the tax system. Much of the document was thoughtful, but its collective proposals were problematic. Essentially, it proposed an increase in a range of taxes, including the skills levy, corporate and income tax, and a wealth tax. The immediate collective tax increase on business would have amounted to more than 10 per cent, which would have accelerated tax avoidance and imploded the economy as in the cases of Venezuela and Zimbabwe. When I called Khaya to engage him, he informed me that I had been sent an earlier version of the model and subsequently sent me the updated version.

The new version was a far more sophisticated policy expression and was testimony to the ability of social movements to make valuable contributions when they take policy and engagement seriously. Essentially, it proposed increasing the state subsidy from 38 to 50 per cent of university financing as had been the case in 2000, and was coupled to a private-sector-funded capital infrastructure fund (in exchange for tax rebates and capital allowances) and an education endowment fund (EEF). The EEF, it was proposed, should be initially capitalised through state resources, including a 1 per cent increase in the skills levy, but was thereafter to be maintained by a graduate tax structured through the payroll. The model did envisage modest corporate and individual tax increases, and a phased-in development of the new financing of the higher education system. These policy recommendations would have pushed the fiscal boundaries, yet were entirely pragmatic and worthy of serious consideration. So, I forwarded the proposal to Dikgang Moseneke's NECF and linked Khaya to the organisers so that the proposal would become the subject of the collective deliberation it deserved.

The common criticism of this financial model and these policies is one advanced against any proposal on the graduate tax – namely, that its payment in perpetuity means that graduates ultimately pay far in excess of the real costs of their programme of study. George Hull, for instance, argues that precisely for this reason a graduate tax violates the principle of fairness. But this is a narrow definition of fairness. It is a principle of many societies that older generations contribute to the costs of the up-keep of their children. A graduate tax simply takes this principle to a higher level by making it a collective responsibility. Such a responsibility would accord with South Africa's notion of ubuntu, a collective solidarity where those in a position to assist others do so with a view to creating enabling conditions for the harmonious life of all.

My concerns about the model revolve around two more practical problems, the first political and the second fiscal. The political problem lies in my uneasiness that this proposal does not command the support of the protesters, as it claims to. I have been struck by how few members of the student leadership have actually read and understood this proposal that they purport to support. Further uneasiness emanates from the sporadic negative commentary by student leaders about a black tax and why should they be subject to carrying an additional tax burden when they graduate. It should be noted that the earlier version of this financial model excluded a graduate tax and replenishment of funds was exclusively based on increases in the skills levy and in corporate, personal and wealth taxes. Moreover, my unease is founded on the explicit opposition to a graduate tax by Salim, Enver, Leigh-Ann, Mondli, Rasigan and Zolisa, some of whom were in the student leadership and all of whom claim to be speaking to the interests of the student protesters. Essentially, I fear that, in their haste to find a policy measure that they can claim as their own, the student leadership have either obfuscated the issues or lowered the bar to enable a limited consensus, to the point where the financial model may no longer carry the support of the very constituency it was said to speak for.

My fiscal criticism is that the numbers of the graduate tax model simply do not add up. Calculations by the National Treasury suggest that the number of graduates in the system in 2011 was in the region of 1.3 million. If you assume a graduate production of 80 000 per annum, you could say that there were just under 1.62 million graduates in society by 2015. On the basis of a 1 per cent tax on all graduates who earn an income higher than R75 000, Treasury estimates that the total tax revenues received would be in the region of R2.2 billion. Even if this tax were to be increased by an additional percentage, the revenues would be less than R5 billion, not even 10 per cent of the total cost of Zuma's programme announced in December 2016 and about 3 per cent of the additional cost required for a comprehensive, free higher education for all students.

The second model to have emerged in the #FeesMustFall era is the Ikusasa model developed by Sizwe Nxasana, the previous chair of NSFAS and former CEO of FNB. The model has an interesting evolution. As indicated in Chapter 1, the idea of a bank-funded but government-guaranteed loan for students in higher education emerged as part of the conversation between USAf and the banks in early 2015. It resurfaced in the deliberations of the Presidential Task Team on Short-Term Funding Challenges, and eventually came out as one of its recommendations for a long-term solution to the problem of funding poor and 'missing middle' students. Sizwe then took the idea and, with partners in the banking sector, developed a financial model for comprehensive funding and wraparound support for students in South African universities and TVET colleges.

The model was premised on a partnership between the public and private sector, with each being incentivised to make a financial contribution to support students in tertiary education. The support was to be a mix of loans and bursaries; the proportion of each, and the resultant interest and tax subsidies, was to be determined on the basis of family income up to a maximum of R600 000. The model was to promote the skills requirements identified by the National Development Plan and the Human Resources Development Council Strategy. Its financing was to be based on a mix of private and public funds, including grants and loans, and resources raised from development finance agencies and the sale of social impact and commercial bonds. Some of this was to be incentivised by a revision of legislation and the black economic empowerment (BEE) codes so that corporates would receive concrete tax and procurement benefits for participating in the scheme. Students would not be required to pay back the loan while they were studying, and would only become liable once they were employed and their income crossed a certain minimum threshold. It needs to be noted, however, that the Ikusasa model has subsequently evolved into a full bursary system, even though there may be a separate subsidised loan product organised by the banks to assist students to complete their study outside the regulated time.

This original Ikusasa income-contingent model was similar to the one proposed by the Heher Commission, whose final report was delivered to President Zuma at the end of August 2017 and publicly released for comment on 13 November 2017. The Commission recognised the crisis in higher education and the need to refinance the post-secondary edu-cation sector. It also recommended the reorganisation of the sector so that TVET colleges became the single biggest component of the system. To enable this, it recommended that R50 billion be ring-fenced in the Unemployment Insurance Fund and invested to expand and modernise the infrastructure of the TVET college sector. Students were to be fully financed in this sector, especially since these institutions serviced the poorest in the country. University education, it recommended, was to be reformed in three distinct ways: first, the subsidy to higher education and training was to be increased from 0.71 per cent to 1 per cent of gross domestic product (GDP); second, the private sector was to be incentivised through tax concessions to invest in university infrastructure, and especially in student accommodation and historically black universities;

and finally, students in both public and private universities were to be fully financed through income-contingent loans that commercial banks would provide but the state would guarantee. The Commission argued that, because these were loans and not grants, it would not aggravate the state's debt-to-GDP ratio, and would therefore not attract the negative attention of international rating agencies. It is worth noting that, while the Commission recommended that a new institution should be established to administer the income-contingent loan scheme, it left open the possibility for the state to allocate this responsibility to the Ikusasa scheme.

There is much to be positive about regarding the Commission's recommendations. First, an increase in the per capita subsidies to universities is long overdue and has to be welcomed. Declining subsidies have been the primary cause of fee increases and have to be the first platform on which to address this challenge. Second, the tax concessions to companies that invest in university infrastructure are eminently sensible and should prioritise historically black universities and student accommodation where there is the greatest need. This could be supplemented by two additional measures: pension regulation and broad-based BEE. Pensions could be regulated, as in Europe, to make it mandatory to direct a small component towards social investment. Again, such social investment could be directed towards addressing the problem of student accommodation, especially by the private sector, if it were supported by our pension funds. This would, however, require there to be rents for such student accommodation, which then could enable the economic returns for the pension investment. In addition, BEE's broad-based component must not be for individual enrichment, but a component of it must be directed towards enabling financially unhindered access to university education. The resources generated from it must be directed to either university infrastructure and/or enabling the progressive realisation of university education to all who want it.

But there are also some elements of the Heher Commission's report that should be subjected to critique. First, it takes an unduly conservative approach to the principle of free higher education by buying too easily into George Hull's philosophical approach, which speaks to the unfairness of the graduate tax and the importance of students paying for higher education simply because they receive significant private returns. The former element was critiqued earlier on the basis that it was too narrow a definition of fairness, and was not sufficiently attuned to the historical realities of South African society. Similarly, on the second element – the private gains of higher education – it could be argued that this applies in many other cases of public social provision. Indeed, educational attainment across the entire system delivers both public and private benefit, yet we have constitutionally obligated ourselves to make primary and secondary education mandatory. The argument here is that the mere presence of private gain is not sufficient to justify the denial of comprehensive funding, especially given that so many of our historical disparities are racialised and that post-secondary education is necessary to allow us to address the skills deficit. If we fail to do this, growth and inclusive development will remain elusive in South Africa.

But perhaps the biggest criticism of both the Commission and the Ikusasa scheme was reserved for their promotion of income-contingent loans. Essentially, this is a deferred-payment loan scheme structured to one's income. Globally, the income-contingent loan scheme has come under severe criticism. It is worth noting that this scheme has been implemented in both the United Kingdom and Australia, and has been experienced differently in the two countries. Andrew Adonis, Director of Policy under Tony Blair in the United Kingdom and the person responsible for the implementation of income-contingent loans, suggests that the loans have essentially become a giant Ponzi scheme that should be done away with. The debt burden they have generated has become onerous for many in the United Kingdom, a source of deep unhappiness in that society. Similarly, student loans in the United States now approximate a $1.3 trillion national debt burden. Many see them as reinforcing inequality within the country. These very real challenges could manifest themselves in South Africa given our history and deep inequalities. It is not hard to imagine that they could become an even greater source of tension in South African society, especially if they were to take a racial form, given our historical trajectory.

But, to be fair, there is the very real problem that we just do not have sufficient resources in state coffers to address the problem comprehensively. While it is easy to criticise the Heher Commission's recommendations in this regard, it is worth noting that they do, in effect, address the immediate problem of cost as a barrier for admission to higher education. Perhaps it is important not to view the solution to the financial woes of our higher education system as a single, Big Bang approach. Rather, it would be useful to imagine the solution as a series of structural reforms that, over many years and decades, increasingly expand the scope of access to higher education and slowly shift the mix between state subsidy and student fees in favour of the former. Not only would this be a measured restructuring of the higher education system, but it would also be one that does not irreparably damage the academic depth and substance of the country's universities.

President Zuma would eventually adopt some of the recommendations of the Heher Commission, in particular the call for TVET colleges to be free and for the subsidy to higher education to be increased to 1 per cent of GDP. But as Chapter 7 indicated, he would not adopt its other major recommendation for an income-contingent loan scheme. Instead, he promulgated free higher education for those with a family income of less than R350 000 per annum through the provision of grants from NSFAS. This measure will have a dramatic, positive impact on the poorest students in the higher education system. As already mentioned, this only covers 40 per cent of students in the system, and not the new 'missing middle', those with a family income higher than R350 000. This means that the financial challenge for the vast majority of students at Wits University and other urban institutions – the ground zero of the student protests of 2015 and 2016 – has not been resolved.

Commentary has questioned whether President Zuma's proclamation is affordable, and it is not unreasonable to take a cynical interpretation of his announcement given its timing, but it also cannot be said that the initial estimate is unaffordable. As indicated, the initial estimate of the full implementation of the programme was an additional R57 billion per annum. Some R23 billion of this has already been raised by the increase of VAT from 14 to 15 per cent, announced by the Minister of Finance in his February 2018 budget speech. While there has been some debate in the country about the regressive nature of the VAT provision, this has been contested by economists like Imraan Valodia who maintain that it is the most suitable mechanism under the circumstances and is far less regressive than other measures, such as cutting expenditure on the budget. It is also worth noting that if the economic growth rate was to increase from the current 1 per cent to 2.5 per cent or higher, there would be more than enough resources to finance comprehensive, free higher education for all students whose family income is below R350 000. Of course, one could ask whether this money should have been spent on higher education rather than other components of the social wage. But this is a different question; it is worth underscoring the point that a democratically elected government made the decision officially. It is therefore perfectly legitimate for it to have decided to dedicate public resources to fund the free higher education provision.

So what, then, is new in this state of affairs? Students with a family income of less than R350 000 per annum, and who are academically admitted to universities and TVET colleges, will effectively receive a grant for their tuition, accommodation and subsistence costs. This leaves the new 'missing middle', those students whose families are above the R350 000 annual income threshold but who still cannot afford higher education. These students should be covered by the income-contingent loan scheme, recommended by the Heher Commission and originally envisaged as being piloted through the Ikusasa programme. There is an urgent need to accelerate, expand and reimagine the Ikusasa programme along its original model to ensure that the financial challenges of the 'missing middle' are addressed. Once this is done, the net outcome would be that poor students would receive a grant, those in the 'missing middle' would receive an income-contingent loan, and students from families with means would be required to pay their fees. The system would still be funded with a mix of subsidy and fees, but as the former increases to reach 1 per cent of GDP, as recommended by the Heher Commission and accepted by government, so too would pressure be reduced on the need to increase fees beyond inflation. In any case, the Heher Commission also proposed a fee capping regime that would govern university fee increases, an intervention that is already being implemented. All in all, the new funding regime that is being born in the wake of #FeesMustFall will be dramatically different from that which prevailed prior to the protests.

Perhaps a caution is warranted. The system that is currently being fashioned must not ossify, for significant negative consequences could still emanate from it. As the experiences of the United Kingdom and the United States demonstrate, a loan scheme can seriously aggravate inequality and provoke deep resentment within society. Given this, and the warnings of many scholars who are concerned about the negative effects of student loans on accelerating and consolidating inequality, it may be prudent to demand that the mix between state funding and fees be regularly reviewed and shifted in favour of the former becoming the primary component of university financing. Indeed, we could tie the proportion of university subsidy to economic growth rates so that, as the latter goes up, so too will the former. In this way, we would have put into motion an evolving agenda of structural reforms where there is a slow systemic creep in favour of comprehensive, free education.

It is also worth noting that, where this has happened, free quality higher education has had an enormous equalising effect on society and has simultaneously enabled the emergence of competitive economies. This is particularly relevant in our current context, being as we are in the midst of perhaps the most fundamental economic transformation in two or three generations. Such a bold initiative could then propel us to the forefront of the digitised era, and enable us not only to address the disparities of our past, but also to create a more socially inclusive future.

9

Seeding a new world

SOCIAL justice has to be advanced in the world that exists, not the one we wish existed. This obvious statement is perhaps the single most important lesson that advocates of social justice need not only to realise, but also to internalise. Radical activists of a variety of ideological persuasions, including the grand masters of the Marxist traditions – Lenin, Trotsky, Luxemburg and Gramsci – devoted more than a century of study to strategies and tactics for challenging the political and economic order and advancing social justice. There is now recognition among many in the social justice community, including theorists, that the overthrow and/or transcendence of the political and socioeconomic order will not be a single event, but a drawn-out process of advances and retreats. Thus, for social activists who are committed to change, strategies and tactics are paramount. We should develop strategies and tactics not from what we think is fair in an abstract worldview, but rather from what will work in the realities of our current context. This means not forgetting our ultimate goal, but rather understanding the possibilities of achieving our goals, not from a rule book or formula from a time that is past, but from the contextual realities of the present. Too often, too many demand reforms that are compatible with an alternative social order, rather than those that are viable in the present and yet push the boundaries of what is acceptable to enable a political dynamic of continuous social change – what Michael Hardt and Antonio Negri describe as a strategy of 'antagonistic reformism'.

Perhaps this has to do with the fact that most activists are often so emotionally invested in their cause that they cannot imagine that there are others who are not the enemy, but may not share the same strategies, or even passion, for the social justice issue at hand. It is often said that anger and rage are essential in mobilising against injustice, but what is often forgotten is that they also blunt actors' ability to dissect the forces arraigned against them critically and determine how to neutralise or demobilise these to register social gains. All of this was evident in the #FeesMustFall movement. It may be valuable to extricate the movement's lessons, not only for the advancement of the struggle for free education, but also for those associated with other social justice causes.

Of course, I do this from a particular vantage point, that of a vice-chancellor confronted with the largest student protests since the dawn of democracy in South Africa. I recognise that, even if I see myself as a progressive who is committed to the goals of social justice and an alternative political and socioeconomic order, my views will inevitably be influenced by my responsibility as an executive to manage these protests. As a result, and to serve as a check on this executive managerial influence, my reflections will be deliberately framed in relation to comparative experiences and the reflections of other scholars who have written on these issues in the past two to three decades.

Perhaps it is best to begin this reflection with an acknowledgement that mass action and social mobilisation are an essential component of the strategic arsenal required for changing our world. This is the most obvious lesson to emerge from the #FeesMustFall movement. As I have explicitly and publicly stated on a number of occasions, the students achieved in ten days what vice-chancellors had been debating for ten years. The difference between these two interventions was that the students' engagement took the form of social mobilisation. In the process, they redefined the systemic parameters of what was possible and opened up policy options and financial concessions that had not been seriously considered in normal daily engagements. In my view, some of these outcomes exceeded those expected by the student leadership themselves. As indicated in Chapter 1, the SRC president's original proposal to Council was not for a 'no fee' increase, but rather for a more measured one in the region of 9 per cent. When the protests kicked off, this demand shifted to no increase; when this was achieved, it shifted again to free university education. This was not the first time that these demands had been made. Indeed, they had been made regularly across the country for some time, but government and, more particularly, Treasury and the Presidency had not been responsive to them. But when the 2015 protests erupted and took on the scale that they did, generating widespread support from stakeholder groups across society, not only was a significant financial concession made, but a policy process was also initiated to change the financing of universities fundamentally.

Similarly, the insourcing of vulnerable workers was never on the agenda until the 2015 protests fundamentally changed the environment. As indicated in Chapter 4, the Wits executive had recognised for years that outsourcing practices were exploitative and incompatible with the institution's human rights obligations. But as I indicated in the Senate meetings where this issue continued to emerge, addressing outsourcing would require trade-offs that internal stakeholders were not collectively willing to agree to at that stage. The student protests changed this, again by opening up the systemic parameters and allowing options to emerge that had not previously been considered. These influenced me as vice-chancellor as much as they influenced other executives, the Council, staff and the entire university community. Recall that insourcing vulnerable workers came at a cost of R130 million, paid for through budget cuts in academic and administrative departments, and senior researchers forsaking the interest on their grants for two years. The collective willingness to incur these costs was not always present; it only emerged in the wake of the #FeesMustFall protests.

In both these cases, then, social mobilisation was essential for putting policy and financial options that had not previously been available on the systemic agenda. But the value of social mobilisation cannot be unqualified. This is where I depart from many of the #FeesMustFall activists and some of their supporters who tend to romanticise social mobilisation. Social mobilisation is incredibly important for opening up systemic parameters. But some forms of mobilisation can also undermine the possibility of social justice being realised. This was also quite evident in the #FeesMustFall movement. As social mobilisation became more violent and increasingly started to violate the rights of the institutional community, it also became more factionalised and lost the broader support of the public. As importantly, it forced authorities, both institutional executives and national government, to begin to activate security protocols in an effort to protect universities and the broader public. The net effect was that, in a number of institutions – including Wits – stringent security measures contained violent social mobilisation. This, of course, created huge controversy, not only between institutional executives and student protesters, but also within the broader progressive community itself, issues to which we will shortly return.

It is also worth saying that social mobilisation on its own does not translate into progressive social outcomes. For such outcomes to be realised, social mobilisation needs to be institutionalised through processes of deliberation and policy formulation. It also requires the presence of intra-institutional actors who are willing to use the opportunities that it enables to craft new social policy. Again, this was quite evident in the #FeesMustFall movement. The fact that it occurred within a democratic society, and in a context where the ruling party was deeply polarised, ensured responsiveness from some institutional actors. The democratic character of South African society and the vibrancy of civil society meant that options such as all-out repression were not on the agenda, as would be the case in more repressive societies. It is also worth bearing in mind that the student protests emerged soon after the Marikana massacre, where police killed 34 workers in a mining labour dispute. This event traumatised South Africans, deeply delegitimised the police and parts of the government, and paralysed the police in their management of the student protests. The democratic character of South African society, the divisions within the ruling party, the widespread support of the social movement and the paralysis of policing in the aftermath of the Marikana massacre all created a resonance for the demands of #FeesMustFall within the institutional apparatus of the state itself.

The same is true of the insourcing movement. It is worth noting again that insourcing was implemented in some institutions, and not others. Part of this had to do with the resources available within different institutions. Government, after all, refused to provide financial support for this reform. Where it was implemented, it was done on the basis of institutional resources. But the success of insourcing was also, in part, determined by the presence of intra-institutional actors who were willing to use the systemic opening to think it through and implement it.

Chapter 4 makes this abundantly clear in the case of insourcing at Wits University. But it also demonstrates the importance of intra-institutional actors determining how best to implement insourcing in a manner that does not harm the academic project. As we discussed, it was executives and Council representatives who insisted that insourcing be managed within the context of available resources and put in place a trade-offs committee to find the resources that would eventually underwrite the implementation of this institutional measure. Without this engage-ment, the social justice outcome would never have been implemented, or it would have been realised with unintended consequences. This suggests that social justice outcomes result from a complex dialectical interplay between social mobilisation and intra-institutional action – between social activists enabling the emergence of social action and intra-institutional actors translating the pressure into policy and/or decisions that culminate in social justice outcomes.

None of what I am suggesting here will be unfamiliar to those well versed in the literature on social movements. Scholars writing in the traditions of political process theory and political opportunity structure, such as Charles Tilly, Doug McAdam, Sidney Tarrow and Donatella della Porta, have for some time been exploring the dynamics of how political systems and institutional actors significantly influence, and are in turn conditioned by, the evolution of social movements and their outcomes. But social movement actors and their leaders have never understood this sufficiently well. Even in the case of their academic supporters, some of whom are familiar with the literature of social movements, it has been neither sufficiently internalised nor allowed to inform their practice. This is urgently required if movements are to become more effective in achieving social justice outcomes.

Effective social struggle depends on more than a simple reflection on the dynamics of the struggle and the complex interplay between social and institutional actors, however. It also requires deep consideration of the strategies deployed by social movements themselves. Perhaps the most important of these for consideration is the use of violence to achieve desired outcomes. It must be said that, at least at the rhetorical level, most of the leaders of #FeesMustFall professed a commitment to peaceful action. Peaceful mobilisation also seemed to be the substantive intent of the vast majority of its supporters. But it is also indisputable that the movement, or at least elements of it, became substantively violent in the course of the struggle itself.

As earlier chapters indicated, activists and even their supporters have suggested that this violence was inspired by the actions of the police and security. But as these chapters also demonstrated, while individual incidents may well have been caused by the behaviour and actions of police and security personnel, the general picture is one of police and security being deployed only when some protesters had begun to perpetrate violence and/or when the widespread abuse of rights was becoming evident. In 2015, for instance, police were only deployed on campus when the bookshop and a vehicle were burnt on the evening of 27 October. In January 2016, private security was only brought in when protesters repeatedly refused to allow registration and continued to assert that if there was 'no free education, there shall be no education at all'. Similarly, Chapter 6 demonstrated that the university only embarked on a comprehensive security response in October 2016 after the failure of repeated attempts to negotiate with the protesters, through the mediation of previous leaders of the SRC and the Black Students Society.

At the end of 2016, I lamented this state of affairs in an essay in the *Daily Maverick* criticising some social scientists, and Jane Duncan in particular, for their suggestion that violence was a result of police and security action – in violation of the empirical facts. In a subsequent response, Jane quoted an interview with Chris Barron in which he essentially harangues me, correctly, to recognise that part of the reason why we had to resort to private security in January 2016 was because we had not dealt with the perpetrators firmly enough previously by acting against them and barring them from the university. She concludes that, instead of calling private security, we should have used 'the least restrictive means [which] would be to prevent the perpetrators from registering, punish them through the disciplinary process and lay charges against those guilty of criminal conduct, to dissuade others from following suit'.

But herein lies the problem with her suggestion. Ignoring the fact that she is using a journalist's criticism of me for not having acted firmly enough while herself accusing me of the direct opposite, the essential problem with what she recommends is that, when we acted along these lines, this same collective of academic supporters accused us of authoritarian behaviour and violating the right to protest action. Indeed, when student activists became violent at the election circus in August 2015 and we suspended them, we were essentially criticised by this same group of far-left academics for acting too heavy-handedly. Just as importantly, when I asked critics in the Faculty of Humanities meeting in January 2016 what they would have recommended as an alternative to deploying private security, the answer was not suspension and rigorous deployment of disciplinary processes against perpetrators, but the closure of the campus and the suspension of activities; in effect, capitulation to the protesters' demands, even if the vast majority of the community was against this and it impacted negatively on the poor.

When I broached this with Jane in a subsequent engagement over lunch on 19 January 2017, she replied, 'I cannot answer for others,' and reiterated the major gripe of her article – which was that our court interdict had been too broad and referred to all forms of protest. I then demonstrated to her that, while it may have been broadly defined, it was never applied in a restrictive manner. At no time in January or even later in the year were protests or meetings not allowed at Wits, as was the case at some other universities. Indeed, we continued to allow for protest and its coverage by journalists; during the events of January 2016, private security was simply mandated to secure the two buildings where registration occurred and to regulate access to them. Private security was deployed, and not police, not only because the latter could not commit for a long period of time, but also because, in the case of private security, we could specify that no serious weapons would be carried. Was this, then, not acting in 'the least restrictive' of ways as required by the Constitution? Yet this same collective group of far-left scholars opposed our measures and tried to disrupt them. Essentially, the problem with Jane's suggestions was that the collective with whom she associates would reject the very measures she was recommending. Their use of her critique was the cynical deployment of an argument for opportunistic reasons when they themselves would refuse to subscribe to the recommendations that she advances.

But the problem is not simply one of coming to terms with the need for security in selected circumstances. It is also some leaders' actual advocacy of violence. There is no doubt that resorting to violence was, in part, facilitated by strands of the movement that deliberately adopted it as a strategy. In fact, violence and arson were particularly romanticised by some of the movement's activists and leaders. This was cogently and evocatively expressed by Leigh-Ann Naidoo, Lwandile Fikeni and Nolwazi Tusini at a Ruth First lecture at Wits University in August 2016. Disgusted by the Ruth First committee's decision to create an enabling environment for the unqualified propagation of violence, and believing that it violated everything that Ruth First stood for, I declined to attend and open the event. Unsurprisingly, the central message of the speakers was that black people are confronted with structural violence daily, as they have to experience the consequences of inequality, poverty and corruption. In their view, it is therefore legitimate to respond with black violence to protest this structural violence. In Lwandile's evocative words, violence is the 'aesthetics of rage'. Although his original reference was throwing faeces at the Rhodes statue at UCT and the 'fuck white people' graffiti at Wits, in the course of the engagement he spoke approvingly of the burning of university infrastructure, seeing all of these acts as 'a common aesthetics' to the movement, 'an insistence on moving beyond the boundaries of "civil" discourse towards attacking the symbols of white supremacy through disruptive acts of rage'.

In discussing rage and violence, Leigh-Ann highlighted 'a generational fault line' in which she held that

> the spectre of revolution, of radical change, is in young peoples' minds and politics, and it is almost nowhere in the politics of the anti-apartheid generation … Many in the anti-apartheid generation have become anesthetized to the possibility of another kind of society, another kind of future … And they can no longer be trusted with the responsibility of the future. When they dismiss the student movement's claim on the future, its experiment with time, when they belittle it, shoot it down, well, then pain becomes anger, anger becomes rage, even fire.

Ignoring the fact that the claim of revolutionary consciousness being present among young people and absent among the anti-apartheid generation has no empirical basis, what is notable in Leigh-Ann's argument is her highlighting of the generational challenge. There is indeed a restlessness among young people across the world – in the Americas, Asia, Europe and Africa – all of which is reflected in contradictory phenomena like #BlackLivesMatter, the Bernie Sanders movement, the rise of the far right, and the migration crisis in the Mediterranean. Some of this restlessness does have structural dimensions, in particular the rise of insecurity among young people as a result of the technological shifts of the global economy and the unemployment it portends for those with no or limited skills. A generational conflict that has not been seen in fifty years is, indeed, possible – and may even be necessary. But it does not have to be violent, yet this is exactly where Leigh-Ann wants it to go. Student leaders are fond of quoting Frantz Fanon's celebrated remarks that 'each generation must out of relative obscurity discover its mission'. However, as Xolela Mangcu reminds us, Fanon follows this statement with another:

> We must rid ourselves of the habit, now that we are in the thick of the fight, of minimizing the action of our fathers or of feigning incomprehension when considering their silence and passivity ... if the echoes of their struggle have not resounded in the international arena, we must realize that the reason for this silence lies less in their lack of heroism than in the fundamentally different international situation of our time.

A humbler and more measured response may be required if student leaders want to honour Fanon's words.

In any case, other leaders have parroted these views on violence on multiple occasions, sometimes implicitly and at other times more explicitly. For instance, in an interview with Kyla McNulty on *South African History Online*, Shaeera Kalla held that violence 'is a build-up of justified outrage, the university is a violent space symbolically for poor students ... Universities have still not acknowledged the silent violence innate in the commodification of our institutions and should be held accountable for inciting this violence'. In a subsequent essay on criminalisation in the *Daily Maverick*, she equated the case of Khanya Tandile Cekeshe, who had been sentenced to eight years' imprisonment (of which three were suspended) for arson and burning a police vehicle, to the case of Ahed Tamimi, a young Palestinian activist charged for assaulting a soldier in Israel. In other cases, the advocacy of violence was accompanied by references to Steve Biko and Frantz Fanon, as in Mbuyiseni Ndlozi's 'In Defence of Black Violence' in the *Daily Maverick*. Provocatively phrasing the challenge by asking what one can do when confronted 'with house nigger collectives who take up arms to kill the revolutionary ... when our state is run by a black collective which presides over colonial property relations and massacres blacks to protect these colonial properties', Mbuyiseni responds by first using Biko to distinguish between blacks (those willing to fight the system) and non-whites (those complicit with the system), then advocating for the right to engage in violence against other political actors when subjected to intolerant behaviour or attacks. Rekgotsofetse Chikane suggests that violence had become an 'addictive reality' for many Fallists, although he goes on to suggest that they 'never dared throw the first stone' – which, of course, does not accord with how developments evolved on the ground at either Wits or many other universities in the country. It is incontestable, therefore, that – at least among a cross-section of student and political leaders – there was an almost infantile romanticising of violence, justified with reference to both existing racial and economic disadvantage and/or the writings of revolutionary leaders.

But the rationality of these arguments for violence breaks down when it is subjected to even a little scrutiny. First, Fanon and Biko wrote about revolutionary violence in the crucible of the colonial struggle. Is it legitimate to transpose these ideas onto a democratic era which, however flawed, provides the space not only for protest, but also the right to vote out the political elite? And even if one did believe in the legitimacy of violence given Fanon's criticisms of the compromising and profiteering character of the newly emergent nationalist elite, what of Hannah Arendt's searing critique of both Fanon and Jean-Paul Sartre's views on violence when she suggested that violence inevitably contaminates and destroys the end for which it was originally deployed? Essentially, the case of comparing democratic South Africa to colonial societies, or even to Israel in the occupied territories, is not only intellectually unsustainable, but also suggests that student leaders are incapable of distinguishing between different types of political systems and the forms of protest that can be legitimately deployed against them.

Second, how is the struggle against structural violence advanced by attacking other students and destroying university property that is intended for housing and teaching the students themselves? If anything, such actions are likely to consolidate the very effects of the structural violence against the poor and marginalised. Indeed, if the presence of structural violence can legitimate individual acts of violence in a democratic society, then the consequences are too horrendous to contemplate: it could justify not only violent attacks on any public authority or its representatives, but also rape and murder against any individual simply on the basis that the perpetrator belongs to a community that is historically disadvantaged, and the act is committed against someone who belongs, by accident of birth, to a community that is historically advantaged. It would, in essence, violate the very social pact on which democratic society derives its philosophical legitimacy. Finally, as a result of this very social pact on which democratic society is founded, violent actions compel the state to respond with force to protect public property and the rights of other citizens, thereby creating a securitised atmosphere that works against the immediate interests of the protesters and the legitimacy of the protests themselves.

We should not only level criticism against the leaders who advocated or romanticised violence, however. We should also direct it against the small group of supporters within the academic community who were sanguine about violence. They often claimed that they were not partial to the violence, but their complicity was evident in their failure to condemn the violence publicly and their deliberate misrepresentations of the events on campus. It must be stressed that the condemnation had to be public. Many have claimed that these criticisms were indeed made, in private. But public criticism was necessary, not only to create awareness that it was only a minority within the movement who resorted to violence, but also because it would have subjected the perpetrators to greater pressure to refrain. It is also worth saying that such individuals essentially became complicit when they demanded the withdrawal of police and private security, while being unwilling to demand publicly that the student protesters renounce violence. What they refused to recognise is that, until violence is rejected, in both rhetoric and practice, there is no moral legitimacy in the demand for a public institution to withdraw security.

Part of the problem with much of the writings and reflections advocating or condoning violence is that they confuse violence with rage. It is important to distinguish between the two. Feelings of rage can be important and useful if they inspire collective action against injustice and drive progressive social change. As Wits University's Hugo Canham argued in a recent essay in the *Du Bois Review*, 'black rage [can be] … seen as an expression of black self-love in that it is the ultimate cry for freedom'. Yet he also cautions against romanticising black rage, because it has the potential to harm the poor and vulnerable, and not only the system. As importantly, one must never confuse explaining and understanding black rage with condoning it, especially when it works against the agenda of freedom. My own view is that black rage need not be violent in our present circumstances to achieve positive outcomes, as the national student protest in 2015 demonstrated. Moreover, rage must not cause leaders to act emotionally and impulsively. It must not blunt them from critically assessing the forces arraigned against the social justice cause, and determining how to overcome these without compromising the end goal itself. Rage is necessary, violence is not; when the two get confused, the cause of social justice itself maybe delegitimised or defeated.

The same can be said of contentious politics and social struggles. Activists and radical scholars often refer to the importance of disruption in enabling change. This is entirely valid. As Martin Luther King Jr's ideas and practices, detailed later, reflect, social activism must impose systemic costs to create the political will among decision-makers to enable social change. But he also states that this must not be violent, for it then becomes immoral and self-defeating. This understanding poses an important question for the leaders and supporters of #FeesMustFall. Would resorting to a permanent shutdown of the university not have entailed a cost that exceeds what is socially acceptable, given the fact that its immediate victims would have been the poorest among the student community and it would not automatically have created an impetus for change among the institutional decision-makers? Moreover, was resorting to violence not unacceptable in these circumstances? Did violence as a strategy not become self-defeating?

It is worth noting that the issue of violence is not only about social movements' deploying it strategically, but also about how the social justice community approaches policing in a democracy. To return to Achille Mbembe's reflections discussed in Chapter 3, are all security arrangements inimical to freedom? The automatic opposition to policing by so many in the social justice community suggests that too many would respond affirmatively to this question. But as Achille suggests, this is untenable – freedom does not automatically lead to security, so there is a need for pragmatism that contextually analyses each moment and incident. A de facto, automatic response is neither legitimate nor appropriate for a democracy for, as suggested earlier, it would violate the very essence of the social pact on which a democratic society itself is founded.

None of this should detract from a realisation that our police force is neither appropriately organised nor adequately trained for a democratic society. Engagements with generals in the police force suggest that we have too few public order police, with the result that the limited numbers deployed rely too heavily on weaponry. As importantly, those who are deployed tend not to be appropriately trained to demobilise and manage protests without resorting to force. It was this realisation that prompted us, as Chapter 6 indicates, to urge the generals of the police force to act with restraint and in a manner that was compatible with the Constitution. But irrespective of our request, we were all too aware of the danger that deploying the police could escalate the violence.

Perhaps our dilemma and how we addressed it can be better understood through a reflection on the scholarly work of Donatella della Porta and Mario Diani, who suggest that social movements become violent under two conditions: when police are deployed and engage in a repressive response, and when movements are factionalised and compete with each other to claim victories. Scholars like Jane Duncan used their work and its conclusions to suggest that police should not have been deployed at the universities, even if violence was being committed. But again, this conclusion was flawed; it was morally problematic and did not logically flow from a nuanced understanding of the empirical facts. As indicated earlier, the violence at Wits preceded the deployment of police, largely as a result of the second factor that Della Porta and Diani identify. But their first causal factor was also evident, because the violence did indeed escalate immediately after the deployment of the police and subsided only a few days later, after those who had committed it had been arrested and restrictive security protocols had been activated, at least temporarily, to stabilise the situation.

The question that emerges is this: what is the responsibility of institutional and societal decision-makers in a context where protests turn violent as a result of the second factor, the factionalising of the movement? Can responsible leadership refuse to deploy the police because of the fear of the first causal factor, the escalation of the violence as a result of the deployment? Our answer as institutional executives to this question was not to concede to the framing of this debate. To refuse to deploy police would have enabled the violation of the rights of the vast majority within the university, and would have made public institutions and society vulnerable to any group that was willing to commit violence to realise its ends, an untenable situation in a democratic society. Even in the context of a lack of adequate training of the police, the answer was not to deny their legitimacy to manage security challenges. Rather, the appropriate strategic response in the medium term is to urge their training and organisation so that they can fulfil their constitutional responsibility in a democratic society. In the interim, the mitigation measure was to urge them to act with restraint through an engagement with police leadership and the political authorities to whom they reported. The mitigation was also in the recognition, publicly expressed in my review of the 2016 protests, that a security solution was not sustainable in the long term, which influenced our interventions to find a political solution through both institutional initiatives negotiated with the SRC and student leaders, and systemic ones such as the NECF and the Heher Commission.

In the middle of 2018, student leaders would canvass for a political solution, but only insofar as it related to some of them being granted political amnesty by President Ramaphosa for crimes they had been found guilty of committing during the #FeesMustFall protests. They motivated this call on the grounds that they had been involved in a progressive struggle, their engagement in violence had been prompted by police action, and their futures as young black men and women should not be irreparably compromised, as they would be if they were to be convicted of a crime. Mcebo Dlamini would petition me to support their call for amnesty on the grounds that Wits University and I had declared the students' demand for free or lower-cost education legitimate. My view, which I expressed in a *Daily Maverick* article, was that I could only support the call for amnesty if it were qualified and the protesters acknowledged that violence and arson are not legitimate strategies for protest in universities and democracies. I expressed concern that protests at universities were continuing to degenerate into violence and burning infrastructure. The assumption implicit in the argument that this was a political act for a progressive cause is that progressive activists are somehow entitled to commit violence and break the law because their cause is legitimate. I held that there cannot be one set of rules for political actors and another set of rules for ordinary citizens – this would create the conditions for the emergence of another generation of unaccountable political elites. When we legitimise violence, we undermine the social pact – the philosophical foundation – on which any democratic society is founded and we enable the beginnings of a gangster state. This is why there have to be consequences for violence and for those who act outside the law. Otherwise, no progressive society is possible. Both USAf and the Minister of Justice, Michael Masutha, responded in a similar vein to the student leaders' call for amnesty. Minister Masutha indicated that, while he would assist the students in the process of engaging the NPA, they needed to follow the correct process and the rule of law must be upheld. USAf further argued that, for amnesty to work, 'the process [had] to be based on specific admissions made by those who caused damage and threatened life and limb and, for such cases, predetermine a clear set of atonements'.

Finally, it is worth noting that the broader progressive community has never developed a coherent approach to the matter of security in a democracy. But this agnosticism is no longer tenable, especially given the violent character of our society and the rising populist threats to it. I am reminded of then Deputy National Police Commissioner Gary Kruser's remark to me during the protests that, while people often criticise the police for their use of force, they seldom appreciate the fact that South African protests tend to be far more violent than those in other parts of the world. Of course, Gary should be aware that, as the South African Police Service is a public institution governed by our Constitution, there can be no equivalence between the violence of the police and that of societal stakeholders. Nevertheless, bringing violence under control in our society, which is essential for the sustainability and vibrancy of our democracy, will require concerted action by both social movements and societal stakeholders, and the police themselves. We all need to become the collective agents of the future we desire and claim to want to build.

The struggle for social justice must contain within itself the imagery of the outcome it desires. This means that it should be framed in a language, and its activities should be organised in a way, that is compatible with the intended social justice outcome. This strategic principle has a particular resonance for #FeesMustFall: it is here where the movement floundered, which influenced its trajectory dramatically towards factionalism and violence. In 2015, the movement was largely framed and organised in anti-racist and non-racial terms. The protests' goal was lowering the cost of higher education, thereby enabling the poor and the middle classes to access universities more easily. Its marches comprised students from across class and racial lines, and drew support from stakeholders across the political spectrum. Earlier chapters have shown how, as political parties tried to intervene to gain control of the movement, it became more factionalised and racialised. As indicated in Chapter 3, some students started to wear T-shirts bearing racialised statements, while others began to frame the movement in explicitly racial terms. When this happened, and other parts of the movement refused to condemn and marginalise these elements, broader groups of students withdrew. The net effect was that the 2016 protests had neither the non-racial flavour nor the broad support that the movement had experienced a year earlier.

This is why it is so important for those interested in social justice to frame their movement in explicit anti-racial or non-racial terms. There are two reasons for this. The first is an instrumentalist rationale. If a social movement is to be successful, it needs to draw on the support of the vast majority of society. In the language of the UDF of the 1980s, one needs to maximise support for the movement and minimise that for the advocates of the status quo. Framing the movement in more racial terms with explicit racist and/or prejudicial statements and activities weakens support for the movement and allows adversaries to caricature it as an agent of division and hatred.

The second rationale is perhaps even more fundamental, for it speaks to the desired social justice outcome. A central political tension that confronts all oppressed communities in their struggle is whether the movement should be framed as a retreat into nativism, where the previously oppressed become the master, or as progress towards the construction of a non-racial, cosmopolitan society in which all have a future. This political divide was perhaps most dramatically evident in the struggle for the allegiance of the African-American community by Martin Luther King Jr's Southern Christian Leadership Conference and the Black Power movement of Stokely Carmichael (Kwame Ture). Too often, however, the divide is caricatured as one between mainstream integration and co-option on one side and radical exclusionary politics on the other. Yet, as *Where Do We Go from Here: Chaos or Community?* demonstrates, King's ideas were much more complex and defied this simple caricature. In this book, King criticises the segregationist and militaristic impulses of the Black Power movement and advances a vision of radical change that is more cosmopolitan and inclusionary. Yet the radicalism of his ideas speaks not only to racial integration, but also to socioeconomic inclusion, calling for a guaranteed income for all citizens in an effort to banish poverty in the United States. Moreover, as indicated earlier, King's mobilisational and organisational strategy was not one of appeasement, as is often suggested. Indeed, his brand of contentious politics recognised the importance of disorder and disruption for there to be systemic social costs to create the impetus for change. But he also drew an explicit boundary at violence, which the Black Power movement too often ignored. This book, King's last, is worth going back to in these fractured times when social inclusion and fundamental change are back on the global agenda.

Scholars in other settings have also reflected on this central political tension in the struggles of oppressed communities. In *When Victims Become Killers: Colonialism, Nativism, and the Genocide in Rwanda*, Mahmood Mamdani tries to develop an understanding of the Rwandan genocide by exploring how colonial authorities manipulated tribal divisions in Rwandan society, framing the Hutus as subjects and the Tutsis as citizens. The Tutsis were thus constructed as settlers by colonial authorities and by the Hutu administration in the postcolonial era. Once this defining and labelling happened, the genocide was a logical consequence. It was, Mamdani maintains, not an ethnic but a racial cleansing in which newly established citizens were ridding themselves of the settler presence. This work is a timely warning of the long-term societal consequences that can emerge from present-day political choices and behaviour.

These cases essentially underscore the fact that the path a society takes – towards nativism or towards a non-racial common humanity – is not crafted at the point of victory when one ascends to political power. Rather, it has its origins in the character of the movement that led to that point, and the strategies and tactics it employed. Michael Hardt and Antonio Negri put it like this:

> Rather than asking only how to take power, we must also ask what kind of owner we want and, perhaps more important, who we want to become … We must train our eyes to recognise how the movements have the potential to redefine fundamental social relations so that they strive not to take power as it is but to take power differently, to achieve a fundamentally new democratic society and, crucially, to produce new subjectivities.

Essentially, the imagination of the new society is seeded in the struggle itself. Acts of racial prejudice, or silence in the face thereof, are not simple theatrics of social struggle – they are the building blocks of consciousness that will ultimately define the very character of the society that is to be born.

It is worth reiterating three of the central messages of Chapter 5. First, the struggle framed in anti-racial or non-racial terms must not ignore, but rather incorporate, the principle of social justice. This requires recognising the importance of affirmative action, black economic empowerment and other redress measures to correct for the historical injustices bequeathed by our past. Second, this programme of redress and social justice must not dissuade us from standing firm against those few individuals who manipulate their victimhood to advance their own personal agendas – agendas that contravene either the social justice outcomes themselves, or the broader constitutional principles of equity and fairness to which we all collectively subscribe. Third, the necessity of a consciousness of whiteness and the privileges associated with it must not translate into white guilt in which principles are abandoned and racism is tolerated. To do this is to patronise, which in the end compromises the socially just outcome itself. Ultimately, the trajectory of the #FeesMustFall movement demonstrates that anti-racist framing and organisation are essential if social justice struggles are to contain within them the non-racial, inclusive community that social justice activists desire.

The final strategic consideration that the trajectory of the #FeesMustFall movement warrants is the argument of some in its leadership that representative institutions and vertically organised structures of leadership are no longer compatible with social justice struggles and outcomes. This was reflected in the demands of some elements of the #FeesMustFall movement to locate decision-making solely in the mass meeting and disband or reform all governance structures, including the Council, Senate and SRC. Part of the motivation for this lay in a deep fear among some of the activists that individual leaders are too easily co-opted by business, government and institutional elites. But, as argued in Chapter 6, the insistence on making decisions in mass meetings was also driven by a political logic in which small, fringe political groups could easily dominate proceedings through a 'politics of spectacle' – one that silenced ordinary, pragmatic voices. Lacking political acumen and experience, the leadership of other student groups were incapable of challenging these voices and repeatedly found themselves on a strategic path more compatible with the agenda of competitor political parties. And so, whether by design or default, an anarchist tradition of decision-making, captured in the language of participatory governance, took root in the #FeesMustFall movement.

This tradition is not as democratic as it professes to be. As Chapter 6 demonstrated, many students who supported the #FeesMustFall campaign but wanted to return to class were harangued and intimidated in mass meetings by a group of self-appointed political commissars. Individuals who proposed measured and pragmatic solutions were labelled as sellouts, betrayers of a generational cause. Extreme choices were deemed radical and were enabled in the meetings through demagogic speeches and rhetorical fervour, where sloganeering dominated and complex issues were trivialised. Essentially, the mass meeting was as much a mechanism of silencing ordinary, pragmatic voices as it was of mobilising others.

But the scepticism about the university's governance structures extended beyond the #FeesMustFall movement to the unions and individual academics. Beguiled by the illusion of the crowd as the only site of participatory traditions, they argued for councils to be comprised of greater numbers of internal stakeholders such as students, academics and union representatives, and the Senate to be less representative of the professoriate and become more of an elected body chosen by staff and students. The challenge of these recommendations was that their advocates were ignorant about the historical debates and experiences with the reform of decision-making and governance in higher education in the country. None of the recommendations was new, they had all surfaced quite early in the debates on transforming higher education in the immediate aftermath of 1994. They were rejected for good, contextually grounded reasons. First, there was a concern that students and professional and administrative staff did not have sufficient knowledge to make informed decisions about matters of academic governance. There were also potential conflicts of interest. Representation from these constituencies was therefore to be limited, although not excluded.

Second, a simple election of academics to the Senate was determined problematic because, unlike North America and Western Europe where almost all of the academics have a doctorate, this was not the case in South Africa. An election of the Senate would inevitably have had the consequence of juniorising the most senior academic authority within the university. Third, councils deliberately consisted of a majority of external stakeholders. When there had been a preponderance of internal stakeholders, many of the governance structures were paralysed as different groups within the university vied for supremacy within these structures to control financial decision-making and the deployment of the institution's resources. As a result, conflicts of interest easily prevailed in decision-making as internal stakeholders prioritised their own collective, short-term interests rather than the universities' long-term mandate.

We should not interpret any of this as suggesting that reforms are not required. Indeed, there are questions to be asked about the efficacy of decision-making in vertically organised representative structures within universities and elsewhere. Similarly, the overwhelming presence of external stakeholders on councils can be questioned on the grounds that these stakeholders do not fully appreciate the academic needs of the university – as can be the dominance of professors on the Senate, because academic seniority cannot simply be equated to a better understanding of teaching pedagogy and students' academic needs. There is no doubt that universities need to reflect far more on the balance they should strike between representative and participatory forms of governance and decision-making – one that eschews both the romanticism ensconced in the critique of #FeesMustFall activists and the arrogance of institutional elites who believe that nothing needs to change.

The lesson to be learnt by the social justice community is that greater thought needs to be given to how to structure decision-making so that it can be more socially accountable. Michael Hardt and Antonio Negri's *Assembly* makes a number of proposals in this regard. While I am especially sceptical of their recommendation to locate strategic decision-making in the multitude and confine leadership to tactical considerations, they do nevertheless enable thoughtful deliberation about the matter. We need further considered engagement along these lines, especially between multiple stakeholders, so that the reform of governance structures within the university does, ultimately, manage the tensions between different forms of decision-making and organisation. Only then will we be able to develop universities and public institutions that are socially accountable, yet progressively pragmatic and practical, focused on being responsive to both the short-term needs of different internal constituencies and the long-term institutional mandates defined by the broader society.

A final set of deliberations that the evolution of #FeesMustFall poses for the advancement of social justice is whether there should be an ethics in the conduct of social justice struggles. In late 2015, I wrote my first reflections on the student protests in which I argued that there cannot be a divorce between means and goals, and that the former are essential for realising the latter. As I have suggested earlier in these pages, I am now even more convinced of the need for this. However, the #FeesMustFall struggle suggests that it needs to be manifested not only by leaders and activists in the movement, but also by supporters inside and outside the university.

Perhaps the most important ethical value to underscore is the importance of movement leaders being consistent in their public and private engagements. In my reflections on the 2016 protests, and in earlier chapters, I detailed the duplicity of too many leaders. Many claimed publicly that executive management was not willing to meet them when they had personally met me and other executives, and pleaded with us not to reveal these engagements. Many who interacted with me face to face were utterly charming and respectful, but their personas seemed to change fundamentally on Twitter. There, they engaged in a most virulent, extreme manner that was frankly reminiscent of far-right behaviour. One student leader repeatedly made the most scurrilous remarks about me and my family, but then sent me an SMS to say that he respected me and that his actions were not personal. In interactions outside the university, other student leaders also suggested that their actions were not personal, apologised for any discomfort that they may have created, and then promptly behaved even more obnoxiously in the months that followed. Some repeatedly criticised the presence of private security and police, but then indicated in personal discussions that they understood why we needed it and felt safer as a result. A few who had called for a boycott of lectures and examinations privately approached individual executive managers and asked whether they could write their examinations in secret, so that other students would not see them. This kind of behaviour was not exclusive to Wits University. Vice-chancellors and executives across the system had similar experiences and interactions with student leaders of all political persuasions.

The problem with much of this behaviour is not simply the individual duplicities, but that it seems to emanate from a belief that astute politics involves saying one thing in public and doing another in private. Student leaders across the spectrum seem to have become captured by a politics of spectacle, believing that they are obliged to be extreme, rude and obnoxious in public, and pragmatic and polite in their engagements outside the public eye. There is also the belief that the overriding goal is to win through any means. As indicated in Chapter 5, student activists would often be willing to make false accusations of sexual and racial harassment against security officials in incidents of eviction or security action without recognising that, by opening the floodgates of false allegations, they were making the struggle to address real instances of these scourges even more difficult. This kind of duplicity should be of particular concern to all of us. It suggests that, despite their criticisms of the existing political elite, some of the prominent leaders among this new generation of activists are displaying behavioural traits that are typical of the most venal of the country's current politicians.

There has also been an astonishing level of intolerance among the leaders and activists of the #FeesMustFall movement. On many occasions, student leaders have tried to implicate one another and get the university to invoke its disciplinary processes against others in an effort to get rid of potential political and electoral rivals. Earlier, I discussed the examples of #FeesMustFall supporters being silenced because they argued for a return to class in October 2016. Students outside the movement were treated with far more disdain, and those who dared to organise formally outside the #FeesMustFall fold were harassed, threatened and often pilloried as stooges of white interests or executive management. This intolerance was also reflected in the disruption of meetings – numerous university executives' meetings were disrupted across the system, as were national meetings convened by government and even the NECF. Essentially, there was a widespread belief among some #FeesMustFall leaders and activists that anyone who did not fully share their views was a legitimate target for silencing.

This intolerance afflicted not only leaders and activists, but also supporters, including some of the university's academics. At a book fair organised by Khanya College, certain student activists refused to continue with the panel discussion until I left. I willingly did so after consultation with the organisers – it was not a university event, after all, and I was merely a guest. The astonishing feature of this incident was the behaviour of some of the other participants, including other academics on the panel, the organisers of the book fair and long-time activist colleagues with whom I had previously collaborated. All of them sheepishly apologised, expressed disquiet and then proceeded with the event when I left. The book fair organisers and the other long-time activists had, on multiple occasions in the past, expressed concern about and been victims of Stalinist behaviour and practices, yet they were now either complicit in allowing it or actively participating in an action of intolerance. In a subsequent conversation with one of the organisers, I was told that had I not offered to leave, they would have 'engaged' the audience and continued the seminar with me. As a result, I would again speak on their platform two years later in September 2018. But this was not an isolated incident. During my sabbatical at Harvard University, where I wrote this book, I was asked to give two lectures on the subject. A few days before the events, a student leader of #FeesMustFall and an academic from Wits University wrote to the organisers, demanding that my invitation to speak be revoked. In their view, those sympathetic to the movement had a monopoly on telling the #FeesMustFall story and anyone else could be stopped from doing so. Ironically, they found no contradiction in appealing to a university to violate both the principles of academic freedom and free speech.

Again, these incidents were not exclusive to Wits University or me. Academic staff, professional and administrative staff, students and executives across the system have increasingly reported similar intolerance. But the challenge also extends to external stakeholders. In Chapter 3, I lamented the case of academics outside South Africa undertaking lazy solidarity action in which they pronounced on a course of action by the university at the prompting of an academic colleague, without any independent investigation of the issues on the ground. When confronted, very few even bothered to engage further. Similarly, in Chapter 6, I criticised progressive public lawyers who refused to think through the political implications of their legal representation, pleading that their profession required a political agnosticism. Finally, I bemoaned how civil society activists, even notable ones who had demonstrated incredible bravery in the struggle against apartheid, remained silent in the face of student leaders' intolerance, while at the same time privately communicating with me about how unacceptable their behaviour was. Most of this was inspired by a mistaken belief that they could earn student leaders' trust and then slowly encourage them to behave in more acceptable and principled ways. These activists had forgotten that, if left unchecked, these behaviour patterns could generalise themselves across society, consolidate a new generation of venal politicians and, in the process, compromise the very social justice outcome that the protest desired.

The challenge of these ethical violations among leaders, activists and supporters of #FeesMustFall is not only that they delegitimise the social movement, but also that they consolidate a cynical view of politics within broader society. People come to see all politics, politicians and political activists as duplicitous and unprincipled, saying one thing and doing another. As I suggested earlier, a movement seeds an imagining of the alternative society that it envisions. This requires not only that its strategies are compatible with the outcome, but also that its participants practise a politics that is distinctive, and more ethical than that which prevails in the current political system – one that can incubate an alternative behaviour that is compatible with the social outcome that the movement desires.

If there is one lesson that the trajectory of #FeesMustFall can impart, it is that the dynamics, strategies and practice of politics in a social justice movement must be very different from what the political system normally practises. This is a lesson not only for South African social movements, but also for social struggles across the globe. It is worth noting that, in many ways, South Africa is two worlds in one: an advanced, competitive and successful world, surrounded by another that reflects underdevelopment's most tragic features. Its contradictions, then, are as global as they are local. It is fair to say, perhaps, that social struggles are more accentuated in South Africa and that, as a result, political fault lines are more dramatically exposed. This makes South Africa a centre of political protest, but also an incredible social laboratory from which to investigate global challenges and potential solutions.

The struggles of #FeesMustFall – the high costs of education, minimum wages and humane working conditions for vulnerable workers, and socially inclusive communities – are not unique to South Africa. Indeed, they are the global struggles of our time. As a result, movements similar to #FeesMustFall have emerged across the world, including in North America and Western Europe. The social struggles that these movements organise, and their success, are essential if we are to heal our world, address its inequalities and political polarisation, and build more inclusive cosmopolitan communities and societies. To do this, we need to learn from past struggles in both the local and global setting. If reflections on #FeesMustFall can help at least a little in this regard, then the protests, and the difficulties that accompanied them, would have been worth it – for South Africa and the rest of the world.

10

A glimmer in the cracks

IN 2017, Jonathan Jansen, the former vice-chancellor of the University of the Free State, published a book – *As by Fire: The End of the South African University* – on the protests that had engulfed the country's universities in the preceding two years. The title spoke to a common fear among many South Africans. But the book was far more nuanced than the title suggests. It did indeed argue that the South African university was under threat, but it did not conclude with a firm pronouncement on its demise. Nevertheless, the future of the South African university is of concern to many stakeholders. In one school graduation after another that I have addressed in the past two years, the most common issue raised by parents and students is the stability of the South African university and its future as a recognised academic entity in the world. Some parents – those with financial means, both black and white – have even begun to explore the option of universities outside of the country.

While these concerns are legitimate, I am not of the view that the South African university is lost. Indeed, I believe that students and academics who opt for universities elsewhere in the world often make a mistake by choosing institutions that are, in many cases, academically weaker, and often cannot provide the contextual grounding that allows graduates to operate effectively in South Africa. After all, skills are important, but so is an understanding of contextual circumstances. Moreover, at university one learns as much outside of the classroom as within. These contextual learnings are what an external institution does not easily provide. I should immediately clarify my argument, lest I be misunderstood. International experience is valuable because it enables a global consciousness and learning from comparative experience, and builds a solidarity that promotes a common humanity. But there are many ways of achieving this; the right mix of foreign and local experiences is important for producing graduates and citizens who are globally competitive and locally relevant, simultaneously African and citizens of our world.

It is also worth noting that, measured against the normal indicators by which university success or failure is determined, many of the South African universities perform really well. Obviously, as in many diverse higher education systems, the performance of individual institutions can vary significantly. But South Africa's top universities compare well against their global peers. Research output is up in many of the universities, as is the number of postgraduate students. Pass rates and student throughput have improved in recent years, even if they may have plateaued in the past year or two. Technology has been widely adopted and there is significant experimentation underway with blended learning. By all these measures, South African universities are doing well. This is before taking cost into account. Even the most expensive of our institutions – UCT and Wits University – cost 10 to 20 per cent of an equivalent institution in the United States or the United Kingdom. The South African university degree is a truly worthwhile investment.

This is not to suggest that there are no problems. Indeed, there are quite significant ones. Too many students still do not graduate. Access is a challenge, particularly for the poor and the 'missing middle'. Social inclusion is an issue. But all these issues – access, inclusion, throughput and protests – are increasingly becoming a feature of higher education institutions around the world, including those in North America and

Western Europe. It is perhaps true that these issues play out in a more accentuated form in South Africa. But all this means is that we are simply a precursor of what is to come. In many of my engagements with universities and their executives elsewhere in the world, I have reminded them that our issues are the same; our current challenges are essentially their future ones.

Yet this must not lull us into complacency. Our challenges may be the world's, but there is an urgency to address them, if only for our own needs, collective ambitions and goals. In a public reflection in the *Daily Maverick* in early 2018, I argued that we would not be able to address these challenges if all stakeholders in the university did not become measured in their expectations and requirements. I lamented that university leaders are caught in a pincer by students who do not want to pay fees, below-inflation increases in government subsidies, and employees' demands for high remuneration. This scenario is just not sustainable. If it persists, the fiscal stranglehold on universities will begin to undermine quality. I urged measured demands on the part of unions, and consideration by union and university leaders of multi-year salary agreements, to protect employee rights while still ensuring that the sector remains stable. There is no doubt that we need to pay competitive salaries, simply because universities need to appoint and retain the best staff. But we also need to do this within our institutional and wider sectoral context. In addition, we may need to consider differential salary agreements that prioritise the poorest among us, although this needs to be time-bound lest we create unintended consequences down the line.

Employees, however, are not the only ones who need to make concessions. All stakeholders need to make contributions that enable the collective's effective functioning. Executives need to go the extra mile, be even more measured in the remuneration that they receive, facilitate the emergence of an environment that enshrines the principles of mutual respect, transparency and learning, and make institutional decisions that are in the broader interests of the university and society. Alumni must remain engaged in the university, support it in whatever way they can, and defend its interests in the wider community. Students also have to engage responsibly. They cannot demand fee-free education while making ever more requests for the provision of services. Most importantly, they have to engage other stakeholders with courtesy and respect. Ultimately, it is essential for all stakeholders – university and union leaders, staff, students and the student leadership – to work together with integrity to achieve the balance between the short-term needs of each constituency and the long-term institutional obligations to our country.

Internal stakeholders cannot guarantee the South African university's future. Broader South African society needs to recognise the importance of the public university and rise to its defence when it comes under threat. In recent years, the defence of the university has become the obligation of the vice-chancellor. But the public university is too precious a resource to be defended by only one of us. Its defence must become the responsibility of each and every member of society. We must collectively hold sectoral interests or politicians with short-term political agendas accountable. It is only our collective might and leverage that can bring to heel many of the powerful individual and political forces that try to use the public university as a football for narrow individual, party or sectoral ends. It is in our collective interest to do so.

Some of our universities are world-class, and play in a league way above the country's level of economic development. Part of the reason for this is our skewed history, which allowed some of our institutions, Wits University included, to receive a greater share of national resources and compete with their peers elsewhere in the world, thereby enhancing our national competitiveness. We must ensure that we never lose this competitive advantage, especially given the digital transformations underway globally. Science and technology have always been important determinants of a society's economic well-being. This is even truer in this new world of ours. The strategic challenge that we confront collectively is how to advance institutional equity and systemic higher education transformation without destroying the competitive national advantage bequeathed to us by our unequal history.

All of our public universities have the potential to be used as instruments either to consolidate a social order or transform it. To do the latter, they have to be reformed – nudged to provide greater access and facilitate greater inclusion. Some among us want to destroy the university as part of the process of social transformation. This will forever condemn many South Africans to perpetual servitude, for universities cannot be easily rebuilt. The destruction of our public universities would put processes in motion that would ultimately lead to the complete commodification of higher education. Local private teaching universities and foreign research universities would provide a quality education for the rich; the poor would be damned to inadequate and ever-declining post-secondary education in public institutions. This has happened before, in our schooling system. We must not repeat this in our university sector. Rather than embark on this destructive path, it would be far better to reform universities slowly, so that they increase access and continue to provide quality post-secondary and postgraduate education.

As we move deeper into the 21st century, it is important that all stakeholders recognise the central importance of public universities. They are essential – not only for training professionals, but also for producing the knowledge and technologies we need to participate and compete as equal citizens in the global community. Strong public universities are the midwives of the society that we want to become. We enter them as individuals, and emerge as part of a community. In a sense, they epitomise that principle of ubuntu, 'I am because we are.' Only through strong public universities, and the social foundation they build, can we achieve the collective progress, prosperity and inclusion for which we have yearned for so long.

Public universities are the *sine qua non* of our collective freedom.

References and selected reading list

BOOKS

Philip Altbach and Jamil Salmi (eds), *The Road to Academic Excellence: The Making of World-Class Research Universities*, Washington: The World Bank, 2011.

Hannah Arendt, *On Violence*, New York: Harcourt Brace, 1969.

Saleem Badat, *Black Student Politics: From SASO to SANSCO 1968–1990*, Pretoria: HSRC Press, 1999.

Steve Biko, *I Write What I like*, Chicago: University of Chicago Press, 2002.

Susan Booysen (ed.), *Fees Must Fall: Student Revolt, Decolonisation, and Governance in South Africa*, Johannesburg: Wits University Press, 2016.

Roseanne Chantiluke, Brian Kwoba and Athinangamso Nkopo (eds), *Rhodes Must Fall: The Struggle to Decolonise the Racist Heart of Empire*, London: Zed Books Ltd, 2018.

Rekgotsofetse Chikane, *Breaking a Rainbow, Building a Nation: The Politics behind #MustFall Movements*, Johannesburg: Picador Africa, 2018.

Crispen Chinguno, Morwa Kgoroba, Sello Mashibini, Bafana Nicolas Masilela, Boikhutso Maubane, Nhlanhla Moyo, Andile Mthombeni and Hlengiwe Ndlovu and contributions from Hugo Canham, Simamkele Dlakavu, C. Anzio Jacobs, Bandile Bertrand Leopeng, Nonkululeko Mabaso, Tebogo Molobye, Ntokozo Moloi, Ashley Nyiko Mabasa, Tebogo Radebe, Neo Sambo and Busisiwe Cathrine Seabe (eds), *Rioting and Writing: Diaries of the Wits Fallists*, Society, Work and Development Institute: University of Witwatersrand, 2017.

Donatella della Porta, *Clandestine Political Violence*, Cambridge: Cambridge University Press, 2013.

Donatella della Porta and Mario Diani, *Social Movements: An Introduction*, Malden: Blackwell Publishing, 2006.

Donatella della Porta, *Social Movements, Political Violence and the State*, New York: Cambridge University Press, 1995.

Jane Duncan, *Protest Nation: The Right to Protest in South Africa*, Pietermaritzburg: UKZN Press, 2016.

Frantz Fanon, *Black Skin, White Masks*, New York: Grove Press, 1967.

Frantz Fanon, *The Wretched of the Earth*, New York: Grove Press, 2004.

Michael Hardt and Antonio Negri, *Assembly*, New York: Oxford University Press, 2017.

Anne Heffernan and Noor Nieftagodien (eds), *Students Must Rise: Youth Struggle in South Africa Before and Beyond Soweto '76*, Johannesburg: Wits University Press, 2017.

Jonathan Jansen, *As By Fire: The End of the South African University*, Cape Town: Tafelberg, 2017.

Martin Luther King Jr., *Where Do We Go From Here: Chaos or Community?*, Boston, MA: Beacon Press, 2010.

Nosipho Majeke (pen name for Dora Taylor), *The Role of Missionaries in Conquest*, Johannesburg, 1953, Cumberwood, APDUSA, https://www.sahistory.org.za/archive/role-missionaries-conquest-nosipho-majeke.

Mahmood Mamdani, *When Victims Become Killers: Colonialism, Nativism, and the Genocide in Rwanda*, Princeton, NJ: Princeton University Press, 2001.

Sizwe Mpofu-Walsh, *Democracy & Delusion*, Cape Town: Tafelberg, 2017.

Musawenkosi Ndlovu, *#FeesMustFall and Youth Mobilization in South Africa: Reform or Revolution?*, London and New York: Routledge, 2017.

Malcolm Ray, *Free Fall: Why South African Universities are in a Race against Time*, Johannesburg: Bookstorm, 2016.

No Sizwe (Neville Alexander), *One Azania, One Nation: The National Question in South Africa*, London: Zed Press, 1979.

Sidney Tarrow, *Power in Movement: Social Movements, Collective Action and Politics*, New York: Cambridge University Press, 1994.

Charles Tilly, *From Mobilization to Revolution*, Reading, MA: Addison-Wesley, 1978.

Charles Tilly, *The Politics of Collective Violence*, Cambridge: Cambridge University Press, 2003.

Zeynep Tufekci, *Twitter and Tear Gas: The Power and Fragility of Networked Protest*, New Haven: Yale University Press, 2017.

ARTICLES AND BOOK CHAPTERS

Stephanie Allais, 'Analysis must rise: A Political Economy of Falling Fees', in Devan Pillay, Gilbert M Khadiagala, Roger Southall and Sarah Mosoetsa (eds), *New South African Review 6*, Johannesburg: Wits University Press, 2018.

ASAWU, 'ASAWU Advocates Measures to Improve Productivity at Universities', *Daily Maverick*, 11 March 2018.

Saleem Badat, 'South Africa: Free Higher Education – Why Not?', *University World News*, 28 March 2010.

Danny Bradlow, 'Perpetual Bonds Can Help Open Universities to All Who Qualify', *The Conversation*, 2 February 2016.

Danny Bradlow, 'South African Universities: Common Problems but No Common Solutions', *The Conversation*, 26 January 2017.

Gregory Dennis Breetzke and David William Hedding, 'The Changing Racial Profile of Academic Staff at South African Higher Education Institutions (HEIs), 2005–2013', *Africa Education Review*, vol. 13, issue 2, 2016.

Hugo Canham, 'Embodied Black Rage', in *Du Bois Review: Social Science Research on Race*, vol. 14, no. 2, 2017.

Nico Cloete, 'For Sustainable Funding and Fees, the Undergraduate System in South Africa Must be Restructured', *South African Journal of Science*, vol. 112, no. 3/4, March/April 2016.

Nico Cloete, 'The Flawed Ideology of "Free Higher Education"', *University World News*, 6 November 2015.

Nico Cloete, 'The Wrong Questions are Being Asked in the Free Education Debate', *The Conversation*, 27 September 2016.

Pierre de Vos, 'No, the Constitution does not guarantee a Right to be Presumed Innocent Until Proven Guilty', *Daily Maverick*, 2 November 2017.

Jane Duncan, 'Playing into the Hands of the Securocrats: A Response to Adam Habib', *Daily Maverick*, 8 December 2016.

Jane Duncan, 'Why Student Protests in South Africa Have Turned Violent', *The Conversation*, 29 September 2016.

David Everatt, 'What Must Fall: Fees or the South African State?', *The Conversation*, 20 October 2016.

Lwandile Fikeni, 'Protest, art and the aesthetics of rage: Social solidarity and the shaping a post-rainbow South Africa', Ruth First Memorial Lecture, 2016.

Nigel Gibson, 'The Specter of Fanon: The Student Movements and the Rationality of Revolt in South Africa', *Social Identities*, vol. 23, issue 5, 2017.

Adam Habib, 'Are South African Universities Under Assault?', *Daily Maverick*, 1 March 2018.

Adam Habib, 'Goals and Means: Some Reflections on the 2015 #FeesMustFall Protests', *Daily Maverick*, 26 January 2016.

Adam Habib, 'Institutional Crisis at the University of Transkei', *Politikon*, vol. 28, no. 2, 2001.

Adam Habib, 'The Politics of Spectacle – Reflections on the 2016 Student Protest', *Daily Maverick*, 5 December 2016.

Adam Habib, 'Transcending the Past and Reimagining the Future of the South African University', *Journal of Southern African Studies*, vol. 42, no. 1, 2016.

John Higgins and Adam Habib, 'Academic Freedom, Affirmation and Violence: A Dialogue', *Kagisano*, no. 1, 2017.

Rebecca Hodes, 'Questioning "Fees Must Fall"', *African Affairs*, vol. 116, issue 462, 2017.

George Hull, 'Reconciling Efficiency, Access, Fairness, and Equality: The Case for Income Contingent Loans with Universal Eligibility', *Kagisano*, no. 10, 2016.

Alan Jacobs, 'Renewing the University', *National Affairs*, no. 35, Spring 2018.

Shaeera Kalla, 'Do Not Criminalise Those Who Are Marginalised', *Daily Maverick*, 23 March 2018.

Brian Kamanzi, 'In response to Adam Habib: #PrivateSecurityMustFall', *Daily Maverick*, 19 January 2016.

Claire Keeton and Tanya Farber, 'Mayosi "was a genius, an A-rated scientist"', *The Times Select*, 6 August 2018.

Matthew Kruger, 'The Cult of Lived Reality: Reflections on the 2016 Ruth First Memorial Lecture', Helen Suzman Foundation, 6 September 2016.

Vladimir Lenin, '"Left-Wing" Communism: An Infantile Disorder', in Robert Tucker (ed.), *The Lenin Anthology*, New York, W.W. Norton & Company, Inc., 1975.

Bertrand Leopeng, 'A Response to Habib', in Crispen Chinguno et al (eds), *Rioting and Writing: Diaries of the Wits Fallists*, Society, Work and Development Institute: University of the Witwatersrand, 2017.

Mahmood Mamdani, 'The African University', *London Review of Books*, vol. 40, no. 14, 19 July 2018.

Xolela Mangcu, 'Imagining our institutions as they should be', Project Rise, 16 February 2017.

Achille Mbembe, 'Decolonizing the University: New Directions', *Arts and Humanities in Higher Education*, vol. 15, no. 1, 2016.

Achille Mbembe, 'Theodor Adorno vs Herbert Marcuse on Student Protests, Violence and Democracy', *Daily Maverick*, 19 January 2016.

Doug McAdam, 'Tactical Innovation and the Pace of Insurgency', *American Sociological Review*, vol. 48, 1983.

Kyla McNulty, 'Interview with Shaeera Kalla, Former SRC President at Wits University', South Africa History Online, nd, http://www.sahistory.org.za/archive/interview-shaeera-kalla-former-src-president-wits-university-interviewed-kyla-mc-nulty.

Enver Motala, Salim Vally and Rasigan Maharajh, 'Education, the State and Class Inequality: The Case for Free Higher Education in South Africa', in Devan Pillay, Gilbert M Khadiagala, Roger Southall and Sarah Mosoetsa (eds), *New South African Review 6*, Johannesburg: Wits University Press, 2018.

Leigh-Ann Naidoo, 'Hallucinations', Ruth First Memorial Lecture, 2016.

Mbuyiseni Ndlozi, 'In Defence of Black Violence', *Daily Maverick*, 31 August 2015.

Greg Nicolson, '#FeesMustFall: UJ's continuing use of violent private security – a dangerous move in dangerous times', *Daily Maverick*, 30 September 2016.

Richard Poplak, 'Trainspotter: Adam Habib – The Rock, the Hard Place, and the Cruel Beauty of an Uncaring Universe', *Daily Maverick*, 4 October 2016.

Jared Sacks, 'Keep Calm and Let the Students Disrupt Injustice: A Response to Achille Mbembe', *Daily Vox*, 27 January 2016.

Jean-Paul Sartre, 'Preface', in Frantz Fanon's *The Wretched of the Earth*, New York: Grove Press, 2004.

Mia Swart, 'Campus Security: Students are not the Enemy', *Mail & Guardian*, 29 January 2016.

Natasha Vally and Sarah Godsell, 'A Response to Wits VCs' Open Letter on University Protest', *The Daily Vox*, 27 January 2016.

Salim Vally, Enver Motala, Leigh-Ann Naidoo, Mondli Hlatshwayo and Rasigan Maharajh, 'Free Education is Possible if South Africa Moves Beyond Smoke and Mirrors', *The Conversation*, 21 September 2016.

DOCUMENTS, LECTURES AND INTERVIEWS

Brian Bruce, Deputy Chairperson, 'Statement from the EXCO of the Council of the University of the Witwatersrand on the Suspension of Students and a Student Society Following the Disruption of an SRC Election Debate Held Earlier this Week', 21 August 2015.

Randall Carolissen, Chairperson, 'Statement from the Council EXCO of Wits University Following a Meeting with Leaders of the National EFF on Monday, 24 August 2015'.

'Report of the Commission of Enquiry Into Higher Education and Training to the President of the Republic of South Africa', www.thepresidency.gov.za/download/file/fid/1075.

'Statement of Council of the University of Witwatersrand, Johannesburg Pertaining to Sexual Harassment', 24 April 2013.

Donatella della Porta, 'Social Movement Studies and Political Science', Lecture at the Centre for Studies in Islamism and Radicalisation at the Department of Political Science at Aarhus University, Denmark, 29 May 2009.

David Dickinson, 'Academics' Council Report: 2nd October 2015', 2 October 2015.

David Dickinson, 'Report Back to Academics from Council: Events of #Fees Must Fall', 2015.

Adam Habib, 'Adam Habib appeals for more respectful interpersonal engagement', Wits University Official YouTube Channel, 21 June 2017, https://www.youtube.com/watch?v=H6P4QcXwA7w.

Adam Habib, 'An Open Letter to Colleagues Critical of Campus Safety and Security Arrangements', Wits Communique, 17 January 2016, https://www.wits.ac.za/media/wits-university/news-and-events/images/documents/An%20open%20letter%20to%20colleagues%20critical%20of%20campus%20safety%20and%20security%20arrangements.pdf.

Adam Habib, 'Message from the Vice-Chancellor on the Outcome of the Application by the EFF Against Wits University', 26 August 2015.

Adam Habib, 'Opening the Conversation: Accelerating Transformation for an Inclusive and Competitive Wits', Wits Communique, 21 May 2015, http://wiser.wits.ac.za/system/files/Opening%20the%20Conversation_Accelerating%20Transformation%20for%20an%20Inclusive%20and%20Competitive%20Wits.pdf.

Adam Habib, 'Wits: Leading a University at the Very Source of Civilization', Installation Address at the University of the Witwatersrand, 24 August 2013, http://blogs.wits.ac.za/vc/2013/08/24/leading-a-university-at-the-very-source-of-civilization/.

'Interview with Adam Habib, Fasiha Hassen, Kefentse Mkhari, Gwebs Qondo', *Dennis Davis: You Be the Judge*, ENCA, 27 September 2016.

'Interview with Julius Malema', *Hard Talk*, BBC, 5 December 2015.

Sizwe Mabizela, 'Rhodes University Presentation to Higher Education Fees Commission', http://www.justice.gov.za/commissions/FeesHET/hearings/set1/day09-RhodesVC-Presentation.pdf.

Sizwe Nxasana, 'ISFAP: Support and Funding Model for Poor and "Missing Middle" Students – A Public-Private Partnership', November 2016, http://acceleratecapetown.co.za/wp/wp-content/uploads/2017/05/IKUSASA-Student-Financial-Aid-Programme-ISFAP-Sizwe-Nxasana-Chairman-NSFAS.pdf.

'Interview with Naledi Pandor', *The Eusebius McKaiser Show*, Radio 702, 8 March 2018.

The Presidency, Republic of South Africa, 'The President's Response to the Heher Commission of Inquiry into Higher Education and Training', 16 December 2017, http://www.thepresidency.gov.za/press-statements/president%E2%80%99s-response-heher-commission-inquiry-higher-education-and-training.

Max Price, 'The Future Funding of Higher Education: A University of Cape Town Submission', https://www.news.uct.ac.za/images/archive/dailynews/downloads/2016/2016-09-06_UCT_FeesPresentation_HeherCommission.pdf.

Mary Rayner, Laurel Baldwin-Ragaven, Steve Naidoo, 'A Double Harm: Police Misuse of Force and Barriers to Necessary Health Care Services', produced by the Socio-Economic Rights Institute (SERI), October 2017.

Khayo Sithole, 'Thuto Ke Lesedi: A Model for Fee Free Undergraduate Higher Education in South Africa', https://drive.google.com/file/d/0B8Okr6IdEwxNcV9tM3dnb0VxekNlYlRGSTBHQjVDb2hBY01R/view.

USAf, 'Statement Prior to the Higher Education Convention Called by the National Education Crisis Forum', 18 March 2017.

USAf, 'Submission to Presidential Commission', 30 June 2016, http://www.justice.gov.za/commissions/FeesHET/submissions/oinst/2016-FHETC-Sub-USAf-30June2016.pdf.

Acknowledgements

THERE are a number of individuals to whom I owe a particular debt of gratitude in writing this book. Skip Gates was an incredible host during my time at Harvard University, as were Jean and John Comaroff and Emmanuel Akyeampong from the Center for African Studies at Harvard University. A seminar with the Hutchins Fellows and a Center for African Studies workshop with students and academics provided valuable insights on different chapters of the book.

Shireen Hassim, who was on her own sabbatical at Harvard University, was valuable in clarifying the train of events and commenting on various drafts of the manuscript. Others who commented on the manuscript and provided valuable insights were Tawana Kupe, Ahmed Bawa, Barney Pityana, Randall Carolissen, Isaac Shongwe, Achille Mbembe, Imraan Valodia, Cheryl de la Rey, Mark Orkin, Tasneem Wadvalla and Max Price. Carol Crosley assisted greatly with correcting facts and sourcing material. Kanina Foss was a fantastic first editor on the manuscript, and supported me throughout the period, as did Shirona Patel, who assisted with fact-checking, sourcing material and editorial comments. Alexandra Leisegang joined the team later, and also provided invaluable assistance in the final editorial stages of the manuscript. Thank you to Sumbul Pardesi for designing the diagram of the major role players.

Finally, and perhaps most importantly, I owe a debt of gratitude to my family: Fatima, who once again uprooted herself and joined me at Harvard University, incisively commenting on all chapters throughout the writing process, and, coining the title of the book, Irfan and Zidaan, with whom we were in touch almost daily and who provided their own unique thoughts on the protests and the challenges that they brought to the fore. This book would not have been possible without the valuable contribution and collegiality of all of these individuals. Yet none can be held responsible for its weaknesses; the ideas and critical reflections are my sole responsibility. It is, after all, a personal memoir of and reflection on the #FeesMustFall protests at Wits and at South African universities between 2015 and 2018.

Index

CPSIA information can be obtained
at www.ICGtesting.com
Printed in the USA
LVHW040846110319
610189LV00029B/1172